FAITH
IN ACTION

NIALL BOYLE

GILL & MACMILLAN

Gill & Macmillan Ltd
Hume Avenue
Park West
Dublin 12
with associated companies throughout the world
www.gillmacmillan.ie

Artwork by Kate Shannon

978 07171 4233 0

Design, typesetting and print origination by Anú Design, Tara
Imprimatur: Most Rev. Michael Smith DCL, Bishop of Meath

The paper used in this book is made from the wood pulp of managed forests.
For every tree felled, at least one tree is planted, thereby renewing natural resources.

Contents

Section a

1

The Search for Meaning

Introduction

From the moment we are born until the moment we die, we try to make sense of life. Often, however, we are so preoccupied with such immediate matters as relationships, study, work and recreation that we give too little time to reflecting on the deeper issues, such as the meaning and purpose of our lives. Sometimes, it requires an experience of just how tenuous and fragile our hold on life is to encourage us to reflect on such issues.

Consider the following instance:

While vacationing in the Swiss mountains, I foolishly made a mountain trip without proper conditioning, without adequate equipment and without companions. The narrow winding trails are fascinating, but often treacherous and dangerous. In one place, the path had totally disappeared under a layer of gravel that had come down from the slopes during the winter. Carefully I stepped on the little stones and was making good progress when suddenly everything started sliding toward a precipice only two metres away. I tried to plant my walking stick through the gravel into the underlying earth, but several times I hit solid rock. Finally, two or three feet from the edge, I got a firm hold and there, behind my walking stick, I experienced

my own mortality. It was no longer an abstract possibility in some uncertain future. It pervaded my whole being, and I lived the fact that at any moment my life line could be snapped.

(From E. Van Croonenberg, *Gateway to Reality: An Introduction to Philosophy*.)

This sort of experience can be profoundly shocking, and people can respond to it in different ways.

For some, any intimation of their own mortality is too disturbing to contemplate. Fearful of it, they recoil into a flurry of activities that occupy their minds and leave no time for reflection. Thus, they cope with life's big questions by striving to ignore them, by pretending that they do not exist.

Others among us react very differently to such 'life and death' experiences. These people find the courage within themselves to consider honestly the implications of such experiences. They abandon the cosy, unreflective self-assurance they once had and begin to ask questions about the place of human beings in the grand scheme of things.

Questions

1. What is meant by a 'life and death' experience? Give an example of your own to illustrate your answer.

2. Examine the two ways in which a person may react to a 'life and death' experience.

Wonder

Consider the following questions:

◆ why do I exist?
◆ how should I live my life?
◆ does my life end at death?

We say that a person who begins asking such questions has begun to *wonder*.

The ancient Greek polymath Aristotle identified wonder as the origin and root of *philosophy*.

The world 'philosophy' means *the love of wisdom*.

A 'philosopher' is one who seeks *wisdom*, i.e. insights into the meaning and purpose of life.[1]

For many centuries the study of philosophy has been considered an important part of education because it encourages:

◆ the development of clear and orderly patterns of thinking; and

The Greek philosophers Plato (*left*) and Aristotle (*right*), as depicted by Raphael in his fresco painting, *The School of Athens*.

[1] See: Louis De Raeymaeker, *Introduction to Philosophy*, New York: Wagner and Co., 1948.

♦ the adoption of a calm, balanced and reflective approach to important life issues.

The formal study of philosophy usually involves delving deeply into the works of the great thinkers of the ancient, medieval and modern periods in order to assess and to understand their distinctive contributions. When doing so, however, people need to remember the warning sounded by St Thomas Aquinas that the focus of studying philosophy 'is not merely to know what great thinkers have said, but to know the truth of things'.

By 'truth' Aquinas means that which is the case, independent of what anyone thinks or wishes.

A study of philosophy's long history shows that a determination to seek out the truth courageously and honestly is the hallmark of an authentically philosophical mind.

Importance

Why should a commitment to seek the truth be so important for us today?

According to philosophers such as Karl Jaspers and Gabriel Marcel, it is important because it goes to the very heart of what it means to *be* a human being. These thinkers make a critical distinction between when a human being *lives* and is *lived*.

When a person *is lived*, his/her life is a thing *shaped entirely* by the surrounding people and events. These external forces dictate what the person thinks and how he/she should act. Thus, the individual is reduced to a piece of flotsam in the ocean of life, always pushed and pulled this way or that by the prevailing current, never setting his/her *own* course.

Contrast this with when a person *lives*. In this case, he/she makes *conscious* (i.e. deliberate) choices. While acknowledging that one is a member of a community and therefore has obligations towards others, a person who *lives* seeks to chart his/her *own* course. Guidance may be sought and received from trustworthy sources, but in the end each person accepts responsibility for his/her *own* actions.

A person who *lives*, rather than is lived, seeks to fulfil his/her full potential as a human being, but not at the expense of others. Such a person sees what is sometimes referred to as '*the big picture*'. He/she neither exaggerates nor underestimates his/her own importance in the grand scheme of things, and strives to achieve a balance between the needs of the self and the needs of others.

Common Human Needs

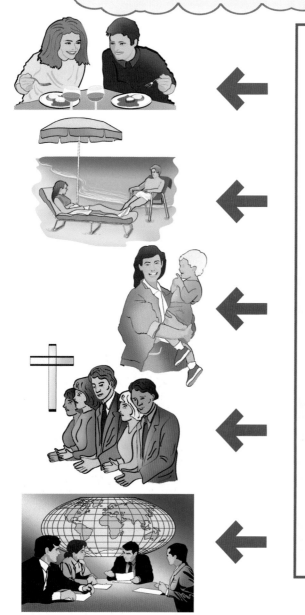

1. Physiological:
satisfied through food, drink and shelter.

2. Psychological:
satisfied through pleasure, rest and relaxation.

3. Social:
satisfied through family, friends and community.

4. Spiritual/creative:
satisfied through knowledge, truth and love.

5. Communication:
satisfied by the ability to express oneself to others.

When seeking things that will fulfil these basic needs, people must be careful to do so in a balanced manner that respects the needs of others. To achieve this, each of us must become, in the broadest sense, *a philosopher*. This involves:

◆ a commitment to search for the truth and *accept* it once one has found it;

◆ the development of one's own *personal* perspective on life's meaning and purpose.

This approach will help us to find the right path through our daily struggles and enable us to *live* rather than *be lived*.

Questions

1. Explain each of the following terms:
   (a) *philosophy* and (b) *a philosopher*.

2. What are said to be the benefits derived from studying philosophy?

3. What is meant by *truth*?

4. Why is the pursuit of truth important?

5. Explain the difference between a person who *lives* and one who *is lived*. Give your own examples of each to illustrate your answer.

Challenges

To achieve a genuinely philosophical outlook, one must face up to reality, i.e. one must see people and the world we share as they *truly* are. This is easier said than done.

In Chapter 7 of his dialogue, *The Republic*, the Greek philosopher Plato sought to illustrate this difficulty in his famous 'Allegory of the Cave'.

According to Plato, many people wrongly believe that their minds are focussed on reality, when in fact they are absorbed by mere *distractions*.

Plato compared most of us to people who dwell in a cave, chained to the one spot in such a way that all we can see is a large, blank wall. Behind us is a permanent fire, which projects onto the wall our own shadows and the shadows of those around us. As we have never seen anything else, we are convinced that these shadows are *the only* reality. We focus our minds on these shadows in the mistaken belief that, by doing so, we will better understand reality.

Plato's Cave.

If, somehow, one of the men in the cave were freed and brought out of the cave into the open, it would initially be very confusing and disorientating because:

◆ his eyes would suffer from the intense sunlight to which he was not accustomed;

◆ he would be told that what he is *now* seeing is the *true* reality.

Not surprisingly, the man would find this difficult to accept. It would challenge everything he has known so far and which he believed to be true.

Initially, the man would probably be very tempted to flee back into the comfort of the cave. There, he could pretend that nothing had changed. He could immerse himself in distractions once more.

Once he sets aside his pride, however, and finds the courage to brave the discomfort and the estrangement from his old, familiar surroundings, the man begins to re-evaluate his ideas about the world. He wants to learn more. He no longer wants to re-enter the cave and he may try to help liberate others, too.

In the light of Plato's work, we can say that we have developed a genuinely philosophical outlook when we are each willing to do the following:

◆ honestly reflect on what we have experienced;

◆ put aside our own pride;

◆ question what we have assumed or been told;

◆ resist pressures to conform, without good reason, to other people's expectations;

◆ calmly evaluate all the facts we have ascertained;

◆ reach our own conclusions about important issues.

Questions

1. What were the key insights contained in Plato's 'Allegory of the Cave'?

2. Why do you think Plato wrote it?

3. What are the *shadows*, i.e. the distractions that consume many people's lives in the twenty-first century?

Approach

The purpose of this book is twofold:

◆ to inform the reader about a wide range of religious and moral issues;

◆ to encourage the reader to critically *evaluate* them and to reach his/her *own* conclusions about them.

But as the eminent psychologist William James once warned:

A great many people think they are thinking, when they are merely rearranging their prejudices.

A philosopher is expected to scrutinise an issue in a fair and impartial manner and *not* allow bias or prejudice to interfere with his search for the truth.

Clearly, it is important that each of us should be able to justify what we *believe*, i.e. what we accept as true. To do so, we need to be able to present *arguments* as to why we hold the particular views we do.

Argument

The word 'argument' is frequently misunderstood. Two people yelling at each other are having a blazing row, *not* an argument. Here we shall define an argument as:

> *A piece of reasoning that aims to convince us why we should accept or reject a particular idea or course of action.*

But how are we to evaluate arguments? Here, *logic* can help.

Logic

'Logic' may be defined as 'the study of arguments'.

Aristotle founded logic as an academic discipline in the fourth century BCE. He was the first person to formally set out the rules for thinking clearly, consistently and effectively.

Evaluating arguments

In an argument we *infer* (i.e. draw out) a conclusion from a chain of connected statements.

An argument is said to be either *sound* or *unsound*.

Sound Argument

Consider the following examples:

A

Statement 1:	**All human beings are mammals.**
Statement 2:	**All mammals are warm-blooded.**
Conclusion:	**Therefore all human beings are warm-blooded.**

B

Statement 1:	**Mr X drove his car at 130 kph on the motorway.**
Statement 2:	**The maximum speed limit on the motorway is 100 kph.**
Conclusion:	**Therefore Mr X drove his car beyond the maximum speed limit.**

Both of the above arguments are sound because in each case:
- ◆ both statement 1 and statement 2 are true;
- ◆ there is a reasonable link between statement 1 and statement 2;
- ◆ the conclusion drawn from these statements can be fully justified.

Unsound Argument

Consider the following examples:

A

Statement 1:	**I like this subject.**
Statement 2:	**The Leaving Certificate exam is easy.**
Conclusion:	**Therefore I do not need to do any study to get an A grade in this subject.**

This argument is *unsound*. Why?
Although statement 1 may be true, statement 2 is *false*. Therefore we are *not* justified in drawing this conclusion.

B

Statement 1:	**All dogs are animals.**
Statement 2:	**All cats are animals.**
Conclusion:	**Therefore all dogs are cats.**

This argument is also *unsound*. Why?
Both statement 1 and statement 2 are true. However, there is *no* reasonable link between them that justifies drawing this conclusion.

> ## N.B.
> It is essential that we listen to or read an entire argument *before* deciding whether it is sound or unsound. We should always hear the other person out *before* making up our minds.

Fallacies

Some arguments give the *appearance* of being sound at first glance or hearing. Only after close inspection do we realise that they are in fact *unsound*. These deceptive arguments contain an error in reasoning called a *fallacy*. Some of the most common fallacies are:

◆ *Argumentum ad hominem*: attacking the person.

For example:

'I wouldn't listen to a word he says because he is a hypocrite.'

Even if he *is* a hypocrite (i.e. someone who does not practice what he preaches), it in *no* way means that whatever he says is automatically false or without any value.

◆ *Argumentum ad misericordiam*: appealing for compassion or pity.

For example:

'She could not have embezzled that money because she is such a nice person.'

She may be a nice person, but then, perhaps she only pretends to be. At any rate, even if she were a *nice* person, it would *not* necessarily mean that it is impossible for her to have committed such a crime. We would have to calmly evaluate the evidence put forward *before* deciding whether she is innocent or guilty.

◆ *Argumentum ad verecundiam*: appealing to the prestige or social status of a person, group or institution.

For example:

'I will give this promotion to Mr X because he went to Cambridge University.'

Mr X may be the right person to be promoted, but *not* for this reason. There may be someone more deserving who fails to be promoted solely due to attending a less prestigious university.

◆ *Non sequitur*: jumping to a conclusion that in no way follows.

For example:

'If I buy lottery tickets for each prize draw, I stand a chance of winning. If I keep doing it for enough years, then I am bound to win eventually.'

Perhaps this person will one day win the lottery, but the reasons offered here do *not* provide solid grounds for accepting this conclusion.

◆ Sweeping generalisations: broad statements that ignore the particulars of a situation in favour of over-simplification and distortion.

For example:

'All tradesmen are wealthy.'

'All dogs are vicious.'

One must exercise considerable caution when using the word *all*.

Questions

1. Explain the following terms:
   (a) *logic* and (b) *argument*.

2. When is an argument said to be *sound*?

3. When is an argument said to be *unsound*?

4. Spot the fallacy in each of the following:

   - 'Oh, I wouldn't listen to anything she has to say about road safety. I mean, she doesn't even own a car!'

   - 'Of course he couldn't have murdered that pensioner. After all, he's very kind to his pets and always treats them so well.'

   - 'Yes, you should follow his advice about which career to pursue. Well, he is captain of our golf club.'

   - 'Don't be ridiculous! Violence has no place in our society. Why, anyone who advocates the use of violence should be shot down like a rabid animal.'

   - 'All important people speak a foreign language. Mrs Y speaks a foreign language. Therefore she must be an important person.'

   - 'Susan and Yvonne are both architects. Susan is wealthier than Yvonne. Therefore Susan must be a better architect than Yvonne.'

   - 'I simply cannot accept the evidence offered by that witness. I find her accent very annoying.'

Contemporary Ireland: A critique

The following excerpt offers an example of the kind of searching meditation on Irish society that deserves close attention and should provoke discussion:

The Celtic Tiger has made a small number of people *immensely* wealthy but it has also enabled many people who were poor and unemployed to *escape* from poverty. They can now live with dignity and pride, no longer having to scrape the bottom of the barrel to put food on the table and to clothe their children. They no longer have to feel that they are a failure, unable to give their family what everyone around them takes for granted.

But *not all* have benefited: some remain unable to take up employment, often through no fault of their own. For example, a single parent who cannot afford childcare, or a single person living in private rented accommodation and who depends on a rent supplement, are trapped in their dependency on the State.

Others remain in poverty despite having a job: one in every six households in relative poverty has a head of household in work. Nevertheless, despite its shortcomings no one wants to turn back the clock and return to the high unemployment and deep poverty which preceded the Celtic Tiger.

However, this Western capitalist economy in which we have so successfully embedded ourselves brings with it certain values on which we need to reflect and which we need to *challenge*.

▶

What brings fulfilment

First, the Celtic Tiger tells us that it is in getting that we find our fulfilment. It is in purchasing and consuming that we find our satisfaction and happiness—the bigger house, the new car, the latest gadget will make a major contribution to our happiness. Indeed, we come to be persuaded they are *essential*.

Advertising, the heart that pumps the money through the system, is successful in selling the products it promotes to the extent that it succeeds in persuading us that those products are necessary to our success or satisfaction. The irony of the capitalist economy is that while it must persuade us that acquiring something new is essential to our happiness, it actually depends on us becoming, in time, dissatisfied with what we have recently acquired, so that we feel the need to go out and purchase yet again.

Not in getting but in giving

I believe that our fulfilment and happiness are to be found, not in getting, but in giving. It is in letting go that we find our fulfilment, not in accumulating. The young homeless people with whom I work regularly remind me of this. Most of the time they are on the receiving end—dependent on others for their accommodation, their income, their food, their clothes, for all the basic needs of their lives. But it is when they have an opportunity to give to others that they find their self-respect and are uplifted. For example, each year a few young people come to us on a social placement, as part of their school programme or work experience. These young people usually come from a very comfortable background. They engage with, and learn from, the homeless people around them. These homeless people discover—through sharing their experiences, their life stories, their struggles, their successes and their failures—that they have something unique to give to those on the social placement. They are making a contribution to the education of those on placement which all their money cannot buy. It is in making that contribution that the homeless feel important.

I believe that what we have is *not* our own. It is given to us to be used for the good of others. The satisfaction we get from buying a new car, or acquiring a new toy, soon fades and cannot compare with the satisfaction we get from meeting the needs of others—be it our children, our families, our friends, our neighbours, or strangers we have never met.

Possessions give security

The *second* value that accompanies the economic system we enjoy is that it must persuade us that our security is to be found in what we possess. Purchasing our own home, building up our bank balance, expanding our shareholdings are essential in order to escape from the insecurity of the future. We have to work hard in order to obtain more so as to cushion ourselves and our families against what might lie ahead. ▶

But we are constantly reminded that possessions may not necessarily bring us the security we seek—ironically, by the economists! They remind us that the threat of higher interest rates could push many families, who now enjoy a comfortable standard of living, into a debt from which they may not emerge. Economists discuss the conditions which could trigger a collapse in the housing market that would plunge many families, who now enjoy a comfortable security, into homelessness.

I believe that our security is to be measured, *not* in material possessions, but in community. Our security is to be found in the knowledge that there are those who love us, who will be in solidarity with us in good times and in bad. In community, we will in good times share with those who have little, while in bad times others will share with us. Our security is to be found in building community, not bank balances; the wealth we create is for sharing, not for hoarding. In that sharing, we find both fulfilment and security.

Excessive individualism

The *third* value that accompanies this economic system is an excessive individualism. This system promotes, encourages and rewards individual effort—this has been the mark of its success. The individual is the source of the innovation which drives capitalism and the individual is the beneficiary of the rewards of capitalism. We are all pushed into a competitive struggle with other human beings to accumulate the material benefits of capitalism which, we are promised, guarantee our security. Others become not the source of our fulfilment, but a threat to that fulfilment. Community becomes an optional extra as we rush to find security and fulfilment in what we, as individuals, can accumulate.

I believe that we are *not* isolated individuals but exist in solidarity with all other human beings. Promoting solidarity is the antidote to excessive individualism.

(Adapted from an article entitled '*The False Values of the Celtic Tiger*' by Peter McVerry S.J. in *Reality*, March 2005.)

Questions

1. What does the author of this article identify as the positive outcomes of '*the Celtic Tiger*'?

2. Who is identified as *not* benefiting from it?

3. The author states that the first value of the Celtic Tiger is that 'it is in getting that one finds fulfilment'.
   (a) What does this mean?
   (b) What alternative does the author propose?
   (c) Do you agree/disagree with him? Explain your answer.

4. It is stated that the *second* value of the Celtic Tiger is that 'one's happiness is in what one possesses'.
   (a) What does this mean?
   (b) What alternative does the author propose?
   (c) Do you agree/disagree? Give reasons for your answer.

5. It is stated that the *third* value of the Celtic Tiger is that of 'excessive individualism'.
   (a) What does this mean?
   (b) What alternative does the author propose?
   (c) Do you agree/disagree? Give reasons for your answer.

6. The author is someone who has dedicated his entire life to helping the poor and championing the cause of those without a voice in Irish society. He admits that many would describe him as an *idealist*.
   (a) What does this mean?
   (b) Do you agree/disagree that he is an idealist? Give reasons for your answer.

The Aspects of Religion

Introduction

Religion often proves to be a difficult subject to discuss because of the contentious and emotive nature of the issues involved. Yet, it is necessary to do so because religion has been, and continues to be, one of the key factors shaping human society.

Scholars generally agree that:

◆ religion has existed, in one form or another, as far back as we can trace the history of the human race;

◆ religion appears to be central to our understanding of virtually every culture on Earth.

Meaning

Our modern English word 'religion' is thought by many scholars to be derived from both the Latin word *religare*, which means literally '*to tie or bind*', and its root word *ligare*, which has the connotation of '*acting with care*'. Thus, the term 'religion' may have its origin in ancient people's sense of being tied and bound by obligation and duty to serve and worship whatever powers they believed guided or governed human affairs.

Christ the Redeemer, Rio de Janeiro, Brazil.

These powers have tended to be understood at different times and in different places as either:

◆ natural (e.g. the sun) *or* supernatural (e.g. a spiritual being);

◆ a personal deity (e.g. Allah in Islam) *or* an impersonal cosmic force (e.g. Brahman in Hinduism);

◆ one God (i.e. monotheism) *or* many gods (i.e. polytheism).

Over time, however, the term '*religion*' has come to be used in a much *broader* sense. Today, it is commonly understood as referring to:

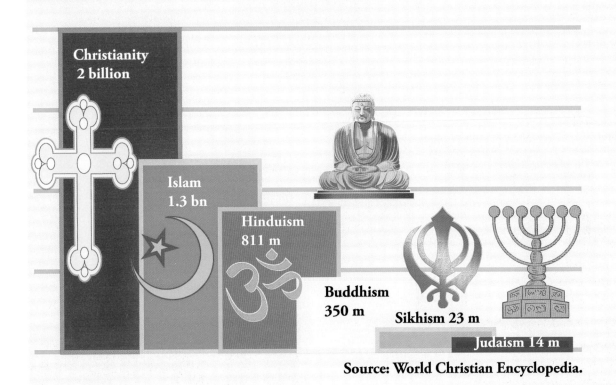

Christianity remains the world's largest religion. However, Islam has shown a notable increase. Hinduism shows a slight gain relative to world population.

Christianity
2 billion

Islam
1.3 bn

Hinduism
811 m

Buddhism
350 m

Sikhism 23 m

Judaism 14 m

Source: World Christian Encyclopedia.

Survey of World Religions.

… an adherence to a set of beliefs or teachings about the deepest and most elusive of life's mysteries.

Religious people are those who join with others in a *shared* quest to gain *wisdom*, i.e. insights into a whole range of perplexing questions, such as:

◆ What is the origin of life?
◆ What does it mean to be a human being?
◆ What is the meaning of evil, suffering and death?
◆ How should a person of good will behave?
◆ Is life as we know it all that there is?
◆ What happens after death?

Perspective

Clearly a religious person seeks answers to many of the same questions as a philosopher. Indeed, it is not surprising to learn that many of the greatest philosophers were deeply religious people.

So what is the difference between philosophy and religion?

Let us begin by recalling that *both* are concerned with truth. They differ from one another in how they approach it.

Religion is based on *divine revelation*, i.e. God communicates truth to human beings, who then meditate upon it and seek to grow in understanding of it.

Allegory of the Old and New Testaments, by Holbein.

Philosophy, in contrast, involves *unaided* human reason engaged in the pursuit of truth.

A philosopher is like a detective who uses all his powers of observation, imagination and reasoning to track down any clues, no matter how seemingly trivial, in order to arrive at the truth.

A religious person, on the other hand, *starts out* from a position of having the truth revealed to him/her and then judges all other things in light of this.

In case one gets the wrong idea here, it must be noted that a religious person (especially one in the Judaeo-Christian tradition) does *not*, in any way, deny or denigrate the role of reason nor consider it

to be in some way superfluous. On the contrary, he/she *welcomes* its assistance and invites its accompaniment throughout life.

Different Paths

Up to this point we have spoken of religion as a general, observable phenomenon. However, it is important to realise that there is no such thing as 'religion in general', any more than there is an 'animal in general'. Though we can form a concept of 'animal' in our minds as '*a living being that can feel and move of its own accord*',

we know that, in *actuality*, every animal is a member of a particular species, each with its own set of distinguishing characteristics.

So it is with 'religion'.

We know that *in actuality* there are only different *religions*. Each one has its own system of beliefs, practices and values. The most important and numerous of these religions include: Judaism, Christianity, Islam, Hinduism, Buddhism, Sikhism, Confucianism, Taoism and Shintoism.

While some people may be tempted to dismiss all religions as essentially the same, any fair-minded study soon reveals this view to be utterly *groundless*. Although, as we shall soon see, one can discern certain

common elements among them, they *differ* considerably from one other. Each major religion offers its own distinctive path towards the truth.[2]

Indeed, it is also tempting to imagine that all the members of each of the major religions listed above believe nearly the same things, but this is true only in a very general way. On close inspection, each world religion contains within it clusters, or families, united by *certain basic beliefs*, but *separated* by others.

For example:

◆ within Christianity there are three traditions: Catholic, Orthodox and Protestant;

◆ within Islam there are two branches: Sunni and Shia;

◆ within Buddhism there are two sub-communities: Mahayana and Theravada.

It would require a whole library of books to describe the similarities and differences between the various traditions contained *within* each of the major religions, never mind to examine the differences *between* each of the religions. This is a vast and immensely complex area of study; in this book we will only be scratching its surface.

Questions

1. Explain the origin of the term *'religion'*.

2. How is the term *'religion'* commonly understood today?

3. What are the questions to which religious people seek answers?

4. What is the difference between religion and philosophy?

5. Explain the following statement:
There is no such thing as religion in general.

[2] This is a topic to which we shall return in Section C of this text.

Key Aspects

Scholars warn us to be cautious when trying to fit the many different religions into a set pattern because this tends to distort our view of them, which can lead us to make over-simplistic generalisations that do *not* reflect the complexity and individuality of each of them. Nonetheless, it is true to point out that all extant religions tend to share certain traits and that identifying these common aspects can help us to better understand the role they play in the human search for meaning and purpose.

What, then, are the key aspects of religion? They include the following:

◆ creed;
◆ sacred text;
◆ code;
◆ symbol;
◆ myth;
◆ ritual;
◆ spirituality;
◆ community.

Creed

The English word '*creed*' is derived from the Latin *credo*, meaning '*I believe*'. It can be applied to religion in two ways:

◆ as a *general concept*, where 'creed' refers to the totality of what members of a particular religion believe;
◆ as a *technical term*, where 'creed' means a formal statement, approved by the authorities of a particular religion, that encapsulates the key points of its belief system.

In the technical sense a creed is:

◆ short enough to be memorised easily;
◆ recited by members of a religion to reaffirm their assent to its core beliefs.

Sometimes a creed may consist of a direct quotation from a sacred text, such as the Shahadah from Islam's holy book, the *Qur'an*. More often than not, however, a creed is a *later* development, the product of several generations of meditation and discussion. Historians have shown that elaborate creeds, such as Christianity's Nicene Creed (which dates from the fourth century CE), are typically formulated when a diversity of views has begun to develop *within* a religion, causing internal divisions and tensions. This leads the majority to feel the need for a clear statement of key beliefs to define themselves against the unacceptable ideas of an emerging minority group.

Some religions, on the other hand, for example Hinduism, see no need to formulate a creed, although they do possess basic beliefs and teachings that we can examine.

Sacred Text

All religions possess *sacred texts*, i.e. holy books, which are commonly referred to as **scriptures**.

◆ Some religions revolve around a single sacred text, composed over a relatively short period of time and associated with one person only.
  For example: Islam's *Qur'an*.
◆ Other religions produced their sacred texts in gradual stages, over a period of time lasting several centuries, resulting in scriptures that are effectively anthologies of separate books of different genres (e.g. poetry, history) bound together in a single volume.
  For example: Judaism's *Tenakh*.
◆ Still other religions revolve around a whole library of sacred texts that have come into existence over as many as 2,000 years.
  For example: Hinduism's vast religious literature.

One of the most interesting, though often highly controversial, aspects of religion is the *interpretation* of sacred texts. Some scholars employ what is called

the historico-critical method, by which they attempt to show that while these sacred texts are *historically conditioned*, i.e.

> *the product of a particular group of people in a particular time, place and culture,*

they may also have a lasting value and enduring authority for all subsequent generations within that religion.

Historico-critical scholars begin by asking:
◆ What kind of a text is it?
◆ What was its original purpose?

If they discover that the historical meaning of the text is that '*X went to visit Y at date Z*', then it is of limited value, such as helping us to understand a set of events that took place long ago.

If, however, scholars discover deeper meanings embedded intentionally in text, then it is of much *greater* importance. These messages discovered in the

text are valid for every time and place since the text was first composed. They are of *continuing* importance for every member of that religion because they have major implications as to how each should live today.

Code

Every religion offers its members a code, i.e.

> *a set of guiding principles for living a truly human life.*

Examples of a code can be found in the following religions:

◆ **Judaism**
It is believed that God gave the Ten Commandments to Moses on Mount Sinai (Exodus 19:1–20:21). These commandments set out the attitudes and values that are consistent with Jewish belief in the one God, Yahweh.

Moses with the Tablets of the Law, by Guido Reni.

- ◆ **Islam**

    For Muslims the teaching of the *Qur'an* and the *Hadith* (stories or traditions about the Prophet Muhammad) set out the moral way of life that Allah expects of human beings.

The code presented by each religion makes clear that one's religious beliefs are not to be boxed away and aired publicly only on special occasions, such as weddings and funerals. On the contrary, such a code provides direction for how to treat others and clarifies what behaviours are to be valued or shunned in all the dealings of daily life.

Being a moral person, i.e. one who honestly seeks to apply the code of one's faith in daily life, is an inherent dimension of an authentic religious faith.

Questions

1. Explain the meaning and purpose of the term '*creed*' for a religion.

2. How are elaborate creeds, such as Christianity's Nicene Creed, formulated?

3. What is a sacred text?

4. Describe how scholars apply the historico-critical method to sacred texts?

5. What is a code?

6. Where can one find the code that guides
   (a) Jews and (b) Muslims?

7. What is a moral person?

8. How do the major religions expect their members to live out their religious beliefs?

Symbol

We live our entire lives in a world of *symbols*. Consider how a smile or a frown, a handshake or a tear communicates a message about us to others.

In order to clarify the meaning of symbol, it will be helpful if we first distinguish between the terms '*sign*' and '*symbol*'.

These terms are often regarded as being interchangeable. They are not. This confusion arises from the fact that both a sign and a symbol share this aspect in common:

Each is a concrete image, word or gesture intended to represent something other than itself.

However, a sign has only *one* specific and unambiguous meaning. **For example:** ➡

No parking! **No overtaking!** **Hazardous material!**

Unlike a sign, a symbol has the following distinctive characteristics:

◆ it has more than one meaning;

◆ it has a richer content than a sign, which can take some time to uncover;

◆ it is more intimately involved and completely identified with that to which it refers;

◆ it cannot be coldly explained in words and still convey the same impact.

For example:

A kiss is a symbol of affection and love. It not only presents these feelings in an abstract way but actually embodies them. A cold, clinical analysis of such an action will utterly miss its significance and fail to explain its meaning.

Religious symbols share these general characteristics. They can have a considerable emotional, intellectual and spiritual impact on the life of believers. This is because such symbols:

◆ enshrine and express the most fundamental beliefs and values of a religion;

◆ have the power to unite people in a community of shared understanding, which encourages and strengthens them in their commitment to live their faith.

As a result, if the symbols of a particular religion are in any way denigrated by others, it can provoke an intense reaction among the faithful.

The following religious symbols command the allegiance of millions of people around the world:

Christianity **Islam** **Hinduism** **Buddhism**

The cross of Jesus Christ The Qur'an The Sacred Cow The silent, seated Buddha

Questions

1. What is a *sign*?
   State any *two* examples of a sign.

2. What are the distinctive characteristics of a *symbol*?
   Explain the meaning of *one* symbol.

3. Why do symbols play an important role in all religions?

4. (a) Name one symbol identified with each of the following major religions:
   Judaism;
   Christianity;
   Islam;
   Hinduism;
   Buddhism.

   (b) Choose any one of these and explain its meaning.

Icons and the Importance of Symbolism

Cultural historians have long noted how central the visual arts have been to Christianity—to expressing the Christian message, but also to influencing and spreading it. The art it has inspired has helped Christianity not only to become rooted in some cultures but to survive when the authorities have turned against it. The classic example is the years of Communist rule in Eastern Europe and the Soviet Union. In these countries the Orthodox Church had been deeply entrenched in society and culture for a millennium. But the Bolsheviks, after

Christ Acheiropoietos, literally 'Christ not made by Hand'. According to legend, King Agbar of Edessa—an independent state halfway between the Roman and Persian empires—asked Jesus to visit him. Jesus wrote back explaining that he was unable to do so, but sent a cloth that he had pressed to his face, leaving a miraculous imprint. This relic, the 'mandylion', was supposed to have miraculous properties and to have inspired icons like this sixteenth-century example from Russia.

coming to power in Russia in 1917, set about trying systematically to eradicate Orthodoxy from the country. Officially, neither Orthodoxy nor any other major religion was forbidden, but ideologically it was incompatible with atheistic Communism, and the authorities hoped to wipe it out as much as possible. Churches were closed and seized by the state, clergy were harassed, imprisoned or executed, and the dissemination of most religious literature was prohibited.

The Orthodox Church had a brief respite during the Second World War, when Stalin re-established it in order to use it to rally the people against Nazi Germany; but Kruschev later clamped down on the religion more harshly than ever. At the same time, other Christian denominations were attacked, to such an extent that the 1,200 Catholic churches that had been there in 1917 were whittled down to two in under thirty years. It is often said that there were more Christian martyrs in the twentieth century than in all the previous nineteen centuries put together, and a good proportion of those who died were killed in the Soviet Union. Little wonder that, as early as 1918, Patriarch Tikhon of Moscow condemned the new Soviet government and oversaw the setting up of the underground Catacomb Church, which operated secretly throughout the Soviet period.

Yet through all this, the values of Russian Orthodoxy survived. The church buildings and monasteries may have been largely empty, but they remained as silent witnesses to the faith that had built them. The great novels of Dostoevsky, Tolstoy and others were read, and the religious questions with which they grappled continued to exercise people. And the icons survived, too.

Icons are among the most distinctive elements of Orthodox Christianity—not simply beautiful expressions of the faith, but central to it. They were first painted in the Byzantine empire in the sixth and seventh centuries, ▶

and they soon became the subject of controversy as some theologians and emperors believed that their use was idolatrous. After the eighth century, however, they ceased to be controversial.

An icon is a painting, usually of Christ or a saint, but it is not meant to be a realistic portrayal, like a photograph. Instead the picture is intended as an aid to worship, and so the artist strives to convey the spiritual nature of the subject. This means that icons have a very stylised appearance, but they are also instantly recognisable. A modern Russian icon, for example, looks much like a medieval Middle Eastern one. Orthodox Christians believe that beauty plays a central role in religion. There is a story that in the tenth century, Prince Vladimir of Kiev decided that his nation needed a religion, and so he sent ambassadors to the Muslims, the Byzantines and the Catholics to decide which religion was best. Those who visited the great cathedral of Hagia Sophia in Constantinople reported that they did not know whether they were in heaven or earth, since they could not believe that such beauty could exist on earth. God clearly dwelt there with the Orthodox, and so Vladimir converted and Russia has been Orthodox ever since.

So, it's not surprising that icons are also intended to be objects of great beauty. They are usually painted on wood, and artists traditionally use layers upon layers of paint—up to thirty—to create the glowing colours that often prove remarkably durable through the centuries. Orthodox Christians believe that

the use of icons in worship reflects a central Christian belief—that in Christ, God became part of the physical world and sanctified it. If the glory of God can be contained within a normal human body, then the holiness of God and his saints can also be accessed through a beautiful image. The Orthodox do not worship the icons, of course, but they do believe that they offer an authentic medium by which we can come into contact with the spiritual world. John of Damascus, an eighth-century Orthodox theologian who strongly supported the use of icons in worship, wrote, 'The beauty of the images moves me to contemplation, as a meadow delights the eyes and subtly infuses the soul with the glory of God.'

But quite apart from being a remarkable aesthetic tradition in its own right, the tradition of icons has played an essential role in preserving and transmitting Christian culture. Icons convey spiritual ideas to those unable to read them in theological tomes; they are spirituality for the people, not for academics or specialists. Gregory the Great, a much-loved pope of the sixth century, once said that 'the picture is to the illiterate what the written word is to the educated'. A good example of this principle in Catholicism is the Stations of the Cross, a series of meditations on the death of Christ, which is often represented in churches by a series of pictures, each one showing a stage in Christ's Passion. In many churches the pictures are found at intervals around the walls, allowing people to physically walk from one station to the next and contemplate each scene as they come to it.

Similarly, icons preserved the spirit and the teaching of Orthodox Christianity, and with it the spirit of holy Russia, throughout the Soviet period. The people remained in touch with their past and their heritage in the form of the saints the icons depicted.

(Adapted from Jonathan Hill, *What Has Christianity Ever Done For Us?* Intervarsity Press, 2005.)

Questions

1. In what way has art been important to the success of Christianity over the centuries?

2. How did the Communist regime in Russia treat both Christian and non-Christian religions following its seizure of and accession to power in 1917?

3. Why did the Communist government react in this way?

4. (a) What is an *icon*?

   (b) When were icons first painted?

   (c) What is the purpose of an icon?

5. Explain Orthodox Christian belief concerning the role of beauty in religion?

6. What do Orthodox Christians believe about the use of icons in worship?

7. How did icons help the values of Orthodox Christianity to survive during the decades of repression in Communist-dominated Russia?

Myth

People like stories—just think about the huge popularity of television dramas and soap operas. We like listening to stories, and stories can have a powerful effect on us.

The English word 'myth' comes from the Greek '*mythos*', meaning 'story'. Myth plays an important role in all religions. Before exploring this, however, we need to distinguish between the different meanings the term 'myth' has acquired in popular usage.

There are four meanings of 'myth':

What is believed to be a statue of Gilgamesh from the palace of Sargon II (722–705 BCE), at Korsabad, Iraq.

1. A popularly accepted falsehood.

> **For example:**
> 'Bad things are more likely to happen to us on Friday the 13th.'

2. Some event that never actually occurred.

> **For example:**
> 'St Patrick drove all the snakes out of Ireland.'

3. A collective name for a variety of timeless stories that have a long-standing tradition in a culture or nation.

> **For example:**
> ◆ the myth of Gilgamesh;
> ◆ the myth of Achilles at the siege of Troy;
> ◆ the myth of King Arthur and the Knights of the Round Table.

We cannot be sure if any of these people actually lived, but that is *not* the point of these myths. We are *not* supposed to ask if they are true. Instead, we are expected to ask what they *mean*. What insights do these stories contain about the human condition?

For example, the myth of Achilles warns us of the terrible consequences that flow from a desire for revenge and a life fuelled by hatred.

4. A collective term applied to stories of profound religious significance.

> **For example:**
> ◆ the story of the Exodus in Judaism;
> ◆ the infancy narratives in Christianity.

Unlike the previous category, these religious myths are said to be based on *real* people and *actual* historical events. Their purpose is to report the *revelation of God* to human beings *not* in the manner of abstract formulae, but in the form of vivid dramatisations of the fundamental beliefs of a particular faith. They express important insights into the most profound mysteries.

For example, the *Exodus* account expresses Judaism's key ideas about God, human freedom and the relationship we should strive to build with God and with one another.

Christians and Jews not only believe that such stories contain profound truths about the meaning of life but that they are inspired by and grounded in *historical reality*.

For example:
Passover Myth and Ritual

Passover is one of the most important holy days in Judaism. At Passover, Jewish families gather for a meal, called a seder, at which they hear the story of the Exodus, the liberation of the Jews from slavery in Egypt. As the story is retold, participants eat certain foods as reminders of what was important in the past. The Passover seder is a symbolic occasion, not a literal re-enactment of the Exodus. Nevertheless, *this symbolic re-enactment is experienced as having the power to make each*

---

seder guest an actual participant in the original event. The distance between past and present is felt to dissolve, and the events of the Exodus are '*happening now*'.

Through participation in the Passover seder, Jews experience who they are—*a chosen people, called by the God of all creation to live justly and to be an example to all nations.* This celebration reminds Jews that God acts in history and will one day overcome suffering and death. Thus each Jew knows that no life is trivial. On the contrary, each life has cosmic significance, helping to bring about the fulfilment of all things. Myth and ritual thus perform a religious function—that is, they 'tie or bind' the life of the individual into a great cosmic drama, serving the highest power—the source of the meaning and purpose of life.

(From J.L. Esposito *et al.*, *World Religions Today*)

Some commentators are concerned that the impact of scientific advances has been to lessen the ability of myths to evoke a response to religious ideas. However, the scholar Mircea Eliade has claimed that, in response to this, some writers have sought to compensate for this by developing new myths in genres such as science fiction, e.g. *Star Trek*, and fantasy, e.g. *The Lord of the Rings*.

Questions

1. What is the origin of the English word '*myth*'?

2. (a) Identify each of the four meanings acquired by the term '*myth*'.

   (b) Give one example in each case.

3. How is one expected to react to a story such as *the myth of Achilles*?

4. Explain the role played by myth in either Judaism or Christianity.

Ritual

In religious terms, a *ritual* is:
> *a formal action or ceremony, performed with words, gestures and sacred objects, according to a set pattern.*

Rituals seem to have been developed quite early in human history. They are depicted on cave walls of the Neolithic period, dating back as far as 25,000 years ago.

The functions of religious ritual are as follows:
◆ to communicate important messages about the meaning of life;
◆ to offer people the opportunity to reflect upon these messages and their implications;
◆ to help believers strengthen their awareness of and relationship with the divine;
◆ to tie and bind those performing these acts to one another and to the divine;
◆ to recall and re-enact important moments in the story of a particular faith, e.g. the resurrection of Jesus Christ, the enlightenment of the Buddha.

Rituals play a central role in almost all religions. This is because most religions have two dimensions, both of which are central to 'being religious'. They are:

◆ **Orthodoxy:** acceptance of certain teachings set forth in sacred texts and formulated by scholars; and

Armenian priest Fr Khad, a Lebanese cleric who serves the American patriarchy in Jerusalem, in the Grotto of the Church of the Nativity in the West Bank biblical town of Bethlehem, the traditional site of Jesus' birth.

◆ **Orthopraxy:** carefully acting in a prescribed manner.

Each religion has its own distinctive set of rituals.
For example:
◆ being baptised in Christianity;
◆ praying five times a day in Islam;
◆ visiting a temple to offer flowers on the day of a full moon in Buddhism.

Many rituals occur in spaces specially designated for religious purposes. Nearly every religion has developed buildings dedicated, to varying degrees, to the conduct of its chief rituals.

Examples of these include:

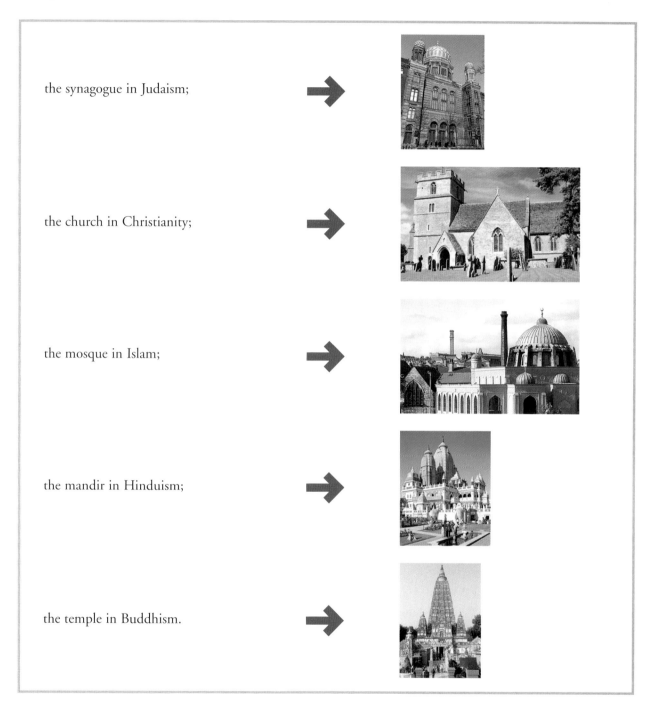

the synagogue in Judaism;

the church in Christianity;

the mosque in Islam;

the mandir in Hinduism;

the temple in Buddhism.

In some religions, however, there is also a tradition of individuals and families performing rituals at home. In such circumstances the followers usually establish a small shrine in a corner of the home, e.g. *puja* in Hinduism.

Many religions also revere certain geographical locations as holy cities, e.g. Makkah for Muslims, and as pilgrimage goals, e.g. Lourdes for Catholics.

Questions

1. Explain the term '*ritual*' as applied to religion.

2. State the functions of religious rituals.

3. Explain each of the following terms:
(a) *orthodoxy* and (b) *orthopraxy*.

4. Identify two contexts in which religious rituals may occur.

5. Explain the purpose of each of the following religious rituals:

(a) baptism;

(b) confirmation;

(c) marriage;

(d) funeral.

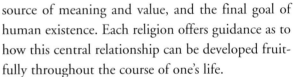

Spirituality

A person is said to be 'religious' insofar as he/she is open to the possibility that, *beyond* that which is tangible and observable by our senses, there exists the *transcendent*, which is usually described as some kind of 'higher power'. Little wonder that the sociologist Émile Durkheim claimed that the *focus of religion* is

things that surpass the limits of human knowledge.

This awareness, or sense, of the transcendent is the root of *spirituality*. We have so far examined how creeds and sacred texts communicate the content of a religion; how myths and rituals describe how believers express all of these beliefs in action; and how morality suggests principles for guiding and evaluating behaviour. Spirituality *presupposes* all of this and goes deeper.

Spirituality concerns what all of these key aspects of religion have to do with the *relationship* between a believer and what he/she perceives to be the ultimate source of meaning and value, and the final goal of human existence. Each religion offers guidance as to how this central relationship can be developed fruitfully throughout the course of one's life.

Community

Religion is essentially a communal phenomenon, i.e.

something shared and lived with others.

Indeed, in order to emphasise this aspect some writers refer to religions as '*communities of faith*'. Historians have shown that, in each case, the major religions began when an inspirational figure built on traditions within his own culture and formed a new community composed of those who had come to share his vision and values. Later, these followers employed myths and rituals to express their beliefs and to set out moral codes to help their members achieve their communal goals—whether they be

'doing God's work' (as in Christianity) or 'spreading enlightenment' (as in Buddhism).

Each religion has its own distinctive term to describe itself as a community of faith:
- in Islam, the *Umma*;
- in Christianity, the *Church*;
- in Buddhism, the *Sangha*.

Every religion teaches that the individual believer requires the support of a religious community to strengthen and sustain his/her belief and practice.

For it is communities that:
- educate the young in the traditions and beliefs of their ancestors;
- build and maintain places of worship;
- feed the hungry and shelter the homeless.

Although most religious communities are willing to integrate themselves into the general culture, some prefer to remain isolated from it. Those who adopt the latter approach do so in the belief that this stance enables them to better preserve their distinctive religious identity.

Questions

1. What does it mean to say that someone has *'an awareness of the transcendent'*?

2. What is the concern of spirituality?

3. Why is religion described as '*a communal phenomenon*'?

4. Read the following saying found in the Jewish Talmud:

   '*Sticks in a bundle are unbreakable. Sticks alone can be broken by a child*'.

   How would you apply this saying to the teaching of all religions that the believer requires the support of a community?

5. Describe how the major world religions have each developed from small founding communities.

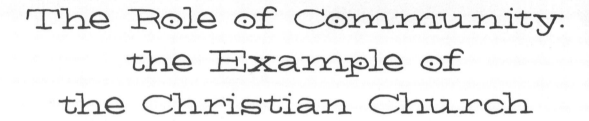

The Role of Community: the Example of the Christian Church

Sally and Tom were interested in Christianity, and when a friend invited them to a Christian meeting they were glad to attend. What they heard made sense and they decided that they wanted to become Christians. But they couldn't understand why they needed to attend church to do this. Why couldn't they be loyal disciples of Jesus without all that …?

Yes, Sally and Tom are an imaginary couple. Or are they? I think that there are many people like them and they want an answer to their question.

My answer would go something like this.

1. *A spiritual hospital*
From personal experience I understand their problem. The Church can be a pretty disappointing outfit and when people accuse it of hypocrisy and draw attention to its failings, we know that what they say has real bite.

Perhaps we shouldn't expect anything else.

Christians are people who admit that they are moral and spiritual failures. That is why we confess our sins and acknowledge our need of Jesus as Saviour. The Church isn't a health

since, it has thrived on *friendship*. We *need* one another.

3. *The Church provides opportunities*

The Church has a much better track record than many people realise. Several of the great caring movements have Christian roots, even though they are *not* limited to Christians in their membership.

For example:

◆ The Samaritans were started by Chad Varah, a London Anglican priest.

◆ The Simon Community started as a result of the vision of one Christian man— Anton Wallich Clifford.

◆ The hospice movement—launched by believers such as Cicely Saunders and Leonard Cheshire—goes from strength to strength.

farm—it's more like a *spiritual hospital*. And you don't go to hospital to show how fit you are.

One church has a large notice outside which declares '*This church is for sinners only*'. That sums it up. If you are a moral and spiritual failure—welcome to the Church!

2. *The Church is people*

The picture of failure is true but *incomplete*. From personal experience I know that the Church rings true in many ways. There is a lot of love and support around.

Without encouragement from Christian friends and teaching from Christian leaders, my faith would soon go cold. At the beginning of his ministry, Jesus chose a *group*. Ever

Mailings continue to arrive in my letterbox from Christian organisations working among the homeless, the starving, among refugees and leprosy sufferers …

Belonging to the Church means that one is part of a network which can get things done. The Church can channel our desire to help. For example, the annual Lenten Appeal raises substantial funds for assisting the developing world. Christians can do *together* what they cannot do apart.

(Adapted from John Young, *Know Your Faith*, Hodder, 1998.)

Questions

1. What does John Young mean when he describes the Christian Church as 'a spiritual hospital'?

2. Read the following story:

> *An old Scot began to miss church on Sundays. One winter evening his minister called. Both were men of few words and they sat by the fire in silence. At length the minister picked up the tongs, took a red-hot coal from the fire and put it on the hearth. It went black and became cool. He replaced it among the other coals and it became red again. The story has a happy ending. The old Scot got the point. He was in church the next Sunday.*

What point does this story make about the need for a believer to participate regularly in communal acts of worship? Do you agree or disagree? Explain your answer.

3. In what ways can membership of a Church provide the source of encouragement to greater social action for Christians?

4. Explain the importance of communal worship in *all* religions.

The Origins of Religion

Introduction

Compared to other species, humans are relative late-comers to this planet. Although the Earth is over four billion years old, people like us (*Homo sapiens*) appeared only about 75,000 years ago. Farming and village life began about 10,000 years ago. Writing was first developed in what is now called Iraq about 5,000 years ago. The period before the invention of writing is known as '*prehistory*'.

Through careful excavation and analysis of artefacts, archaeologists have sought to piece together the surviving evidence to recreate the lives and values of the people who lived in prehistoric times. Given the paucity of the evidence so far uncovered, however, the conclusions they offer must be treated as provisional and speculative, i.e. open to correction or rejection in the light of future discoveries.

To help fill in the gaps in our knowledge of prehistoric hunter-gatherer and early agricultural societies, anthropologists have studied the beliefs and practices of primitive tribal societies still extant in this era, e.g. the Aborigines of the Australian outback and the bushmen of Africa's Kalahari Desert. They have sought to compare these people's lives with the ancient remnants discovered by archaeologists so as to discern the elements common to both modern and ancient tribal cultures. Although no absolutely certain conclusions can be drawn from such comparisons, they do help scholars to form some ideas about what prehistoric people believed.

A Copper Age village priest leads a burial ceremony.

Religion in prehistory

The evidence so far amassed would strongly suggest that our prehistoric ancestors were, like us, deeply concerned about the ultimate explanation of the world's existence, their own role within the world and their ultimate destiny. To this end, they probably constructed elaborate myths to offer answers to these questions, which were then handed down carefully, at first orally, to succeeding generations. We also know that they developed religious rituals regarding fertility, hunting and initiation into adulthood. Their some-times elaborate burial sites tell us that they were deeply concerned with death and the afterlife.

The fact that prehistoric people developed a notion of the afterlife is more important than is commonly realised. The sort of *imagination* involved in this conceptualising depends on what psychologists call '*decoupled thinking*', i.e. the capacity to think of situations that are *not* actually happening in front of you, but *might* happen. The addition of this capacity to the human mental repertoire has been a key factor in the development of human civilisation, making possible our achievements in art, philosophy and science, in addition to religion.

However, there is a general consensus among scholars that prehistoric people most likely experienced the world as a hostile, frightening place. The forces of nature, e.g. floods, drought, earthquakes and storms, would have been terrifying either in their own right or as events triggered by some strange, mysterious beings or forces who lurked unseen and caused them. As the people could not control these recurring natural events, they probably reasoned that their best course of action was to find some way either to appease or to influence these forces, or the spirits (i.e. unseen beings) who controlled them. To this end they devel-oped rituals designed to persuade the forces, or the beings who wielded the forces, to treat them more kindly. In time, every facet of nature, such as the wind and the rain, and each stage of human life, such as childbirth and hunting, fell within the juris-diction of some particular minor deity or god. A belief in and worship of many different gods is called *polytheism*.

Until recently it was thought that prehistoric people were totally preoccupied with a vast array of minor deities, each of whom were believed to control some aspect of human life or the world. However, the anthropologist Mircea Eliade has now claimed that, over time, people began to develop a more sophisticated outlook. They remained polytheists, but developed the notion of a single Supreme Being standing over this multiplicity of minor gods. They seem to have believed that humans could *not* approach

Questions

1. What methods are used to attempt the reconstruction of the religious beliefs and practices of our prehistoric ancestors?

2. (a) What is *decoupled thinking*?
   (b) Why is it important?

3. Describe the development of *polytheism*.

4. What has Mircea Eliade claimed about polytheism?

such a Being directly, but should adopt an indirect approach by asking lesser deities to intercede on their behalf; … as such … a Supreme Being would have no interest in the paltry concerns of human beings.

Monotheism

The origins of *monotheism, that is a belief in and worship of one, supreme, creator God,* can be traced back to a particular time, place and person. Around 1800 BCE a man named Abram led his small tribe, the Hebrews, away from Haran in ancient Iraq and across the fertile crescent to settle in what is now Israel. Abram had grown up in a strongly polytheistic religious environment where, in addition to the major deities, each tribe or clan had its own god. All of these deities were believed to be fearsome and selfish beings, who warred continually with one another, causing natural disasters in the process. These gods treated human beings as mere playthings.

Abram decided to swim against the prevailing religious current. He rejected polytheism and embraced

The Hospitality of Abraham (fifteenth century).

monotheism. He declared that the vast array of gods worshipped by his people were just human inventions. He told them that there was only one God, *Yahweh*, who *loved* humanity. To demonstrate how his new understanding of God had changed everything for him, Abram took a new name—Abraham.

Abraham's conversion is the basis of Jewish, Christian and Islamic monotheism. These three religions are sometimes referred to as *the Abrahamic faiths*.

Historians believe that Abraham did not succeed immediately in converting his fellow Hebrews from polytheism. However, by wooing sufficient numbers he laid down a strong foundation upon which others built. The Hebrews gradually abandoned polytheism and evolved towards the full adoption of monotheism, which is expressed clearly in the Ten Commandments given to Moses on Mount Sinai.

All of this now raises an important question: why did Abraham reject his polytheistic inheritance and advocate monotheism?

The Abrahamic faiths all teach that this was due to God's *revelation*.

Revelation

The world '*revelation*' is derived from the Latin *revelatio*, meaning *to uncover or to draw back the veil*. In everyday speech we use the term 'revelation' to describe some situation where we experience a moment of insight that transforms our outlook either of some particular person or thing, or of life in general. For example, the discovery that someone we previously had little time for turns out to be a real friend in a time of need usually forces us to reconsider

Creation of Adam (1510), by Michelangelo, on the ceiling of the Sistine Chapel in the Vatican.

and change our view of that person and our relationship with him/her.

In a religious context, the term 'revelation' refers to *God's free and loving self-disclosure to humanity*. As with all such moments of revelation, this too *invites a response* from those who receive it. (This is a topic to which we shall return later.)

According to the Abrahamic faiths, revelation is *necessary*. Although we humans may be able to discover God's existence and some of God's attributes by our own unaided reasoning powers, this is as far as we can go. To enable us to know more, God must *intervene* in human history and give us knowledge about God and human destiny that we could *never* otherwise have attained. However, God's greatness *transcends* (i.e. goes far beyond) all our mental categories and therefore cannot be contained within the boundaries of the human mind. Thus, while human beings may come to know God better through prayer, study and good moral actions, they will *never* fully understand God.

Distinction

A distinction must now be made between two kinds of revelation:

◆ *natural* or *universal* revelation; and
◆ *historical* or *particular* revelation.

Natural revelation refers to the way in which God has made himself generally known to all peoples, at all times and in all places through the wonders of his creation and the patterns within them that people can discern. This form of revelation is very important for eastern religions such as Hinduism, Shintoism and Taoism. These faiths teach that the divine is an impersonal cosmic force that is composed of the forces and laws observed to be at work in the universe.

Historical revelation refers to the way in which God has specifically made himself known to a particular people (e.g. the Hebrews) at a particular time, in a particular place and made his will known to them by saying or doing something that was neither said nor done before. This form of revelation is central to the three Abrahamic faiths: Judaism, Christianity and Islam. All three agree that God's self-disclosure to humanity has been mediated via a series of messengers at particular moments in human history, beginning with Abraham.

Differences

It is at this point that the Abrahamic faiths diverge sharply from one another.

◆ Christians believe that Jesus of Nazareth is the Messiah and that Judaism's sacred text, the Tenakh, points towards him. Through his life, death and resurrection, Jesus fulfilled the revelations of God to the Jewish prophets.

◆ Jews reject Christian claims that their faith is fulfilled in the revelations recorded in the Christian New Testament.

◆ Both Jews and Christians reject the Islamic claims that Muhammad was the last prophet of Allah (God) and that the Qur'an corrects the revelations of both the Jewish and Christian faiths.

Further, as one commentator notes:

Islam places a unique emphasis on scripture as the means of God's revelation, and indeed views Judaism and Christianity alongside Islam as the three great 'religions of the book'. However, in the sense that Muslims understand it, Judaism and Christianity are not religions of the book. Unlike Muslims who believe that the Qur'an was actually dictated word for word by God, neither Jews nor Christians believe that a heavenly author has actually written the Bible; the Bible is the inspired word of God, but it is through the many different human authors of the Bible that we find the one Word of God. In addition, Jews and Christians would be slow to accept the Muslim designation as religions of the book because it might be seen to neglect their belief that God reveals himself primarily in and through

history. Not only is this a core tenet of the Judaeo-Christian view of revelation but also it is not to be found in any of the other great world religions.

(from John Catoir, *World Religions.*)

Questions

1. Explain the term '*monotheism*'.

2. Why did *Abram* change his name to *Abraham*?

3. What did Abraham teach his fellow Hebrews?

4. How influential has Abraham been in human history?

5. Explain the term '*revelation*', both generally and in a specifically religious sense.

6. Why do the Abrahamic faiths teach that revelation is *necessary*?

7. Explain the differences between (a) *natural revelation* and (b) *historical revelation*.

8. In what ways do the Abrahamic faiths differ among themselves regarding revelation?

One God

The most famous argument in favour of monotheism is that advanced by St Thomas Aquinas. Here is a summary of his argument:

◆ God must be *one* because by '*God*' we mean a Being who is completely perfect in every way, that is, *unique*;

◆ if another god existed, then that god would have to be perfect in a way that God is *not*. This would mean that God would be lacking in some way, as God would *not* be completely perfect, and so would not really be 'God' at all;

The Eternal Father, by Veronese (Paolo Caliari).

- God must, by definition, be completely perfect, unique and therefore *one*;
- consequently, there can be only *one* God.

But what kind of God?

Talking About God

A difficulty now arises: how can human beings say anything worthwhile about God if God is so unique, so unlike anyone or anything else?

St Thomas Aquinas offered an answer based on an analysis of the way human beings use language, which most thinkers ever since have found both useful and convincing.

He divided words up into three different types:

1. *Univocal:* where two words are used in exactly the same sense, e.g. John is tall; Mary is tall.
2. *Equivocal:* where two words are used in altogether different senses, e.g. Peter types an e-mail; a cat is a type of animal.
3. *Analogical:* where two words 'share' a sense of meaning, e.g. God is good; Susan is good.

Here, Susan is *not* understood to be '*good*' in exactly the same way as God is '*good*'. Jews, Christians and Muslims believe that God's goodness must far surpass human goodness. Yet Susan's goodness does point towards, and help people to appreciate, something of the truth of God's goodness.

This type of analogy is called a *metaphor* (unlike a simile, it does not use the words 'like', 'as' or 'than').

The New Testament makes extensive use of metaphor. Jesus told his listeners that God is '*our Father*'. Analogy, therefore, allows human beings to talk about God in a meaningful, albeit limited, way.

The sacred texts of the Abrahamic faiths make extensive use of metaphor. These three religions use the following words to describe God:

- **Transcendent:** God is utterly beyond anything we know. God's greatness surpasses human imagination.
- **Immanent:** God is present in and involved with life in the universe.
- **Omnipotent:** God is all-powerful.
- **Omniscient:** God is all-knowing.
- **Omnipresent:** God is present everywhere.
- **Eternal:** God has always existed and will always exist.

Above all, they emphasise that God is a *person*, *not* an impersonal cosmic force, who has infinite love for human beings. It is because God possesses the personal attributes of goodness, intelligence and freedom that human beings are able to communicate with God through prayer and meditation.

N.B.

The Christian View of God

Judaism, Christianity and Islam are all firmly monotheistic. However, Christians differ from other monotheists in that they believe there are three divine persons—the Father, the Son and the Holy Spirit—in the one God. This is known as the Doctrine of the Trinity.

Questions

1. Why does St Thomas Aquinas claim that there can be only *one* God?

2. Explain each of the following ways of using words:
   - univocal;
   - equivocal;
   - analogical.

3. (a) What is a *metaphor*?
   (b) Why is the use of metaphor important when talking about God?

4. Consider the *positive* and *negative* aspects of Christians using the metaphor '*God is our Father*'.

5. Explain the following terms as applied to God:
   - transcendent;
   - immanent;
   - omnipotent;
   - omniscient;
   - omnipresent;
   - eternal.

6. How is Christian monotheism *different* from that of Judaism and Islam?

Prayer

So far we have considered how the world's religions each offers its own set of insights into the origin, meaning and purpose of life. But they also seek to meet people's need *to love* and to *be loved*.

Traditionally, religions have provided a response to people's desire for perfection, their longing for peace, harmony and happiness, their need for comfort and their wish to have someone to thank for the beauty of nature. Prayer springs from all of these different aims, needs and desires. It is an ancient and distinctively human practice.

Essentially prayer involves:

the raising of the mind and heart to God (or to gods) in an attitude of trust and humility.

Prayer is of central importance in the Abrahamic faiths. It is a way of turning the self towards the divine presence in one's life and entering into some form of relationship with God. The goal of prayer is not only to connect with the divine but also to *transform* the life of the one who prays. *Genuine* prayer is always characterised by honesty and sincerity and always accompanied by good moral actions. Indeed, within the Abrahamic faiths the most authentic prayers are said to be those which put the welfare of *others* ahead of one's own.

Prayer and worship are closely *connected*, for one cannot pray without worshipping, and any form of worship includes some sort of prayer. Worship is not just participation in a communal ritual, it is also an entire attitude of mind and heart that is rooted in a profound love and respect of God (or gods).

Prayer may be:

- vocal or non-vocal;
- spoken or sung;
- private or communal.

↓

Different circumstances give rise to different kinds of prayer.

1 Worship
When we experience a sense of mystery and wonder, either in nature or the love of another person, and glorify God.

2 Petition
When we acknowledge how frail our lives are, how quickly they can end and acknowledge our need for God.

3 Intercession
When we witness another's suffering, wish to help, but are unable to improve matters and ask for God's aid.

4 Confession
When we realise that we have failed to do the right thing and ask for God's forgiveness.

5 Protection
When we are faced with the threat of being overpowered by evil and ask for the strength to endure and not be overcome.

6 Thanksgiving
When we want to offer our gratitude for something, but find words inadequate to express it.

Prayer and Symbolism in Judaism

In Judaism, daily prayers are said both at home and in the synagogue. Jewish beliefs about prayer are symbolised by the wearing of special clothing. **For example:**

(1) It is traditional for practicing male Jews to wear a *yarmulke* (small round cap) to show reverence for God above all else.

(2) The Jewish male also attaches two *tefillen* (phylacteries—small leather cubes containing the *Shema*) to two parts of the body, i.e.
- to the forehead, to remind him to concentrate his mind on serving God;
- to his left arm, to remind him to put his faith into action by pursuing justice, showing kindness and being faithful to God and to others.

Jews do not wear *tefillen* on the Sabbath or on festival days.

THE LORD'S PRAYER
Matthew 6:9–13

Form	Prayer	Focus	Christian Explanation

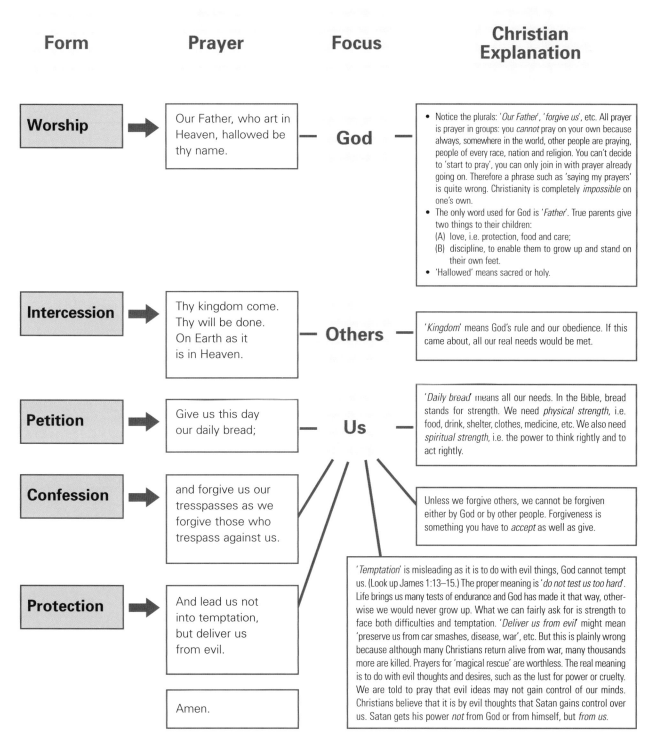

Worship → Our Father, who art in Heaven, hallowed be thy name. — **God** —

- Notice the plurals: '*Our Father*', '*forgive us*', etc. All prayer is prayer in groups: you *cannot* pray on your own because always, somewhere in the world, other people are praying, people of every race, nation and religion. You can't decide to 'start to pray', you can only join in with prayer already going on. Therefore a phrase such as 'saying my prayers' is quite wrong. Christianity is completely *impossible* on one's own.
- The only word used for God is '*Father*'. True parents give two things to their children:
  (A) love, i.e. protection, food and care;
  (B) discipline, to enable them to grow up and stand on their own feet.
- 'Hallowed' means sacred or holy.

Intercession → Thy kingdom come. Thy will be done. On Earth as it is in Heaven. — **Others** —

'*Kingdom*' means God's rule and our obedience. If this came about, all our real needs would be met.

Petition → Give us this day our daily bread; — **Us** —

'*Daily bread*' means all our needs. In the Bible, bread stands for strength. We need *physical strength*, i.e. food, drink, shelter, clothes, medicine, etc. We also need *spiritual strength*, i.e. the power to think rightly and to act rightly.

Confession → and forgive us our tresspasses as we forgive those who trespass against us.

Unless we forgive others, we cannot be forgiven either by God or by other people. Forgiveness is something you have to *accept* as well as give.

Protection → And lead us not into temptation, but deliver us from evil.

'*Temptation*' is misleading as it is to do with evil things, God cannot tempt us. (Look up James 1:13–15.) The proper meaning is '*do not test us too hard*'. Life brings us many tests of endurance and God has made it that way, otherwise we would never grow up. What we can fairly ask for is strength to face both difficulties and temptation. '*Deliver us from evil*' might mean 'preserve us from car smashes, disease, war', etc. But this is plainly wrong because although many Christians return alive from war, many thousands more are killed. Prayers for 'magical rescue' are worthless. The real meaning is to do with evil thoughts and desires, such as the lust for power or cruelty. We are told to pray that evil ideas may not gain control of our minds. Christians believe that it is by evil thoughts that Satan gains control over us. Satan gets his power *not* from God or from himself, but *from us*.

Amen.

Questions

1. What is *prayer*?

2. Why is prayer of central importance in the Abrahamic faiths?

3. What is the goal of prayer?

4. In what way are prayer and worship closely connected?

5. Identify the different situations that give rise to prayer.

6. Read the following extract:

   When you pray, do not imitate the hypocrites: they love to say their prayers standing up at the street corners for people to see them. I tell you solemnly, they have had their reward. But when you pray, go to your private room and, when you have shut your door, pray to your Father who sees all.

   (Matthew 6:5–6)

   What advice does Jesus of Nazareth offer people here about *authentic* prayer?

7. Read the following extract:

   Unanswered Prayer
   Sometimes we think prayer is not answered. This is because most of us cling to a childish view of prayer. We think of it as a set of requests followed by answers or refusals. But true prayer is finding out about oneself and finding out about God; then trying to fit oneself round God and not bend God to one's own ideas.
   Prayer may seem unanswered because:
   1. Our prayer may be meaningless nonsense, asking for magic, e.g. praying for a successful exam result when we've done no work. But God does not do such things.
   2. Our own personal sins may be in the way of an answer, e.g. it's

foolish to pray for a recovery from a lung cancer, if we go on smoking.

3. *We may not be willing to pay the price, i.e. to get what we want, our characters would have to change and we won't.*
4. *The general sins in our society, school, factory, or nation may make our requests unrealistic, e.g. the bad behaviour of a school may simply be due more to overcrowding than to deliberate wickedness.*
5. *What we want might hurt people of whom we know nothing.*
6. *There is more to it than we realise. Some things can't be changed; God has made his laws and keeps them. Our prayer may involve changing things which can't be changed, e.g. you can't pray for a new leg to grow. True prayer is asking for a sense of responsibility, so that you will trust that Love will find a way through the situation (not out of it, but through it).*

(E.J. Taylor, *Problems of Christian Living*.)

How would the author of this extract respond to someone who claims that *'Prayer is a waste of time because even if you ask for something, nothing changes'*?

8. How would you respond to someone who asserts that *'Prayer is a waste of time because you are just talking to yourself'*? Explain your answer.

Religious Faith

Introduction

In common parlance to believe something means to accept that it is true.

Beliefs of every description rule our everyday lives. They are all the many things we take for granted, such as:

◆ the sun will rise tomorrow morning;
◆ the law of gravity always prevails;
◆ there is an explanation for everything that happens.

Consider how often we believe things because we accept the authority of another person's statement on the matter. For instance, if I want to know the average distance between the Earth and its moon, I consult an astronomer. She informs me that it is approximately 238,800 miles. Not only do I not have the specialist knowledge or instruments needed to personally verify the truth of what she says, I do not even intend to do so. As she is an authority in the field, I accept her word. In other words, I believe her because I have faith in her expertise.

Belief and faith are closely inter-related:

◆ belief involves acceptance that some idea or thing is correct;

◆ faith indicates trust that what one is told is, in fact, true.

Clearly belief and faith are vitally important for us. What we accept and who we choose to trust has an enormous impact, both on our own life and on the lives of others, too. It shapes our decisions about how we should think and act.

Christ on the Sea of Galilee, by Jack Hayes. Faith provides encouragement and strength in troubled times.

Importance

One of the highest compliments we can pay another person is to say, 'I have faith in you'. Faith is an essential ingredient of all meaningful human relationships. Not surprisingly, it is also fundamental to those religions that invite people to enter into a relationship with God.

A preliminary definition of religious faith would be:

a willingness to trust in God, a willingness to trust that God exists and is near, whatever the appearances to the contrary may indicate.

(Maurice Reidy, *The God I believe in and why*)

Psychologists and sociologists note that religious faith appears to meet a number of basic human needs:

- it provides people with a sense of meaning and purpose in their daily lives and personal choices;
- it offers comfort and hope when people experience uncertainty and tragedy;
- it encourages people to believe that they can direct their own lives and that their actions will have some predictable outcome now or in the afterlife;
- it offers guidance and rules according to which people can conduct their lives in the belief that, by so doing, their actions will be more often right than wrong;
- through public rituals it forges and renews communal bonds by bringing people together to celebrate life's most important moments;
- in its shared belief system and public expression it meets a deep human need for a positive feeling of identity (Who am I?) and belonging (with whom can I feel a sense of community?);
- it helps people to interpret phenomena that are not explicable in terms of the empirical sciences.

Questions

1. In what way are belief and faith closely inter-related?

2. *'Faith is an essential ingredient of all meaningful human relationships.'* Do you agree or disagree? Explain your answer. ➡

3. What is meant by *'religious faith'*?

4. Identify any *four* human needs that are said to be met by religious faith.

The perceived importance of religion and its impact on adolescents

Researchers from Albert Einstein College of Medicine, Yeshiva University, New York, conducted a study of a sample of 1,182 adolescents (i.e. those in the stage between childhood and adulthood). They surveyed them on four different occasions from 7th grade through 10th grade and tracked these adolescents' alcohol consumptions, cigarette smoking, marijuana use and perception of religion through early to late teens. This enabled the researchers to take into account any developmental changes that occurred during these years that might influence their use of these substances.

They concluded that when adolescents perceive religion to be a meaningful and important part of their lives

◆ they were half as likely to use these substances than adolescents who did not view religion as important

Pilgrims attend the World Youth Day opening Mass at the RheinEnergie Stadium in Cologne, Germany, 2005.

◆ it provided them with a way to cope with life stressors or hardships such as having an unemployed parent or being ill themselves.

This phenomenon is known as a 'buffering effect', from the concept that something about religiosity (i.e. the condition of being religious) serves to reduce or lessen the impact of adverse circumstances.

The effect of religiosity was not limited by ethnicity, as comparable effects were for adolescents from all of the ethnic groups in the study (African-Americans, Hispanics and Caucasians).

According to team leader Dr Thomas Wills:

These buffering effects could be occurring because religiosity may influence a person's

attitudes and values, providing meaning and purpose in life. It could also help persons to view problems in a different way ... besides offering coping techniques, being involved in a religion can also create more healthy social networks than adolescents would have if they got involved in drugs to find social outlets.

(This research was supported by the US National Institute on Drug Abuse. Adapted from 'Buffering Effect of Religiosity for Adolescent Substance Use', *Psychology of Addictive Behaviours*, Vol. 17, no. 1 (2003).)

Questions

1. What were the consequences for those adolescents who perceived religion to be a meaningful and important part of their lives?

2. Describe the phenomenon known as *'the buffering effect'*.

3. What did Dr Wills conclude were the reasons for this buffering effect due to religiosity? Do you agree or disagree with him? Explain your answer.

Criticism

A. Religious faith is childish

In his book *The God Delusion*, Professor Richard Dawkins, a noted atheist, asserts that religious faith is essentially *childish*. He claims that to believe in

God is as immature as believing in the existence of the Tooth Fairy or Santa Claus.

Professor Alister McGrath, a former atheist who converted to Christianity, *rejects* Dawkins' claim that religious faith is infantile. He responds:

... the analogy is obviously flawed. How many people do you know who began to believe in

Santa Claus in adulthood? Or who found belief in the Tooth Fairy in old age? I believed in Santa Claus until I was about five (though, not unaware of the benefits it brought, I allowed my parents to think I took it seriously until rather later). I did not believe in God until I started going to university. Those who use this infantile argument have to explain why so many people discover God later in life, and certainly do not regard this as representing any kind of regression, perversion or degeneration. A good recent example is provided by Anthony Flew, the noted atheist philosopher who started to believe in God in his eighties.

(Professor Alister McGrath, *The Dawkins' Delusion*.)

B. Religious faith is irrational

Professor Dawkins also claims that religious faith is *irrational* because, in his view, it involves *blind trust in the absence of evidence.*

However, Professor Keith Ward, another former atheist who became a Christian, rejects this claim. He argues that Dawkins' criticism is based on *a far too narrow idea of reasonableness.* He writes:

Some critics of religion think that the only reasonable beliefs are those that can be confirmed by the methods of science—by public observation, measurement and experiment.

The trouble with that statement is that it is self-refuting. It is not itself confirmable with observation and experiment. So, according to its own criterion of reasonableness, it cannot be reasonable.

This is admittedly a very short argument. But it has the advantage of being absolutely conclusive. If only scientifically testable state-

A man prays at the Wailing Wall (in Hebrew: *Hakotel Hama'aravi*) in Jerusalem. The wall was built in 20 BC to support the Second Temple, which was destroyed by the Romans in AD 70. The wall remained as a site of pilgrimage, a place where Jews could come to lament the loss of the Temple, hence 'Wailing' Wall.

ments are reasonable, then this statement (that 'only scientifically testable statements are reasonable') is not reasonable. Conversely, if this statement is reasonable, then some statements are reasonable that are not scientifically testable. So the statement is either unreasonable or false.

Many of the most important beliefs we have in life are not scientifically testable, but we still live our whole lives by them. I have beliefs about what happened in history, about whether my partner loves me or not, about what sorts of act are morally right, about what sort of music is of the greatest worth, about what political policies we should adopt, about whether I can trust my friends. There are thousands of things I believe that are not scientifically testable. Quite a lot of them, I hope, are reasonable.

(Professor Keith Ward, *Is Religion Dangerous?*)

C. Religious faith is anti-scientific

Professor Dawkins further declares religious faith to be inherently *anti-scientific* and cites as evidence the opposition of religious fundamentalists, both Christian and Muslim, to Darwin's theory of evolution.

However, as Seamus Murphy, a Jesuit philosopher, points out:

The problem with this view is that it is selective to the point of falsehood. It forgets the development of the modern Gregorian calendar by the Vatican. It ignores so much else: the thirty craters on the moon named after Jesuit astronomers, the fact that the father of genetics was a Catholic monk named Gregor Mendel, the role of Fr Georges Lemaitre in the emergence of 'Big Bang' cosmology, and much more. In any case this distorted view ignores the fact that many, possibly most, of the great names in science (e.g. Galileo, Newton and Faraday) were committed Christians. This must count as over-whelming evidence of Christianity's support for science.

Even if it is accepted that many distinguished scientists have also been religious believers, it is still hinted that their science and their religion had to be kept apart, since religion's influence on science, where it occurs, is necessarily negative. Yet this claim won't stand up to close examination either.

What we call 'science' emerged in Europe between 1600 and 1900, i.e. in a socio-cultural world where the Judeo-Christian ethos was all-pervasive. So, those who insist religion is anti-scientific are committed to the odd and implausible thesis that modern science emerged from an inherently hostile matrix. If Christianity had any effect, it is historically more likely to have helped science to emerge.

Christian faith has no direct connection to science. But some of its philosophical assumptions cleared the intellectual space within which science became possible. The Church taught that the physical world is not an illusion, and so there is something to study; that it is not evil, and so not likely to contaminate; that it is not divine and hence not blasphemous to investigate. It taught that the world is the product of a rational mind, and hence supports the belief of the scientist that the universe is intelligible and that there are scientific truths to be found.

(Adapted from 'Secularism and Religion: Time for Dialogue' in *Doctrine and Life*, Vol. 55, No. 6.)

Sir Isaac Newton (1710), by Sir James Thornhill.

Questions

1.　(a)　How does Alister McGrath respond to Richard Dawkins' claim that religious faith is *childish*?

　　(b)　With whom do you agree? Give reasons for your choice.

2.　(a)　How does Keith Ward respond to Richard Dawkins' claim that religious faith is *irrational*?

　　(b)　With whom do you agree? Give reasons for your choice.

3.　(a)　How does Seamus Murphy S.J. respond to Richard Dawkins' claim that religious faith is inherently *anti-scientific*?

　　(b)　With whom do you agree? Give reasons for your choice.

D. Religious faith is a form of escapism

In his book *The Future of an Illusion*, Dr Sigmund Freud (d. 1939) caused considerable controversy by declaring that religious faith is a form of *neurosis*, i.e. a treatable mental disorder. He elaborated on this by describing religious faith as essentially both *a defence mechanism* and *wish-fulfilment*.

1.　A defence mechanism
Freud claimed that all religious faith is the product of:
◆　the human experience of helplessness in a hostile world;
◆　the human desire for some all-powerful being who will intervene and rescue those who worship him.

2.　Wish-fulfilment
Freud claimed that religious belief was merely:
◆　a symptom of immaturity on the part of people who cannot accept the limitations of their actual

Sigmund Freud (1856–1936).

'*earthly*' parents and so dream up a perfect '*heavenly*' parent instead;

◆ a flight from reality and an acceptance of an illusional reassurance that there is justice in an unjust world, meaning in a meaningless world and an eternal reward for enduring suffering in this life.

Some people still claim that Freud explained away religious faith, revealing it to be nothing more than a form of escapism that is practised only by those who are insecure and delusional.

Response to Freud

Freud himself believed he had inflicted a death blow to all forms of religious faith. However, he failed to realise that there were a number of key weaknesses in his work. Critics of Freud's work have pointed out that:

◆ Freud *assumed* that *all* religious faith in God was a neurosis. He never seems to have considered that this might apply only to the particular beliefs of some people;

◆ although a person's attitude to his/her father/mother might influence his/her attitude towards God, this does *not* necessarily lead to the conclusion that God is only a figment of the human imagination and does not exist;

◆ to say that many people *wish* that a loving God exists no more automatically means that such a God does *not* exist than it means to say that such a God does exist. It does *not* decide the issue one way or the other;

◆ Freud thought that if faith in God was revealed to be nothing but an illusion, then all religions would eventually fade away as people came to realise that their only hope for salvation lay with the advance of scientific knowledge. However, Freud never appeared to question his own faith in the capacity of the natural sciences to answer all of humanity's most profound needs;

◆ indeed, it is now recognised that Freud's rejection of religious faith owes more to private speculation than to scientific observation. He did not present a decisive argument for rejecting religious faith. He merely cast light on how some people's faith is built on inadequate foundations;

◆ Freud never made a secret of the fact that he was an *atheist*. However, he was an atheist *before* he ever made a study of religious faith. He did *not* become an atheist because of it. In fact, his biographer, Ernest Jones, discovered a letter Freud wrote in which he made clear his unhappiness at having to read through books on religion *before* writing on the subject. Freud considered this a waste of time because he *already* knew the answer as to why people believed in God. He wrote: '*I am reading (religion) books without being really interested in them, since I already know the results*' (Ernest Jones, *Sigmund Freud*, Vol. II, p.394);

◆ finally, Freud seems to have been unable to recognise that genuine religious faith is anything but an exercise in escapism or is easier than facing up to reality. He did not take into account how it has motivated so many people to perform extraordinary acts of goodness. One outstanding example would be the devotion of Mother Teresa of Calcutta to caring for the homeless, rescuing abandoned babies and giving the terminally ill a dignified death.

Freud's critics maintain that he was quite wrong. Authentic religious faith does *not* involve people hiding behind illusions. Indeed, it can fill people's lives with real meaning and purpose and can direct them towards the achievement of true and lasting happiness.

Questions

1. Explain what Sigmund Freud meant when he described religious belief as (a) a defence mechanism and (b) wish-fulfilment.

2. Did Freud offer a decisive argument for rejecting all forms of religious faith? Explain your answer.

3. Some of Freud's critics claim that his rejection of religious faith stemmed primarily from his own atheistic prejudices rather than hard experimental evidence. What evidence is there to support such a claim? Do you agree/disagree? Explain your answer.

Religious Faith in Action: Dom Helder Camara

One of the most famous and relentless advocates of social reform throughout the world was Helder Camara, who in 1931, as he celebrated his first mass at the age of twenty-two, tried to preach in the most elegant and learned words he knew. One of his teachers told him to stop being foolish—that from now on he was to speak for simple and humble people. As priest, bishop and later archbishop of Olinda and Recife in Brazil, he spent his life doing just that.

Camara was desperately concerned about human rights and spoke out against oppression throughout the world, especially that of the rich nations against the poor ones. The arms trade and destruction of the environment were, in his eyes, all part of the same problem, and he strongly criticised the Brazilian government for its human rights' abuses, earning their hatred. Not only did he spend nine years officially not existing, with all references to him in the media forbidden, but there were assassination attempts made against him. Many of the assassins sent against him could not bring themselves to kill him and instead confessed all and asked his forgiveness. The government nicknamed him 'the Red Bishop'. Camara commented once, 'When I give food to the poor, they call me a saint. When I ask why the poor have no food, they call me a Communist.'

To the people, the physically tiny bishop was known simply as Dom Helder. He identified with their simplicity to such a degree as to share it: as archbishop he renounced the palace that went with the post and lived instead in a single back room of the church, furnished with little more than a table, a sink and a hammock. Instead of using an official car, he hitchhiked around the city.

Like Mahatma Gandhi in India, he was deeply committed to peaceful protest and the repudiation of violence. He organised the movement Justice and Peace Action to promote these ideals. The movement was made up in part of what were known as 'Abrahamic minorities'—small groups at the local level that were committed to observing and understanding the plight of the poor and helping them in their own areas. These groups tran-

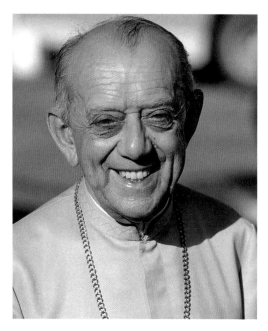

Dom Helder Camara.

scended the Catholic Church to include members from all faith traditions and none.

Dom Helder was nominated four times for the Nobel Peace Prize, and when he died in 1999, the Brazilian president declared three days of national mourning.

(Adapted from J. Hill, *What has Christianity done for us?*)

Questions

1. What were the issues that concerned Dom Helder Camara?

2. How did the Brazilian authorities initially react to his statements and actions?

3. What was *'Justice and Peace Action'*?

4. Could Dom Helder Camara's religious faith be described as *'childish'*, *'irrational'* or *'escapist'*? Explain your answer.

5. Did his religious faith show evidence of true *'personal engagement'*? Give reasons for your answer.

6. Do you agree or disagree with his actions? Explain your answer.

7. What might Dom Helder Camara's life story be said to reveal about the value of religious faith in today's world?

Meaning and Implications

For Jews, Christians and Muslims religious faith involves:

◆ belief in one God, who is the creator and sustainer of all things;

◆ love of God;

◆ acceptance of all God has revealed, as recorded in their sacred texts;

◆ trust in God's plan for creation.

Religious faith is not, by any means, blind. True, it does involve a degree of risk: one's faith could be misplaced; one's beliefs could be mistaken. However, those with religious faith have confidence that God is reliable. This is based partly on their own personal life experiences and partly on what they consider to be the veracity of the stories recorded in their sacred texts.

Non-religious commentators sometimes equate religious belief with an unfounded, unrealistic optimism

Parents and children praying and holding hands at table.

that is expressed in a relentlessly simplistic outlook on life. Neither Judaism, Christianity nor Islam (certainly not in their mainstream varieties) could be accused of this. Each in its own way offers a perspective on life that seeks to transform people's understanding of themselves and help them to work out the implications

Sunday service at Westminster Cathedral, London.

and comforts them when the situation seems bleak.

Jews, Christians and Muslims agree that it is not possible for human beings to achieve religious faith purely by their own unaided efforts. Communication between God and human beings cannot occur without God's assistance. This is why faith is described as a 'gift', or 'grace', given by God to human beings. It is God, not us, who initiates the relationship. God offers us an invitation, which we are free to accept or reject.

The implications of accepting God's invitation are enormous. Religious faith demands personal engagement—it is active, not passive. To truly be a Jew or a Christian or a Muslim is to adopt a completely distinctive way of thinking and living.

The members of these religions are called upon to:

◆ develop their relationship with God through frequent prayer and meditation;

◆ share and strengthen this relationship through regular participation in communal worship;

◆ educate themselves so as to deepen their appreciation for and understanding of the mysteries of God and creation;

◆ commit themselves to live out the love of God by treating others and the world we all share with love and respect.

of this. Thus, although religious persons may be as distressed as anyone else by the suffering experienced in this world, their distress is experienced within a God-believing context. This challenges them to do something positive to help, encourages them not to lose hope

Questions

1. According to Judaism, Christianity and Islam, what does *religious faith* involve?

2. How would mainstream members of these religions respond to the claim that *religious faith is blind*?

3. What does it mean to describe religious faith as a *gift*?

Abolition of Slavery's Faith-based Roots

In the fierce struggles of the 19th century to abolish slavery, Abraham Lincoln remains the mythic American champion. On this side of the Atlantic, however, that honour belongs to William Wilberforce, the Christian activist and member of Parliament who thundered against the slave trade for 20 years.

When Wilberforce first raised his voice in the House of Commons for the cause of abolition in May 1789, he spoke for three and a half hours. Yet the absence of partisanship must have taken his colleagues by surprise. 'I mean not to accuse anyone,' he insisted, 'but take the shame upon myself, in common indeed with the whole Parliament of Britain, for having permitted this horrid trade to be carried on under their authority.'

Wilberforce built a human rights coalition that cut across political and ideological lines, uniting Whigs with establishment Tories and Anglicans with evangelicals and Quakers. His success, it seems, owed much to his genuine devotion to the plight of African slaves, regardless of the political costs.

British traders who raided the West African coast captured 35,000 to 50,000 Africans a year, but the wretched conditions of slave ships bound for the Americas, France, Portugal and Spain were not widely known. Thousands perished from disease or starvation. 'So much misery condensed in so little room,' Wilberforce said, 'is more than the human imagination has ever before conceived.'

The lure of profits and cheap supplies of sugar and tobacco kept the chattel machine running. Historians estimate that in Liverpool alone, a commercial hub for the

Portrait of William Wilberforce (1759–1833), by William Lane.

trade, about 17 million pounds changed hands in a single year. Wilberforce, himself a man of privilege, understood the entrenched economic interests involved yet somehow managed to win many of them over.

A convert to evangelical Christianity, Wilberforce is greatly admired in religious circles today, if not always imitated. Early in his parliamentary career, he made a vow to avoid the corruptions of political influence —and kept it. He was known for his intellectual seriousness and personal charm. French author Madame de Stael confessed her surprise after dining with him: 'I have always heard that he was the most religious, but I now find that he is the wittiest man in England.'

Wilberforce sought to change hearts and minds, not just laws. So he organized boycotts and petitions, staged demonstrations and commissioned artwork to mobilise public opinion on a national scale. Wilberforce suffered many setbacks—his abolition bills were repeatedly killed in committee or defeated in the House of Commons—but he kept on.

Most important, he was unafraid to invoke the moral obligations of the Gospel to challenge the consciences of slavers and their supporters in Parliament. In his Letter on the Abolition of the Slave Trade, published in January 1807, Wilberforce placed the brutish facts of human trafficking against the backdrop of Christian compassion and divine justice. 'We must believe,' he warned, 'that a continued course of wickedness, oppression and cruelty, obstinately maintained in spite of the fullest knowledge and the loudest warnings, must infallibly bring down upon us the heaviest judgments of the Almighty.' A month later, on February 23, the House of Commons voted 283 to 16 to abolish the slave trade.

In our post-9/11 era, there's suspicion and antagonism toward religious faith, especially when it mixes with politics. Writers such as Richard Dawkins and Sam Harris describe the beliefs of the faithful as a 'delusion' and akin to 'insanity'. Wilberforce endured similar scorn. He was lampooned for his 'damnable doctrine' and dismissed as a 'treacherous fanatic'.

Modern sceptics should remember that the great campaign against the international slave trade was led and fought by people with deep Christian convictions about the dignity and freedom of every person made in the image of God.

Today, we face our own assaults on human rights—including the sexual trafficking of women and girls, genocidal violence in Sudan and the prison camps of North Korea.

Surely we need more of Wilberforce's brand of faith today, not less.

(Adapted from Joseph Loconte, 'British Abolition's Faith-Based Roots', *Los Angeles Times*, 21 February 2007.)

Questions

1. Who was William Wilberforce?

2. How large and lucrative was the slave trade when he began his campaign to have it abolished?

3. Describe Wilberforce's personality.

4. How did he finally convince the British parliament to outlaw slavery?

5. How might the statement *'religious faith demands personal engagement'* be said to apply to William Wilberforce's life? Explain your answer.

The Existence of God

Introduction

Over the centuries many religious thinkers have tried, with varying degrees of success, to demonstrate that there are sound reasons for belief in the existence of God. *Before* we consider what some of these writers have to offer, it is necessary to do five things:

1. Clarify what is meant by '*God*'.
2. Explain *the method* by which one should approach the question of God's existence.
3. Examine *the limitations* one faces when exploring this issue.
4. Consider *the appropriate attitude* to adopt.
5. Be aware of *the importance* of the issues at stake.

The meaning of God

Thinkers in the Jewish, Christian and Islamic faiths use the term '*God*' exclusively in reference to the Being who possesses the following characteristics:

1. **Uniqueness**

   God alone is:

   ◆ eternal—having neither a beginning nor an end;
   ◆ infinite—without limitations of any kind;
   ◆ omnipotent—all-powerful;
   ◆ omniscient—all-knowing.

Man and Woman Gazing at the Moon, by Caspar David Friedrich.

2. Transcendence

God is greater than, independent of and distinct from the world he created.

3. Immanence

God is the one who sustains all things and is presently active in bringing his plan for creation to fruition.

4. Ultimate Mystery

God's truth and goodness are vast beyond compare. Nothing greater than God can be conceived. One can only seek to gain insights into and grow in understanding of God through prayer, study and the pursuit of goodness.

Method of approach

Over the centuries numerous religious thinkers have devoted considerable effort to examining the grounds for belief in God's existence. One of the most important and influential of these figures was the medieval philosopher and theologian, St Thomas Aquinas.

Before beginning his own investigation, St Thomas asked himself two important questions:

1. *Is it self-evident that there is a God?*
2. *Can God's existence be made evident?*

In answer to the *first* question, St Thomas declared that God's existence was not self-evident. The reasons for this were:

- if God's existence were self-evident, then no one would ever raise such a question in the first place;
- as God is believed to be a pure spirit (i.e. a being without a physical body), God cannot be observed directly by human beings (i.e. they cannot hear, see or touch God).

The Apotheosis of St Thomas Aquinas, by Francisco de Zurbaran. St Thomas Aquinas, one of the most influential scholars in the history of the Catholic Church, wrote on issues of wide-ranging philosophical importance.

In answer to the *second* question, however, St Thomas stated his conviction that although there was no direct evidence to support belief in God's existence, there was *indirect* evidence to support such a belief. St Thomas claimed that if people reflected on what they experience and observe happening in the world around them, they would find good grounds for believing that God does indeed exist.

Limitations

Any discussion of God's existence quickly stretches the human imagination and the language used to express it to the very limit. Indeed, the great philosophers who strained their intellects on this question were only too aware of the limitations of the different arguments they formulated in favour of God's existence. It is now generally accepted that no single thinker has succeeded in advancing anything like a clear-cut, undeniable proof of God's existence—but neither has anyone succeeded in denying it.

People are sometimes disappointed to discover that there is no neat, watertight formula that can offer them an undeniable solution to the question of whether or not God exists. This reaction is perhaps understandable given the all-pervasive influence of the methods of the natural sciences on most people's outlook. Most are used to thinking of life as a series of problems to be confronted and solved, whereas the question of God's existence is a *mystery* to be encountered and explored.

Religious thinkers claim that the best they can

'There are answers to be found, but our capacity to unlock them is limited.'

offer are strong reasons to justify one's belief in God. They readily admit that asserting God's existence is an act of faith, but insist that it is one grounded in reason, not in fantasy.

Attitude

People are sometimes surprised to discover that those with a deep, mature religious faith are not only aware that there may be legitimate grounds for challenging the arguments in favour of God's existence but are unafraid to *admit* it openly. Nonetheless, a number of religious thinkers have voiced their concern about the growing number of people in our society who, without realising it, have fallen into a mindset that *assumes* that it is impossible to offer rational grounds for belief in God's existence. Such an attitude prevents any discussion on the matter from ever starting.

Religious thinkers such as John Haldane and Richard Swinbourne ask people to adopt the same attitude when debating God's existence as they would on other key issues—that is, to approach the question in a fair, respectful and open-minded way.

Importance

At this point one might ask:

> Don't I have *enough* things to think about?

> Why devote time and effort to the question of God's existence?

> After all, suppose God did not exist. Would it really make any *difference*?

One writer who set out to answer the last question was a convinced atheist named Bertrand Russell. With chilling clarity and brutal honesty, Russell set out the consequences for human beings of living in a universe in which God does not exist. He wrote:

> No heroism, no intensity of thought and feeling can preserve an individual life beyond the grave … all the labours of the ages, all the noonday brightness of human genius are destined to extinction in the vast death of the solar system, and … the whole temple of humanity's achievements must inevitably be buried in the debris of a universe in ruins.

(Bertrand Russell, *Sceptical Essays.*)

The question of God's existence is therefore of utterly *fundamental* importance. It goes to the very heart of the most profound question one can ask:

Does my life have a meaning and a purpose?

Religious writers assert that:
◆ the existence of God is *inextricably linked* to the question as to whether or not there is life after death. The strongest arguments for eternal life presuppose the existence of a benevolent God who rewards the good and punishes the wicked;
◆ it is because God exists and that there is a life after death that people have genuine reason for hope when facing life's challenges and so are encouraged to do good and avoid doing evil.

It is little wonder, then, that people are asked to approach the question of God's existence with due care and respect for the serious issues it raises.

Questions

1. Explain the meaning of the following terms as applied to God:
   (a) unique;
   (b) transcendent;
   (c) immanent;
   (d) ultimate mystery.

2. Is it self-evident that there is a God? Explain your answer.

3. How does St Thomas Aquinas recommend that God's existence can be made evident?

4. Why do religious thinkers claim that there is no possibility of a clear-cut, undeniable proof of God's existence?

5. What is the attitude to the question of God's existence that is recommended by thinkers such as John Haldane and Richard Swinbourne? Why do they recommend it? ➡

6. The French philosopher Voltaire once remarked: *'If God did not exist, it would be necessary to invent him.'*

(a) What difference does the existence or non-existence of God make?

(b) Why is this question considered to be so important?

The arguments for the existence of God

Over the centuries Jewish, Christian and Muslim thinkers have offered a variety of arguments to support belief in God's existence. None of them has ever claimed to achieve certainty on this matter. Instead they have sought to demonstrate that the existence of God is more probable than not.

Among the most widely debated and hotly contested of these arguments are the following:

◆ The cosmological argument.
◆ The teleological argument.
◆ The religio-empirical argument.
◆ The moral argument.

All of these are referred to as *a posteriori* arguments because they take our experiences of the world around us as their starting-point and reason from these experiences to the existence of God.

The cosmological argument

Cosmology:
The study of the origin, evolution and large-scale structure of the universe.

Experience shows us that things do not 'just happen' of their own accord. Every event that occurs does so only because someone, or something, *makes* it happen. Consider this equation:

$$0 = 0$$

If one starts out with nothing, one ends up with precisely *nothing*. Only nothing can come from nothing.

Something can only come about if something is added by someone.

Consider the origin of the universe:
After centuries of viewing the universe as static, scientists came to realise that, on the contrary, the universe is *expanding*. They claim that this is due to '*the Big Bang*'—an explosion of almost unimaginable power that occurred about 14 billion years ago and scattered matter across the universe, leading to the development of everything in existence, from snowflakes to stars. It would seem, therefore, that the universe had a beginning. If so, it can reasonably be argued that the universe required an *originator*, i.e. one who caused it to begin. This *first cause* of all that exists is referred to as 'God'.

Objection

Having read the cosmological argument, a person might be inclined to ask:

If God made all things, then who made God?

Canada, Alberta: Crowfoot Mountain and Bow Lake at sunrise.

Such a question involves a fallacy (i.e. an error in reasoning) known as compound questions.

This comprises of combining several questions in such a way as to preclude all opposing arguments and thus place one's opponent in a self-incriminating position.

So to ask 'Who made God?' is like a cross-examining lawyer asking the accused, 'Have you stopped beating your wife?' The only permissible answer to such a question is either 'yes' or 'no' because of all the implications built into the question.

That sort of loaded question is not appropriate here, however. Why?

Two reasons can be given:
1. The question 'Who made God?' assumes that the creation of God is a proven fact (when it is not) in order to justify the search for God's maker.
2. The antecedent to the pronoun 'who' is lacking. If the antecedent *is* God, then the conclusion would be that *God made God*. If the antecedent is not God, then the Being in question *must* be God, while the second 'God' must be an impostor— only a creature and not *the* Creator.

Thus the question 'Who made God?' involves a serious fallacy and therefore does *not* provide a basis for denying God's existence.

Questions

1. What is *cosmology*? ➡

2. Briefly state the cosmological argument.

3. Read the following statement:

> *The Big Bang cries out for a divine explanation. It forces the conclusion that nature had a defined beginning. I cannot see how nature could have created itself. Only a supernatural force that is outside of space and time could have done that.*

(Dr Francis Collins, Director of the Human Genome Project.)

Do you agree/disagree? Give reasons for your answer.

4. How do religious thinkers in the Jewish, Christian and Muslim faiths answer the question, *'Who made God?'*

The teleological argument

> **Teleology:**
> **the explanation of something in terms of its intended aim or purpose.**

Scientists have discovered that a number of factors are necessary for the existence of life on Earth. Consider:

◆ *The size of the Earth*
If the Earth were much smaller, it would not have sufficient gravity to hold the air around it.

◆ *The position of the Earth*
If the earth were nearer to the sun, its inhabitants would be incinerated. If it were farther from the sun, they would freeze.

◆ *The size of the moon*
If the moon was either nearer or bigger, it would cause catastrophic tidal waves to rage across our oceans.

◆ *The position of the planet Jupiter*
If Jupiter—with its massive size and huge gravitational pull—were not in place, then the Earth would be bombarded frequently and devastated by large meteors.

It is due to a combination of these and many other factors that the conditions for the development and continuation of life on Earth exist. The discovery of these factors has led many to wonder *why* this is the case.

The eighteenth-century philosopher William Paley was struck by the order he detected in the natural world. He concluded that this order was more than likely *designed*, rather than the product of pure chance. A design requires a *designer*. This designer is called God.

Modern advocates of Paley's conclusion, such as mathematician John Polkinghorne, claim that evidence of a design or plan can be traced back to the very origin of the universe itself.

The world of the inner solar system.

Consider:

- if, after the Big Bang, the universe had expanded at a rate of 1 per cent faster than it did, it would have been *too fast* for galaxies to form and for life to emerge;

- if, on the other hand, the speed of the universe's expansion had been 1 per cent slower, the universe would not have reached the size it is today. Indeed, it is believed that all the galaxies would by now have been pulled back together by the power of gravity in what is termed 'the Big Crunch'.

It is thus argued that, from the very outset, the universe was designed with precisely the structure and conditions required for the evolution of life, particularly intelligent life, to emerge.

Though not religious, the scientist Freeman Dyson has admitted that:

The more I examine the universe and the details of its architecture, the more evidence I find that the universe in some sense must have known that we were coming.

Theists contend that none of this would be possible without God.

Questions

1. What is *teleology*?
2. Identify four factors that are necessary for the existence of life on Earth.

3. What conclusion did William Paley reach about the evidence for order and design he observed in the natural world?

4. Read the following statement:

The universe we observe has precisely the properties we should expect if there is, at bottom, no design, no purpose, no evil and no good, nothing but blind pitiless indifference.

(Professor Richard Dawkins, Oxford University.)

Answer the following questions:

(a) Why, do you think, Professor Dawkins holds this view?

(b) Having considered the teleological argument, do you agree/disagree with him? Explain your answer.

The religio-empirical argument

> **Also known as the argument from religious experience.**

A religious experience is one that involves:

- a dramatic, sudden and unanticipated awareness of a spiritual or holy presence;
- an inner assurance about the meaning and purpose of life.

The most famous study of this phenomenon was written by the psychologist William James and entitled *The Varieties of Religious Experience* (1902). More recently, the zoologists Alister Hardy and David Hay have conducted extensive research into this area.

William James claimed that all human knowledge of the world is based on experience. This led him to assert that religious experiences should be considered to be as valid as any other form of human experience and treated with an open-minded seriousness. He was struck by the fact that religious experiences can be found in the folklore, religious and social writings of societies across the globe and in every era of human history, both ancient and modern. Such experiences are recorded as having occurred to people of every racial group and social class, both religious *and* non-religious.

Consider the story of Anthony Bloom. As a teen-ager he was deeply sceptical about the existence of God. One day he decided to prove to himself that Christianity was a complete fraud. He began reading the Gospel of Mark. Bloom later admitted that he had chosen this particular Gospel because it was the shortest and he had decided not to waste too much time on this exercise. However, before he had reached the third chapter of Mark, he claimed that he had an

William James, America's greatest philosopher and psychologist.

the course of human history. Indeed, James believed that if the experiences of such people were deleted from the annals of the history of human civilisation, the record would exclude most of the world's greatest achievements in the fields of art, literature, sculpture, architecture and music.

For James, the very idea of God harmonises and enhances human understanding of the world by presenting it as orderly and purposeful. It also renders life more meaningful because it gives people a reason to live and the inspiration to live well.

Thus the religio-empirical argument states that it is much *more reasonable* to assert that God exists as the basis for religious experience than to attribute the remarkable consequences of religious experience to belief in an imaginary being.

extraordinary and totally unexpected experience that would change the whole course of his life.

> I suddenly became aware that on the other side of my desk there was a presence. And the certainty was so strong that it was Christ standing there that it has never left me.

Bloom described this event as '*the real turning point*' in his life. He went on to become a surgeon and fought as a member of the French Resistance in the Second World War. After the war he was ordained a priest of the Russian Orthodox Church and later became its leader in Britain and Ireland.

Writers such as William James and Alister Hardy were struck by the potency of religious experiences to change the direction and purpose of people's lives. They pointed to the profound religious experiences of people such as Gautama, Moses, St Paul, Muhammad and Gandhi, all of whom went on to radically affect

Anthony Bloom.

Questions

1. What is a *religious experience*?

2. (a) What is the title of the most famous study of this phenomenon?
   (b) Who wrote it?

3. How did he recommend people approach the subject of religious experience? Why did he do so?

4. What fact about religious experiences struck him as worthy of study?

5. What is your reaction to Anthony Bloom's own account of his religious experience?

6. Why did William James and Alister Hardy consider religious experiences to be of enormous significance in human history?

7. Why did James consider the very idea of God to be important?

8. Briefly state the religio-empirical argument.

The moral argument

> **Moral:**
> **concerning the good or evil of voluntary human actions.**

Disagreements are part of daily life: some are trivial, such as a child complaining that '*it's not fair*' when a sibling is given a bigger toy or a larger portion of food; others are over much more significant matters. For example, in the area of medicine there is serious disagreement as to whether or not it is acceptable to carry out research on human embryonic stem cells. Consider:

◆ some claim that such research is a violation of the sanctity of human life and therefore is morally *unjustifiable*;

◆ others claim that such research offers people an opportunity to develop treatments that could do much to alleviate human suffering and therefore is morally *justifiable*.

Whether a disagreement is trivial or important, people —whichever side they take—try to appeal for justification to some *unstated* higher standard. This standard is referred to by C.S. Lewis as '*the Moral Law*'. Its existence is practically assumed by people, whether they believe in God or not, although the latter may be reluctant to admit it.

What *is* usually debated, however, is whether one person's actions or another's is a closer approximation to the demands of this moral law. When people are accused of having fallen short of it, they usually try to offer excuses as to why they should *not* be held blameworthy. Rarely do they simply reject the

The Eternal Father, by Guercino (Giovanni Francesco Barbieri).

notion that their actions should, in some way, be evaluated.

This is a remarkable phenomenon. The idea of right and wrong would appear to be *universal*, i.e. shared by all members of the human community, even though they may disagree sharply as to how it should be applied in particular situations. Writers such as C.S. Lewis and John Henry Newman have argued that the most plausible explanation for the universal human awareness of a fundamental higher standard called the Moral Law is that there exists a Supreme Being who:

◆ established this Moral Law;
◆ gave human beings a general, in-built sense of it;
◆ obliges people to live according to it.

This Supreme Being is called *God*.

Reflection

Religious thinkers admit that:

◆ they cannot offer undeniable proof that God exists;
◆ each of the arguments for God's existence is open to challenge in various ways.

But they claim that they can offer strong defences of these arguments, which effectively counter any objections raised against them. Further, when combined, these arguments do have a cumulative force that amounts to a strong probability that God exists. Above all, they are determined to show that contrary to what some have claimed, religious faith does not involve holding onto an irrational view of life. There are sound reasons why so many people believe in God and from this draw confidence that there is a meaning and a purpose to human life.

Questions

1. Explain the term *moral*.

2. Give your own example of where there is a serious disagreement over the acceptability of a particular course of action or research.

3. What did C.S. Lewis mean by '*the Moral Law*'?

4. Briefly state the moral argument for the existence of God.

5. What are religious thinkers determined to show by presenting arguments *for* the existence of God?

Evil and Suffering

Introduction

There is a great deal of beauty, goodness and joy in the world. Those who are fortunate enough to enjoy it all too often take it for granted. However, we also encounter moments when all these positive experiences are overshadowed by events that both confuse and shock us, such as either witnessing or being a victim of cruelty, dishonesty, grief or violence. These negative experiences usually lead us to ask *why* such things happen. To answer this question we must explore the nature of evil and suffering and the issues they raise.

Meaning

There is a clear link between evil and suffering. Consider:

◆ *evil* is a word generally used to describe *that which is bad in itself because it is harmful or tends to cause harm*;

◆ *suffering* refers to *our experience of the physical and/or psychological pain and injury caused, in varying degrees, by evil.*

The Scream, by Edvard Munch (1893).

Questions raised about God

The Abrahamic faiths claim that God is:

◆ *benevolent*, i.e. utterly good;

◆ *omnipotent*, i.e. all-powerful;

◆ *omniscient*, i.e. all-knowing;

but when people pause to consider the impact of evil and the truly awful suffering it can inflict, they often wonder if such a God really does exist.

Critics of the Abrahamic faiths frequently raise the following objections to the latter's claims about God:

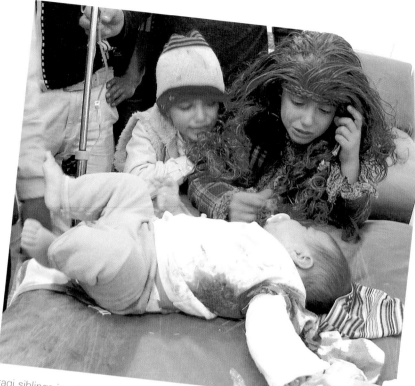

Iraqi siblings in a hospital in Kirkuk, with their one-year-old sister, who was wounded in a rocket attack.

1. God's benevolence

If God is completely good and loving, then God would only want *good* things to happen. Yet the world is in a terrible mess. Why does God not sort it all out? Is it because God is *not* really good and loving? Could it be that such a God does *not* actually exist in the first place?

2. God's omnipotence

If God really is all-powerful, he could use his power to either prevent or eliminate all suffering. Yet he does *not* intervene in this way. Is it because God is actually weak? Is it because God does *not* exist?

3. God's omniscience

If God really is all-knowing, then he must know how people suffer in so many places around the world. Indeed, such a God would have to have known that all this suffering would occur even *before* the world was created. Why would God make a world knowing from the *outset* that so many people would have to endure so much suffering throughout history? Is it possible that God is cruel? Or could it be that there is *no* God at all?

In order to answer such robust challenges to the Abrahamic notion of God, religious thinkers claim that we must begin by exploring and clarifying the meaning of evil and the *purpose* of suffering. They believe that only when this has been done will we understand how the existence of evil and suffering does *not* necessarily undermine belief in the existence of a benevolent, omnipotent and omniscient God. They assert that, paradoxically, such an understanding can actually strengthen and enrich one's religious faith.

Questions

1. Broadly speaking, what is meant by (a) evil and (b) suffering?

2. Describe the God of the Abrahamic faiths.

3. Why does the existence of evil and suffering cause some people to doubt the existence of a loving God?

The nature of evil

A distinction must be made between two kinds of evil:

◆ *Moral evil*
This refers to any action a human being *deliberately* does or fails to do that inflicts harm and causes suffering, e.g. murder, rape, theft.

The Devil presenting St Augustine with a Book of Vices (c. 1455–98).

◆ *Non-moral evil*
This refers to any *naturally occurring event*, one that is *beyond* the power of any human being to control or prevent, which inflicts harm and causes suffering, e.g. an earthquake, a tidal wave, a volcanic eruption.

We shall examine each of the above in greater detail.

Moral Evil

Moral evil and the suffering it causes can exist in many forms. It can either be self-inflicted or due to the action or inaction of others.

1. **Self-inflicted suffering**
Consider the following examples:
◆ where someone drives recklessly at high speed, loses control of the vehicle, crashes and dies of his injuries;
◆ where someone, despite knowing full well the risks associated with over-indulging in alcohol and tobacco, continues to do so, until he develops a serious medical condition, such as cancer or heart disease.

2. Other-inflicted suffering

Consider the following examples:

- where someone is physically, psychologically or sexually abused by another;
- where someone is discriminated against on grounds of gender, sexuality, disability, age, appearance, race or colour.

In each of the above situations someone has deliberately *chosen* a course of action that has harmful consequences. This is why religious thinkers in the Abrahamic faiths make a clear connection between human *freedom* and the existence of evil and suffering in our world.

Freedom may be defined as:

the capacity to weigh possibilities, choose among them and act on this choice.

Alone among the creatures on this planet, human beings are free to:

- love or hate;
- give generously or act selfishly;
- show compassion or demonstrate anger.

As such, human beings are held to be *morally responsible* for their actions, while animals are *not*. In the Abrahamic faiths, freedom is viewed as a *gift* from God and *not* some form of punishment inflicted upon humanity. As with any gift, however, it is given with the intention that it be used *constructively*, not destructively. Some people have raised an objection to this view. They ask:

Why did God not '*programme*' human beings from the very outset not to abuse this gift, but *only* to use it wisely and well?

This is an understandable reaction from someone who has experienced the harm that can all too often result from the choices people make and act upon. However, if God were to '*programme*' human beings to do only good, it would reduce us to little more than his *puppets*. We would no longer have the capacity to think and act for ourselves. We would be deprived of the very thing that makes us *unique*. We would cease to be human because freedom is an *essential* part of our nature.

The Abrahamic faiths teach that God does not want to control us. Rather, God asks *us* to control *ourselves*.

The gift of freedom is an awesome responsibility, which sadly all too many people take too lightly. It is not easy for some people to accept that the source of moral evil is *human* rather than divine. It is *our* greed, our hatred, our lust, our negligence and our pride and short-sightedness that cause so much unnecessary and avoidable suffering in the world.

Non-Moral Evil

Even if one sets aside the suffering caused by moral evil, one is still left with the pain, hardship and death that results from *non-moral* evil, i.e.

those situations where people are *not* responsible for any harm inflicted, such as in the case of natural disasters.

Television news broadcasts have made people very aware of the extent of the suffering endured by victims of:

- drought, which leads to crop failure, famine and disease;
- earthquakes, floods and tornadoes, which destroy homes and wreck infrastructure;
- volcanic eruptions, which devastate the landscape and have a negative effect on climate conditions.

Religious thinkers have sought to utilise our growing understanding of *how* the Earth functions *as a whole* to help people put such tragic events in a perspective that does *not* imply that God put human beings on this planet with the deliberate intention that they should suffer. They argue that, regrettably, such natural disasters are an *unavoidable* part of the workings

Earthquakes and Tsunamis

Under the surface

Around the solid core of the planet is a layer of molten magma called the mantle, through which currents flow. The surface of the Earth, known as the crust, is divided into plates. They float on the mantle and slide against each other.

Tectonic plate boundaries

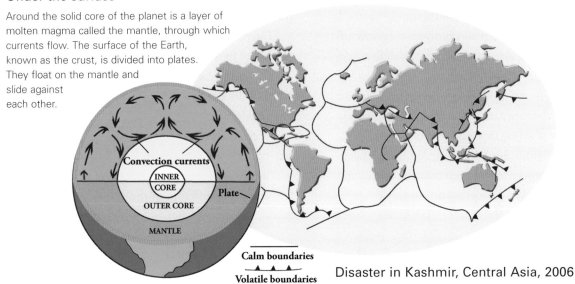

Calm boundaries

Volatile boundaries

How an earthquake happens

1. The edges of two plates that are locked together can move suddenly, releasing devastating energy. Friction between the Indian and Eurasian plates caused the creation of the Himalayan mountain range many millennia ago.

Himalayas

INDIAN PLATE

EURASIAN PLATE

Disaster in Kashmir, Central Asia, 2006

2. The earthquake was caused when the two plates slid against each other, sending shockwaves out from the main point of friction through the surrounding landscape, to devastating effect.

Epicentre

How a tsunami happens

1. The tidal wave that hit South-east Asia in December 2006 began when an earthquake under the sea caused sudden movement of water upwards and downwards along the length of the Java Trench.

2. Within moments of the earthquake, an enormous ripple of water was moving away from the epicentre in all directions. This tsunami moved through the deep ocean at hundreds of miles per hour.

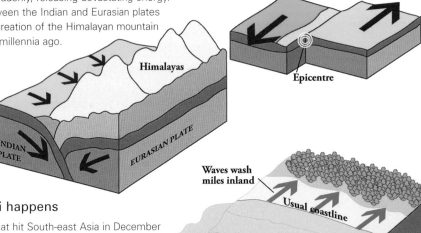

Waves wash miles inland

Usual coastline

Wave movement away from the earthquake's epicentre

3. As the wave approached land and hit shallower seas over the continental shelf, it began to slow down. This loss of speed caused the height of the wave to increase. By the time it hit the human settlements along the coast, the tsunami was a huge wall of water.

of nature. Consider the cases of earthquakes and volcanic eruptions:

◆ geologists study how the Earth was formed;

◆ they say that in order for living things to have ever emerged and survived on it, the Earth had to reach, and stay at, just the right point between molten hot and cooled solid;

◆ the Earth's crust has cooled to just the right point where it can, and continues to, support life;

◆ but it is only a crust, i.e. a cooled outer layer. It rests on top of a molten core;

◆ from time to time this crust moves, cracks and buckles, causing *earthquakes*;

◆ when the molten inner core of the planet breaks through the crust, there are *volcanic eruptions*; these events are called *natural disasters*;

◆ tragically, they can cause great harm to many people;

◆ they are, however, *unavoidable* consequences of how the Earth *must* work if it is to continue to sustain life on its surface.

Of course, none of this can in any way lessen the horrors unleashed upon local populations by such events. Nevertheless it is important to remember that many lives could be saved in such circumstances if certain steps were to be taken. Consider:

◆ the technology to provide advanced warning of impending catastrophe could be developed and put in place;

◆ governments could then evacuate people from areas most likely to be devastated;

◆ governments could relocate people away from known earthquake faultlines, active volcanoes and areas prone to flooding;

◆ international relief and rescue agencies could be better funded to provide aid to those facing a crisis.

All of these measures would require two things: money, and the political will to do what is necessary; neither has been forthcoming thus far. At the same time, there has been no shortage of expenditure on armaments and warfare by most of the world's richest nations. It is a matter of *priorities*.

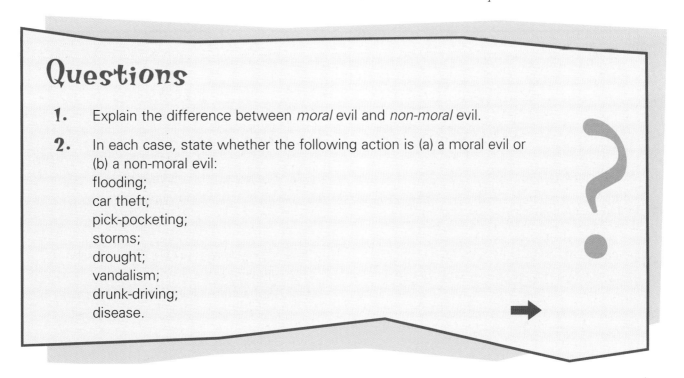

Questions

1. Explain the difference between *moral* evil and *non-moral* evil.

2. In each case, state whether the following action is (a) a moral evil or (b) a non-moral evil:
   flooding;
   car theft;
   pick-pocketing;
   storms;
   drought;
   vandalism;
   drunk-driving;
   disease.

3. Explain the meaning of *self-inflicted* suffering and *other-inflicted* suffering.

4. What is meant by '*freedom*'?

5. Why do thinkers in the Abrahamic faiths believe that God *refuses* to programme human beings to *only* do good?

6. Examine the claim that natural events, such as earthquakes and volcanic eruptions, are a tragic but necessary part of how the Earth must function if it is to sustain life on its surface.
   (a) What reasons do the Abrahamic faiths offer to support this claim?
   (b) Do you agree/disagree? Explain your answer.

7. According to the Stockholm International Peace Research Institute, world military spending has reached an estimated *$1,000 billion per annum*.
   (a) How could this money be *better* spent on alleviating human suffering caused by natural disasters?
   (b) Why is this *not* being done?

You Ignored Whose Warning?

On September 11, 2001, terrorists rammed their stolen jetliners into the World Trade Center, Manhattan, New York City, killing 3,000 people. But compared to another much more destructive force, their efforts pale.

GALVESTON, TEXAS, 1900

Let's turn the clock back over a century, and move the locale from Manhattan to Galveston, Texas.

The United States government had a relatively new agency: the US Weather Bureau. The same one you get on your cable TV, or that your local newscast quotes when telling you to wear your raincoat. That weather bureau.

It was a new science, forecasting the weather. Oh, people had been predicting the weather for centuries. See a hairy caterpillar in October? Bad winter coming. Did the June bugs show up in late April? Long, dry summer on tap.

But then, in 1900, weather forecasting was finally recognised as a science. They used instruments. They studied the barometric reading. They contacted outposts in all directions to track storms. They were the newest of the new, these weather forecasters. And

they protected their turf.

We'll get back to them in a minute, but first let me tell you a little bit about Galveston, because these days it's dwarfed in its own home state by Dallas and Houston and San Antonio—but back then, in 1900, it ranked behind only Houston as the major city of Texas. Not only that, but in the entire country it was second only to New York City as an entry point for immigrants. In fact, it was nicknamed the 'Western Ellis Island'. ▶

How big was it? Well, the population was always in flux due to immigration, but the best estimate was 30,000, give or take. The climate was pleasant, the land was lovely, property was inexpensive, and though it was on the water everyone knew it was safe from typhoons and hurricanes and the like. And if they didn't know, the Weather Bureau was only too happy to tell them so.

The shining light of the Galveston Weather Bureau was a gentleman named Isaac Cline. He was their superstar. Cline was quoted as saying that it was 'an absurd delusion' for anyone to think Galveston could possibly ever suffer serious damage from a hurricane.

He based this conclusion on two erroneous beliefs: first, that any high surf or storm tide would flow over Galveston into the bay behind it and then into the Texas prairie, doing no lasting damage at all; and second, because of the shallow slope of the Gulf coastline, the incoming surf would be broken up and made much less dangerous.

Cline was so sure of this that he ridiculed the notion of building a seawall to withstand storms, and because he was, for all practical purposes, the voice of the US government on this particular subject, the wall was never built.

Now the Weather Bureau was still in its infancy, but the people manning the Galveston division were pretty confident in their skills. Certainly more confident than they were of the skills of the Cubans they had defeated just two years earlier in the Spanish-American War. The Cuban weathermen meant well, decided the Galveston Weather Bureau, but

after all, they were just illiterate peasants, right?

Of course not. But the Cubans' wise warnings fell on deaf ears.

So when, on September 7, 1900, Cuba began reporting that the biggest storm anyone had ever seen was heading right toward Galveston, the Weather Bureau was so sure they were totally mistaken and panicking needlessly that they refused to make the Cubans' warnings public.

After all, everyone knew that Galveston couldn't suffer serious damage from a storm. Either it would turn away before reaching shore, or it would pass right over and blow itself out somewhere over the vast Texas prairie.

But by the morning of September 8, it became apparent to Cline and his co-workers that the storm wasn't going to turn away and miss Galveston. In fact, it was apparent to everyone in the city. All they had to do was look to the south and east and see what was approaching.

Should they evacuate the city? They wanted to know. Certainly not, Cline and the Weather Bureau assured them. This is Galveston, not some shantytown that's likely to get blown away by a strong wind. Our houses are well built, we're sitting right on the slope of the Gulf coastline, and haven't you ever seen a thunderstorm before?

So the people—most of them, anyway—trusted their government bureaucrats and stayed put.

At least until the water became knee-high, and then waist-high, and then neck-high.

Pretty soon those who hadn't fled the town were perched on their roofs.

And pretty soon after that there weren't any roofs, because the houses began collapsing, and boats capsized, and bodies—infants and the elderly at first, then men and women in their primes—began floating down the streets, through the windows, over the vanished roofs.

And still the storm continued.

At one point a train from Beaumont entered the town but halted well short of the station. The passengers wanted to leave and find some high ground, or at least some rooftops, for safety. The conductors, hearing the reassurances of the Weather Bureau, urged the passengers to remain where they were. After all, this was a train, a massive thing of steel. Surely no storm could harm it or wash it away, and you don't have to take our word for it; just ask the Weather Bureau.

Ten passengers looked out the window, said, in essence, 'Nonsense'.

They waded and swam through the rampaging water to try to find some safe haven. Eighty-five passengers believed the bureaucrats of the Weather Bureau and stayed with the train.

By the next morning, all eighty-five were dead.

I should add that this wasn't entirely the fault of Cline and his Galveston bureaucrats. They were in contact with a branch of the bureau in the West Indies, which was anxious to show up the Cubans—their recent enemies—and to prove that these Cubans were pressing the panic button needlessly.

Of course, back in Galveston, by the time it became clear that, if anything, the Cubans were underestimating the danger, no one could find the panic button. It was hidden under tons of water.

So did help rush in, as Americans have always helped their own and others?

NO!

You see, Cline was in control of the forecasting, but his immediate superior, Willis Moore, was in control of the whole Galveston Bureau, and Moore was more concerned with Galveston's—and his bureau's—image than with saving citizens that he had convinced himself weren't really in all that much danger to begin with. So a call for help never went out.

The city's newspapers colluded with the bureau, and down-played the story. In fact, an unpublished editorial in the *Galveston Tribune* the morning after the storm hit assured the public that there was very little danger from the storm, and 'no possibility of serious loss of life.'

Why (I hear you ask) was it unpublished?

Because the press floated out to sea before the issue could be printed.

All the phone and telegraph wires were dead by 4:00 p.m., and Galveston was effectively cut off from the rest of the world. By 7:00 p.m. the winds were over 120 miles an hour, and some were as high as 200 miles an hour before midnight. Contact wasn't re-established with Galveston for another 28 hours, at 11:30 p.m. on September 9. In the interim, the closest any train had been able to approach the ▶

city was six miles. Anything beyond that was too dangerous.

When it was over, it was estimated that Galveston had lost between 3,000 and 4,000 houses and buildings.

It was always going to lose them. The people were something else again. If the bureaucrats of the Weather Bureau had simply told the truth, had shared the information they'd been sent from Cuba, had not been so pigheaded in their certainty that no storm could ever damage Galveston …

No one knows exactly how many people died in New York on September 11, 2001. The best estimate is 3,000, out of a population of more than seven million. That comes to four ten-thousandths of one per cent.

No one knows exactly how many people died in Galveston on September 8 and 9, 1900. The best estimate is 10,000, out of a population of about 30,000. That comes to 33 per cent.

It should be obvious at this point that the destructive force greater than any terrorist's bomb was an arrogant bureaucracy, not the hurricane. Which is rather a pity, as we can at least predict the course of hurricanes.

(Adapted from an essay by Mike Resnick in B. Fawcett and B. Thomsen (eds), *You Did What?*, Perennial Currents/Harper Collins, 2004.)

Questions

1. What was the population of Galveston, Texas, USA, in 1900?

2. Who was Isaac Cline?

3. Why did he wrongly believe that Galveston could *never* suffer serious damage from a hurricane?

4. What *precaution* against hurricane damage did he ridicule and persuade the US government *not* to build?

5. Why did the US Weather Bureau *dismiss* warnings about a massive hurricane by Cuban weather forecasters?

6. Why was *no* warning given to the population of Galveston *before* the hurricane's arrival?

7. Describe the effects of the hurricane once it struck Galveston.

8. Who colluded with the US Weather Bureau to *downplay* the danger posed by the hurricane? Why?

9. What was the estimated death toll from this disaster?

10. A hurricane is a *natural* event that can, and in this case *did*, inflict enormous suffering and death. Yet so many of these lives *could* have been saved. Identify the actions that *could* have been taken to *save* lives at Galveston in 1900.

11. Why, in your opinion, were so many lives *lost*? Explain your answer.

Searching for answers

Whatever about the reasons *why* they exist, one is still left with the suffering caused by both *moral* and *non-moral* evil. This has led some people to question the existence of a loving God.

The Christian writer C.S. Lewis had a deep appreciation of the impact of suffering on people's lives. The death of his beloved wife from cancer left him utterly distraught and inconsolable for some time. Reflecting on his own experience, Lewis phrased the argument about God and evil thus:

> If God were good, he would wish to make his creatures perfectly happy, and if God were almighty, he would be able to do what he wished. But we are not happy. Therefore, God lacks either goodness or power or both.
> (C.S. Lewis, *The Problem of Pain.*)

Lewis told his readers that there were no easy answers to be found to the serious questions raised by evil and suffering. However, he began by pointing out that a large portion of human suffering is the result of what *we* do, or fail to do, to one another. It is *people* who invent instruments of torture and weapons of mass destruction. Why should we blame God for the harmful consequences of *our* actions?

At this point it is sometimes asked:

Dr Harold Shipman, a serial killer who murdered many of his elderly patients.

Should God not have *restrained* our free will in such a way as to *prevent* us from choosing to do such things?

Lewis made clear that such a proposal quickly runs into serious difficulty.

Consider:

- human beings have a capacity for *learning*. Generally speaking, this is a good and necessary thing, but we can learn both helpful and harmful things. If a person studies medicine and becomes a doctor, he/she can use this knowledge to heal others and alleviate their suffering. In the wrong hands, however, such knowledge can be used to destroy lives and inflict injury;

- human beings have a talent for *creativity* and invention, which is why we have art and technology. But some discoveries can have *more* than one application. For example, the ancient Chinese discovered *gunpowder* and used it to propel fireworks. Later, Europeans used their discovery to invent *firearms*, which have been used ever since with devastating effect.

The human capacity for learning and for creativity is an expression of our *freedom*. Theists believe that freedom is a *gift* from God. Were God to withhold his permission for us to act freely, he would *deprive* us of an essential part of what it means to *be* human. That would be both nonsensical and tyrannical, which is why God does *not* do it.

Yet none of what has been said so far makes the reality of evil any less awful, nor the suffering it inflicts any easier to bear. Rational arguments offer little comfort when one is forced to deal with the impact of a terrible tragedy. Understandably, a person may ask:

Why did God not intervene to save me, or someone I love, from harm?

There is no easy answer to this question.

True, the Abrahamic faiths teach that God has, on certain occasions, worked *miracles*. These are said to be *rare* events, however, performed for very specific reasons. Such miracles must remain the *exception* rather than the rule. Why?

C.S. Lewis answered this question by asking people to remember two important facts:

1. Freedom of choice is an *essential* part of what it is to be a human being. Without it, we *cannot* live a truly human life.

2. There is a way in which all events in the universe *must* occur if the universe is to make sense. Reality *must* function according to certain laws or else there will be *chaos*.

Bearing this in mind, let us now conduct a thought experiment. Let us try to imagine a world *without* suffering.

In such a world …

- God would stub out a carelessly placed lit cigarette before it could cause a fire;

- God would stop an improperly positioned ladder

from slipping and thereby prevent injury;

♦ God would guarantee that no matter how fast we drive a vehicle, we are always within our stopping distance;

♦ God would guarantee that no drunken driver would ever knock down and kill a pedestrian, a fellow passenger or the occupant of another vehicle.

Clearly, in such a universe the basic physical law of *cause and effect* would no longer apply. Our every mistake would be immediately put right by God. Now consider the consequences of this:

♦ without the principle of cause and effect, the universe would no longer be rational. We could no longer predict anything because God's constant miracle-working would *prevent* us from doing so;

♦ as a result, our whole lives would be an experience of utter unpredictability and chaos. Science, technology and therefore human progress would be impossible.

But what of natural disasters?

As was pointed out earlier, they seem to be an unavoidable by-product of living on a planet that is engaged in an evolutionary process. God, it is argued, does *not* intervene because such miraculous interventions would reduce reality to chaos.

C.S. Lewis admitted that all of this reasoning still falls short of providing a justification for the suffering endured by so many people. He himself came to the conclusion that although God loves us and wishes the best for us, God's plan is *not* the same as our plan.

Human beings have an understandable desire to experience perpetual happiness. God wants more for us than this. God wants each person to grow and develop into his/her full potential as a human being. To do so, each of us must experience things that *make this possible*. Many of these situations are often the *negative* aspects of life. These situations can demand great courage and resourcefulness. They can ask us to put self-sacrifice before self-fulfilment. But at the same time they can help us to develop into more open, thoughtful, loving and resilient human beings.

Questions

1. Why do theists, such as C.S. Lewis, *reject* the idea that God should restrain human freedom and thus prevent us from ever causing suffering?

2. Imagine a world *without* suffering and death.
   (a) At first glance, it might seem a wonderful place, but what would this mean for us in practice?
   (b) What price might human beings have to pay for living in such a world?

3. Read the following extract by the Irish writer John Connolly:

   What matters is that you understand that others suffer … some … worse than you could ever do. The nature of compassion isn't coming to terms with your own suffering and applying it to others:

it's knowing that other folks around you suffer and, no matter what happens to you, no matter how lucky or unlucky you are, they keep suffering. And if you can do something about that, you do it, and you do it without whining or waving your own … cross for the world to see. You do it because it's the right thing to do.

(John Connolly, *Dark Hollow*.)

(a)   What does the author mean by '*compassion*'?

(b)   In what way does he suggest that suffering may actually offer each of us the *opportunity* for real *growth* in our humanity?

(c)   Do you agree/disagree with him? Why?

The Story of Bill W.

Alcoholism is an addiction to the regular consumption of alcohol.

There is no single cause of alcoholism. It is believed to be the result of an interaction of three factors:

◆   The physical and psychological make-up of the individual.

◆   Ready access to alcohol in his/her environment, i.e. where he/she lives and works.

◆   The addictive nature of alcohol.

Unfortunately, Second Lieut. Bill Wilson didn't think twice when the first butler he had ever seen offered him a drink. The 22-year-old soldier didn't think about how alcohol had destroyed his family. He didn't think about the temperance movement of his childhood or his loving fiancée Lois Burnham or his emerging talent for leadership. He didn't think about anything at all. 'I had found the elixir of life,' he wrote. Wilson's last drink, seventeen years later, by which time alcohol had destroyed his health and his career, precipitated an epiphany that would change his life and the lives of millions of other alcoholics. Incarcerated for the fourth time at Manhattan's Towns Hospital in 1934, Wilson had a spiritual awakening—a flash of white light, a liberating

Bill W.

awareness of God—that led to the founding of Alcoholics Anonymous and Wilson's revolutionary Twelve-Step program, the successful remedy for alcoholism. The Twelve Steps have also generated successful programs for eating disorders, gambling, narcotics, debting, sex addiction and people affected by others' addiction. Aldous Huxley called him 'the greatest social architect of our century.'

William Griffith Wilson grew up in a quarry town in Vermont, USA. When he was ten, his hard-drinking father headed for Canada, and his mother moved to Boston, leaving the child with her parents. As a soldier, and then as a businessman, Wilson drank to alleviate his depressions and to celebrate his Wall Street success. Married in 1918, he and Lois toured the country on a motorcycle and appeared to be a prosperous, promising young couple. By 1933, however, they were living on

charity in her parents' house on Clinton Street in Brooklyn, New York. Wilson had become an unemployable drunk who disdained religion and even begged for cash.

Inspired by a friend who had stopped drinking, Wilson went to meetings of the Oxford Group, an evangelical society founded in Britain by Frank Buchman. And as Wilson underwent a barbiturate-and-belladonna cure called 'purge and puke,' which was state-of-the-art alcoholism treatment at the time, his mind spun with phrases from Oxford Group meetings, Carl Jung and William James' book *Varieties of Religious Experience*, which he read in the hospital. Five sober months later, Wilson went to Akron, Ohio, on business. The deal fell through, and he wanted a drink. He stood in the lobby of the Mayflower Hotel, entranced by the sounds of the bar across the hall. Suddenly he became convinced that by helping another alcoholic, he could help himself.

Through a series of desperate telephone calls, he found Dr Robert Smith, a sceptical drunk whose family persuaded him to give Wilson fifteen minutes. Their meeting lasted for hours. A month later, Dr Bob had his last drink, and that date, 10 June 1935, is the official birth date of AA, which is based on the idea that only an alcoholic can help another alcoholic.

'Because of our kinship in suffering,' Bill wrote, 'our channels of contact have always been charged with the language of the heart.'

The Burnham house on Clinton Street became a haven for alcoholics. 'My name is Bill W., and I'm an alcoholic,' he told ▶

assorted houseguests and visitors at meetings. To spread the word, he began writing down his principles for sobriety. Each chapter was read by the Clinton Street group and sent to Smith in Akron for more editing. The book had a dozen provisional titles, among them 'The Way Out' and 'The Empty Glass'. Edited to 400 pages, it was finally called *Alcoholics Anonymous*, and this became the group's name.

But the book, although well reviewed, wasn't selling. Wilson tried unsuccessfully to make a living as a wire-rope salesman. AA had about a hundred members, but many were still drinking. Meanwhile, in 1939, the bank foreclosed on the Clinton Street house, and the couple began years of homelessness, living as guests in borrowed rooms and at one point staying in temporary quarters above the AA clubhouse on 24th Street in Manhattan. In 1940, millionaire philanthropist John D. Rockefeller Jr held an AA dinner and was impressed enough to create a trust to provide Wilson with $30 a week—but no more. The tycoon felt that money would corrupt the group's spirit.

Then, in March 1941, the *Saturday Evening Post* published an article on AA, and suddenly thousands of letters and requests poured in. Attendance at meetings doubled and tripled. Wilson had reached his audience. In *Twelve Traditions*, Wilson set down the suggested bylaws of Alcoholics Anonymous. In them, he created an enduring blueprint for an organisation with a maximum of individual freedom and no accumulation of power or money. Public anonymity ensured humility.

No contributions were required; no member could contribute more than $1,000.

Today more than 2 million AA members in 150 countries hold meetings in church basements, hospital conference rooms and school gyms, following Wilson's informal structure. Members identify themselves as alcoholics and share their stories; there are no rules or entry requirements, and many members use only first names.

Wilson believed the key to sobriety was a change of heart. The suggested Twelve Steps include an admission of powerlessness, a moral inventory, a restitution for harm done, a call to service and a surrender to some personal God.

Influenced by AA, the American Medical Association has redefined alcoholism as a chronic disease, not as a failure of willpower.*

As Alcoholics Anonymous grew, Wilson became its principal symbol. He helped create a governing structure for the program, the General Service Board, and turned over his power. 'I have become a pupil of the AA movement rather than the teacher,' he wrote.

He died of pneumonia and emphysema in Miami, where he went for treatment in 1971. To the end, he clung to the principles and the power of anonymity. He was always Bill W., refusing to take money for counselling and leadership. He turned down many honours, including a degree from Yale. And he declined Time magazine's offer to put him on the cover—even with his back turned.

(Adapted from an article by Susan Cheever that appeared in *Time* magazine, 14 June 1999.)

Questions

1. Why did Bill Wilson begin drinking alcohol?

2. What conclusion did he reach while resisting the temptation to enter the bar of the Mayflower Hotel?

3. Why is 10 June 1935 a significant date?

4. What is the idea on which Alcoholics Anonymous is based?

5. What did Bill Wilson believe was *the key to sobriety*?

6. How did Alcoholics Anonymous influence the American Medical Association?

7. Christian writers, such as C.S. Lewis, have observed that suffering is *an expert teacher*. The experience of suffering can:

   - make one confront one's own human frailty;
   - force one to ask honestly whether or not one has lived up to one's potential as a human being;
   - bring a realisation of how far short one has fallen;
   - lay the foundation for a new and better way of thinking, living and hoping;
   - provide an opportunity to experience spiritual growth.

   How might the story of Bill Wilson be said to bear out these insights into the redemptive power of suffering in some people's lives?

Reflection

C.S. Lewis was well aware that the notion that God can work through adversity is *not* an easy one for us to accept. Perhaps it makes sense only within the context of a belief that human life does not end in this world. If it did, it would be hard to see any convincing reasons for enduring suffering.

Imagine a vicious crimelord who evades prosecution and dies peacefully in his old age, surrounded by all his ill-gotten gains. Then compare his case with that of the poor parents who devote their lives to caring for their seriously intellectually-disabled child. The former is utterly *selfish*, while the latter are *selfless*. Yet in the long run, why should we ascribe any meaning or value to the actions of either of them? Why should a person be wicked rather than benevolent?

The Abrahamic faiths have taught that we are called to live truly human lives, i.e. lives built on love and compassion. This *unavoidably* involves suffering, to a greater or lesser degree. The faiths tell us that we do not face this alone, however, because God is there to guide and strengthen us in times of suffering. If we bear our suffering with dignity and courage, we open ourselves up to others and to God. In this way we *prepare* ourselves to share an afterlife with God, one in which the good are *rewarded* and the wicked are *punished*. (In the next chapter we shall explore this belief in the afterlife.)

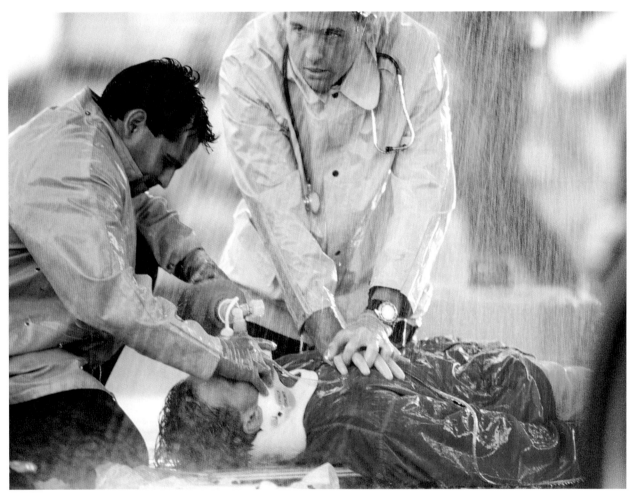

Paramedics at work.

Questions

1. Why do the Abrahamic faiths teach that belief in an afterlife is important when searching for the meaning and purpose of evil and suffering in our lives?

2. Read the following extract:

   In Tomás Ó Criomhthain's classic account of the closing decades of life on the Blaskets, there is a stoicism and resilience in the face of adversity that are extremely rare in the Ireland of today. This man lost his wife and children, sometimes in tragic circumstances, and yet his unflinching faith in an all-powerful God gave him the strength to keep going. As he wrote after one of the many crosses that came his way: 'It was imprinted on my mind that there was no cure for these things but to meet them with endurance as best I could.' Such fortitude is not as easy to come by in a society which has turned its back on the concept of a loving God.

   (Eamonn Maher, 'Where to now for Irish Catholicism?', in *Reality*, September 2003.)

   (a) What point is being made here about the role of faith in a loving God in a person's life when he/she is faced with suffering and death?

   (b) Do you think such a faith still has anything to offer today? Explain your answer.

Afghan Children dispel Myths of War Trauma

Resilience refers to the capacity to recover from some misfortune or harmful event.

At the individual level, resilience is a common characteristic of *all* human beings. Yet what is regarded as hardship in one context may ▶

be simply a way of life in another. For example, power cuts across Europe and North America during the summer of 2003 created serious disruptions to everyday life. Those who depend on electricity for cooking or cooling had *no* alternative provisions and found it difficult to adjust. In many other parts of the world, however, searching for the raw materials with which to cook a meal is a daily chore rather than a disaster. Clearly, supporting disaster resilience requires *different* kinds of intervention in *different* contexts.

These varying examples point towards a common issue: the importance of understanding the ability of individuals, communities or businesses not only to cope with, but also to *adapt* to adverse conditions and to focus any interventions at building on these strengths. The development community has made sig-

nificant shifts towards people-centred policies and approaches based on local capacities. Yet, how far has the disaster community—in its delivery of humanitarian assistance or promotion of disaster risk reduction—moved in this direction?

While conceptually the importance of people and their strengths are understood, there is little analysis of how people survive in the face of disasters. And there is even less programming that builds on the resilience strategies of disaster-prone communities. Afghanistan is a case in point. Despite 25 years of conflict and four years of drought, Afghans have dispelled the myth, subscribed to by many in the West, that they are helpless victims, and have shown astonishing resilience in the face of crisis.

One Western aid co-ordinator has written of his experiences working with Afghan children:

What has been the impact of 24 years of war on children's mental health? How can they be healed when there are so few psychiatrists? Is Afghanistan now burdened with a generation of children who know only what it is to kill and take revenge? These questions – frequently asked by international journalists and aid workers alike – spring from assumptions that reflect only *a fraction* of the reality in Afghanistan.

Of course, Afghan children have lived through events that most of us would not wish upon any child. There is something about children that makes us want to protect them and assume that any harm will affect them negatively. But, as I work with Afghan children, I am constantly amazed at their resilience and fortitude. They have experienced terrible suffering but are still able to live as children, to play, to learn and to laugh. I do not, generally, find children overwhelmed by trauma but children who have come through suffering with their humanity and hope intact. Much of the credit must go to Afghan parents. They bear the brunt of difficult events to shield their children, while teaching them how to cope when bad things do happen. Research among children and their families in Kabul during 2002 revealed that children are taught several key qualities to help them cope:

◆   First is *courage*. Children are expected to learn how to overcome fear – by confronting their fears and by being reassured when they are afraid.

◆   Second, they are taught how to be *thankful* – for still being alive after an attack or for being better off than others around them.

◆   Third, children are encouraged to be *happy* through playing, joking, picnicking, going to school, being with friends. Afghans understand that if children have happiness in their lives, they are much more able to cope with sadness.

◆   Fourth, children are expected to have *religious faith*. They are taught prayers to say when they are scared. They are encouraged to understand that everything that happens to them is in the hands of God, beyond their control and therefore to be accepted.

◆   Finally, children are taught *morality*. As parents in Kabul note, it is one thing to be exposed to bad events but it is another to know right from wrong. Children need not automatically follow the paths of the wrong.

Afghans believe that children who develop such qualities will be affected by violence but not permanently scarred by it. Exposure to war might even enhance these positive traits. Certainly in Afghanistan, the thirst for peace, the hunger for knowledge, the strength and motivation among young people will prove to be a major resource in a country struggling to get back on its feet for many years to come.

(*World Disaster Report – From Risk to Resilience*, United Nations: Department of Public Information, 2004.)

Questions

1. Explain the term *resilience*.

2. The concept of *hardship* is a relative term. What would be considered a hardship in the developed world but merely a daily chore in the developing world?

3. Read the following statement:

   It is important for the developed world to better understand how people in the developing world cope with challenging situations on a daily basis. Only then can they best assist the latter when they must adapt to and deal with the conditions created by natural disasters or wars.

   Why is this necessary if aid is to produce worthwhile benefits to people suffering from the effects of either moral or non-moral evil?

4. Identify:
   - the coping strategies taught to; *and*
   - qualities of character encouraged in Afghan children to help them deal with and grow beyond their experiences of evil and suffering in their community.

5. It is stated in the article that:

   Afghans believe that children who develop such qualities will be affected by violence but not permanently scarred by it. Exposure to war might even enhance these positive traits.

   (a) What is meant by this?
   (b) Do you think this claim is justified? Give reasons for your answer.

Life after Death

Introduction

Mostly people prefer to avoid thinking about and talking about death, but when a loved one dies, we are forced to confront it. Death has been described as '*the great leveller*' because it stalks both rich and poor, young and old, religious and non-religious alike. Death is no respecter of race, creed or colour. It brings all humans to the same level. It is *inescapable*.

Once a person dies, is that it? Does the individual cease to exist? This is a question people have reflected upon and struggled with since the dawn of human history.

Early evidence of belief in an afterlife

The archaeological record would appear to indicate that the human belief in some form of life after death is quite ancient. Excavations in the Skhul and Qafzeh caves in Israel have uncovered a burial site for men, women and children dating back to about 100,000

BCE. It was noticed that some of the skeletons had a few simple possessions placed alongside them, such as stone tools and deer antlers. The precise meaning attached to such items by ancient people is a matter of some debate among archaeologists and anthropologists. Nonetheless the presence of such items would seem to suggest that those who buried them may have believed that the deceased would, in some way, still '*need*' those things in some form of afterlife.

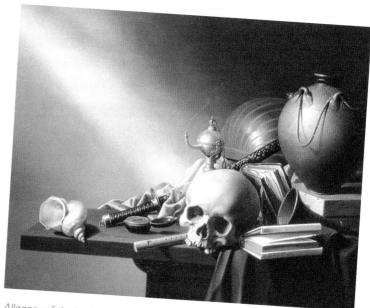

Allegory of the Vanities of Human Life by Steenwyck.

The ancient Egyptians built pyramids and embalmed bodies in order to preserve their dead pharaohs for life after death (*left*). In China, Emperor Shih Huang Ti died *c.* 210 BCE. He was buried with 6,000 terracotta soldiers, horses and chariots (*right*) to protect him on his journey to the afterlife.

By the time of the New Stone Age (*c.* 5000 BCE), there is clearer evidence that our ancient ancestors believed in life after death. They buried their dead with great reverence and conducted elaborate funeral rites. The precise nature of their beliefs regarding the afterlife remains a matter of considerable speculation, however. It is not until the rise of the ancient Egyptian kingdom (*c.* 3000 BCE) that we can detect the beginnings of a more systematic account of what a life after death would be like. The archaeological record has helped us to trace the gradual development of these people's beliefs over the centuries:

◆ initially, the Egyptians believed that only the pharaoh would have a life after death;

◆ later, they believed that their noble class would also survive death;

◆ finally, they came to believe that *every person* would experience an afterlife.

This belief that *all* members of the human race will in some way endure after death is a key aspect of each of the major world religions that have emerged over the centuries since then.

Questions

1. The subject of death, what it means and what may or may not lie beyond it is not a popular subject for discussion in our society. Why might this be the case?

2. What evidence exists to show that people in prehistoric times believed in some form of afterlife? ➡

3. (a) How did Egyptian views on life after death evolve over time?
  (b) Why was this significant?

Common ground

Every religion is concerned with life; every religion is concerned with death. It is because of this that they unanimously reject the doctrine of materialism, i.e.

the belief that only physical bodies or quanta of physical energy exist.

Religions claim that materialism offers an inadequate and incomplete explanation that utterly *fails* to account for not only the complexity and richness of life in the universe but also for the tragic reality of death. While having due regard for the obvious importance of the physical dimension of existence, the major religions essentially agree that:

◆ human life has *a higher purpose* than just meeting physical needs, such as eating, sleeping, reproducing and working, before finally dying;

◆ dying is *not* the end of human life but a moment of *transition* from one way of existing to another;

◆ this is possible because a human being is composed of both a *body* (physical aspect) and a *soul* (spiritual aspect);

◆ at the moment of death only the body dies, while the soul *continues*;

◆ the afterlife provides some form of *completion* of what was begun *in* life but interrupted by death, namely a movement by the person either *towards or away from* God (as each religion conceives of God).

Questions

1. What is *materialism*?

2. Read the following extract:

A materialist is someone who believes that a human being is simply an animal, a kind of self-replicating electrochemical machine, a machine capable of writing and reading Shakespeare.

It is noteworthy that those holding such views rarely draw out their implications.

Machines are there to be used, so on this view society soon

becomes a collection of machines using and manipulating each other.

And morality is reduced to measuring how useful people are.

When machines are no longer of use they are discarded. Will the elderly, the disabled child, the ageing husband or wife and the replaceable worker go the same way?

One may dismiss this as off-the-wall nonsense. But it is the nonsense of highly qualified individuals whose views impress politicians and policy-makers.

It opens the way for many things.

There is a high price to be paid when people lose sight of their dignity as children of God.

(Adapted from 'Editorial Jottings', *Alive*, February 2006.)

(a) What does this writer identify as the *implications* of the materialist view for the ways in which people *understand* and *treat* one another?

(b) The author of this extract asserts that '*There is a high price to be paid when people lose sight of their dignity as children of God*'. Do you agree/disagree? Give reasons for your answer.

3. Read the following statement:

Some great Buddhist masters will ask a visitor who comes to see them, 'do you believe in life after death?' They do this because someone who does have this belief will live life differently and see life differently from those who believe that this life is all that there is.

(Peter Vardy, *The Puzzle of God.*)

Do you agree/disagree with this? Explain your answer.

4. What do all the major world religions essentially agree on regarding human life?

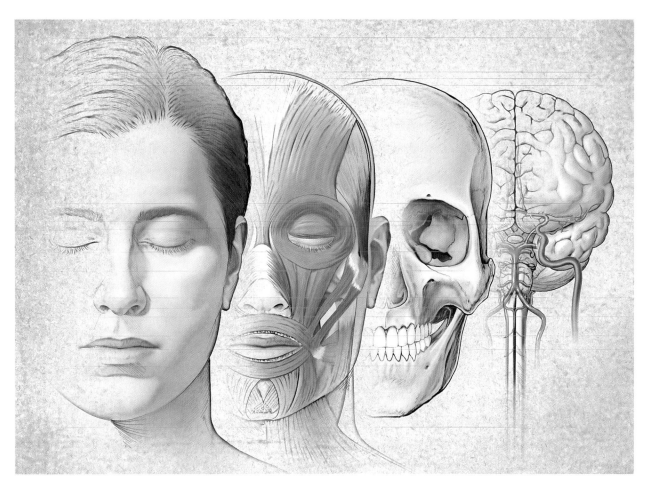

'More to us than meets the eye?'

Different views of the soul

At this point it is important to make clear that the major world religions are divided into two groups on the question of the precise nature of the soul:

1. **The Abrahamic faiths**—Judaism, Christianity and Islam—teach that the soul of each person is created by, and is separate from, God. The soul is the source of each person's individual life and unique identity. After death, the soul will continue to have an individual existence.

2. **The Eastern religions**—Hinduism and Buddhism —teach that the soul of each person is neither unique nor separate, but is actually a fragment of an impersonal *World Soul* that has somehow become trapped in a human body. Upon the death of a person who has achieved a state of complete spiritual enlightenment (*nirvana*), the soul will be released from a cycle of birth and rebirth (reincarnation) and will be re-absorbed into the World Soul and lose its individual existence.

Clearly, the Abrahamic and Eastern forms of religion do *not* share the same understanding of human nature, nor do they agree as to how we will exist in the hereafter. However, both *do* share a strong conviction that our human actions in *this* lifetime profoundly affect our destiny in the *next*.

Criticism and response

Thinkers such as Sigmund Freud and Karl Marx have claimed that the idea of an afterlife:

◆ has been a fundamental element of religious belief from the very *outset*;

◆ was *invented* as a means by which a social elite could control the mass of people by winning them over with promises of '*pie in the sky when you die*'.

Detailed historical studies have shown these claims to be quite *incorrect*.

Consider:

◆ Christianity and Islam both sprang forth from Judaism. Although Judaism was founded by Abraham *c.* 1800 BCE, it was not for another 1,000 years that they began to develop any notion of an afterlife. The earliest expression of such religious aspirations can be found in their Psalms (religious poetry);

◆ belief in life after death is rarely a strong motivating factor in religion. Where it does exist, it is usually as a consequence of other, *more* important beliefs—chiefly those about the nature of God (i.e. God as loving and just) and our relationship with God (i.e. God wishing to share his love and reward the good in the afterlife);

◆ certainly there have been cases where unscrupulous people have sought to, and sometimes succeeded in, taking unfair advantage of people's deeply held religious convictions about the existence of an afterlife. However, this only shows how such a belief is capable of being distorted and abused. It does *not* prove that the belief itself is mistaken.

Contrary to what is sometimes claimed, the major religions do not consider a belief in life after death as being like a drug they offer to people to numb the pain and suffering that is an integral part of life in this world. Rather, belief in an afterlife should make one appreciate how precious each moment of life is and resolve not to waste any of it.

Why? Because how one lives in *this* world influences or determines one's ultimate destiny in the *next*.

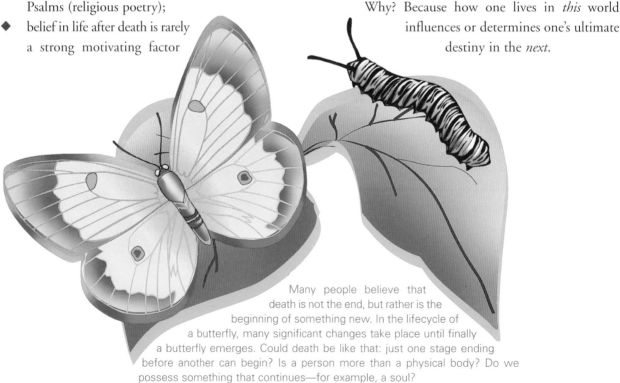

Many people believe that death is not the end, but rather is the beginning of something new. In the lifecycle of a butterfly, many significant changes take place until finally a butterfly emerges. Could death be like that: just one stage ending before another can begin? Is a person more than a physical body? Do we possess something that continues—for example, a soul?

Consider how the Abrahamic faiths teach that:

◆ each person has only one opportunity of life in this world;

◆ the focus of this life is to prepare for eternal life;

◆ a good and wise person is one who lives with this in mind and so always seeks, to the best of his/her ability, to do good and to avoid evil.

Thus, belief in life after death need *not* be understood as stemming from a desire to avoid accepting one's own mortality. Rather, it can be seen as a very real source of inspiration and hope that encourages people to live life to the full.

Questions

1. Explain the view of the soul in both (a) the Abrahamic faiths and (b) the Eastern religions.

2. What did Freud and Marx claim about the idea of an afterlife?

3. In what ways is it claimed that both were incorrect?

4. Read the following statement:

   Belief in an afterlife is dangerous. It may make people care less about what happens in this life.

   How might a Jew, a Christian or a Muslim respond to such a statement?

Human destiny

From the very outset Christianity has taught that death is *not* to be feared. It is viewed as the gateway to eternal life. If one reads the New Testament, one finds many descriptions of the afterlife. These are intended to act as useful images and metaphors, however, and should *not* be taken as literal descriptions. They were never intended as such.

Upon death, each person must face judgment. Christians make a distinction between two kinds of judgment:

◆ *the individual judgment* of God on each person when he/she dies and the soul separates from the body;

◆ *the final judgment* of God on all people at the end of human history as we know it (i.e. '*the Day of Judgment*').

There are differences of opinion among the Christian traditions regarding what happens thereafter. For Catholics, there are *three* possible fates that await a human being in the afterlife, whereas for many Protestants, there are only two possible fates.

The Last Judgement, by Jan van Eyck.

Catholic teaching identifies the following possible destinations for the soul after death:

Heaven

- a *timeless* state in which those referred to as '*the blessed*' enjoy *the Beatific Vision*, i.e. perfect peace and joy in the presence of God;
- in Heaven, the soul of the individual is united with a new and glorified body;
- only those who have led exemplary lives (i.e. pure, unselfish and loving) may enter heaven immediately after death;
- most people require a form of preparation *before* entering Heaven.

Purgatory

- a state in which the individual soul must spend an *undefined* period of time undergoing a process of purification;
- only when it is finally purged of sin will the soul be ready to enter Heaven.*

Hell

- the place where the soul endures a state of *permanent* separation from God.

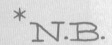

*

Many Protestants do *not* accept the idea of Purgatory, i.e. that there is an in-between state of preparation for Heaven. They believe that our opportunity to respond to God's love is limited to *this* earthly life.

All the Christian traditions believe that God wants to welcome everyone into the Beatific Vision. However, God extends an *invitation* to do so, *not* a command. People are free to choose either to accept or to reject God's offer. We are free to choose our own eternal destiny. Thus, in a very real sense God does not judge us. Instead, by the way we live our lives, *we judge ourselves.*

As one Eastern Orthodox writer puts it:

> *Judgement, as St. John's Gospel emphasizes, is going on all the time throughout our earthly existence. Whenever, consciously or unconsciously, we choose the good, we enter already by anticipation into eternal life; whenever we choose evil, we receive a foretaste of hell. The Last Judgement is best understood as the moment of truth when everything is brought to light, when all our acts of choice stand revealed to us in their full implications, when we realise with absolute clarity who we are and what has been the deep meaning and aim of our life. And so, following this final clarification, we shall enter – with soul and body reunited – into heaven or hell, into eternal life or eternal death.*
>
> *Christ is the judge; and yet, from another point of view, it is we who pronounce judgement upon ourselves. If anyone is in hell, it is not because God has imprisoned him there, but because that is where he himself has chosen to be. The lost in hell are self-condemned, self-enslaved; it has been rightly said that the doors of hell are locked on the inside.*

(Adapted from Bishop Kallistos Ware, *The Orthodox Way.*)

Questions

1. What do Christians mean by the term '*judgment*' in the context of the afterlife?

2. Read the following quotation:

   Death is the one experience when we leave behind everything we have and take with us what we are.

   (Ravi Zacharias, *The Shattered Vision*.)

   (a) What does Zacharias mean by this?
   (b) How would you apply this to your own life?

3. Outline Catholic teaching on the three possible fates that await a human being after death.

4. In what way do many Protestants differ from Catholics regarding the afterlife?

5. What is the central point made by Bishop Kallistos Ware?

The soul in western thought

The question as to whether or not there actually is a soul is one that has occupied some of the greatest philosophical minds in human history. Most of them—notably Plato, Aristotle, Thomas Aquinas, René Descartes and Immanuel Kant—have taught that *the soul exists*. But as in the case of the major world religions, these thinkers also *differ* regarding its precise nature and its relation to the material world.

Initially, the most influential account of the soul was that offered by Plato (fifth century BCE), but his influence was later eclipsed by that of Aristotle (fourth century BCE). It is difficult to overestimate the impact of Aristotle's writings on the development of western civilisation. He discussed topics ranging from astronomy to politics to literary criticism. One area in which he has profoundly influenced western thought is in relation to the soul. In this examination, as in so many other areas of research, he sought to base his conclusions on direct observation of the world around him.

The nature of the soul

Consider the following question:

What is the difference between a *dead* human being and a *living* human being?

A quick examination of a deceased person's body

From conception to old age.

immediately after death will show no material difference in either the body's size or weight. Yet there is an obvious difference: *life is missing*. Life is what makes a human being breathe. The word for '*soul*', '*life*' and '*breath*' is the same in many ancient languages.

Soul is *not* air that is still in the dead person's lungs. Rather, *soul* is *the power, or means, by which a human being lives*. It is for this reason that Aristotle referred to the soul as *the life principle*, i.e. that which makes a human person a *living* being.

Clearly, then, the soul is *not* a material thing. It is not an organ of the body. Rather, the soul is *the life* of the body's organs. It is for this reason that the soul is referred to as *immaterial*.

To say that the soul is *immaterial* means that:
◆ it does *not* have quantifiable (countable) parts, e.g. a body can be cut in half, but a soul cannot;
◆ it is *not* extended in space, e.g. a person does not lose an inch of his/her soul when having a haircut.

As a result, the soul plays a key role as the *source* of each person's unique individual *identity*. Consider the process of maturity that each and every human must undergo during the course of his/her life:
◆ a person's *appearance* as a baby or a child may have nothing in common with the same individual when he/she is elderly. Yet, he/she would still be deemed to be the *same* person;
◆ a person's *character* may change radically—for better or for worse—during the course of his/her life. Yet he/she is still recognised as the *same* person;
◆ more tragically, consider how a physical trauma to the brain or an illness such as Alzheimer's disease can cause a person to have *no memory* of him/ herself as a child. Yet he/she is still said to be the *same* person.

It is the soul that acts as the constant, unchanging core of each individual human being's unique identity. However, this uniqueness extends to more than just separating one individual human being from another. It also sets the human species apart from all other forms of life on Earth.

The human soul is also the source of all those unique capacities of the human mind, which neither plants nor animals share—namely the potential for understanding, imagining, inventing, remembering, reasoning, choosing and loving.

The relationship between body and soul

All this talk of the soul can be misleading. It may seem too otherworldly. After all, experience shows that we human beings are very much part of the material world in which we live. Aristotle would have agreed. He readily admitted that while one can *mentally* draw a distinction between the body and the soul, in reality *neither is by itself a human being*.

The soul on its own is *not* complete. It *needs* the body:
◆ to draw information (via the senses) from the world around us to provide us with the material and stimulus for thinking;
◆ to provide a way of expressing ourselves and interacting with others.

In other words, the body and the soul *belong together*. Therefore, when one says that '*Susan has a capacity to think, choose and love*', one does not mean that it is her soul alone that does these things. Rather, these are capacities of the *whole* person. '*Susan*' is a single, unified being who is a *fusion* of body and soul. This is why philosophers who follow Aristotle's lead refer to the human person as a *psychosomatic* being, i.e. a body-soul unity.

Questions

1. What did Aristotle mean when he described the soul as 'the life principle'?

2. Why did he conclude that the soul is *immaterial*?

3. What does it mean to say that the soul is *immaterial*?

4. In what way can it be said that *the soul plays a key role as the source of each person's individual identity*?
   Give examples in your answer.

5. In what way is it also claimed that the soul is *the source of human uniqueness*?

6. Why did Aristotle believe that the soul on its own is *not* complete and so needs the body?

7. Explain the term 'psychophysical unity' as applied to human beings.

The immortality of the soul

Scholars disagree as to whether or not Aristotle believed that the soul survives the death of the body.

Aristotle's account of the soul has been studied carefully by Christian thinkers, most notably by St Thomas Aquinas.

St Thomas was particularly interested in Aristotle's assertion that as the soul is *not* a material thing, it cannot decay or dissolve into smaller parts as does a physical body after death. This led St Thomas to conclude that the soul is *immortal*, i.e. it does not die when the body dies, but goes on existing *forever*.

St Thomas realised that this raised a serious question:

If only the soul is immortal, what kind of life can one expect after death?

He admitted that:

Anima mea non est ego : My soul is not I

Like Aristotle, St Thomas thought that the body and the soul of a human being *belong together*. When *united*, they give each person his/her own unique identity. As a Christian, however, St Thomas believed that he could draw upon sources of wisdom *other* than Aristotle's philosophy to help him gain insights into what life after death would be like.

St Thomas read the New Testament closely, particularly the post-resurrection accounts in the Gospels and St Paul's *First Letter to the Corinthians* (15:12–19/35–55). The conclusions he arrived at were not based on a philosopher's reflection on the world around him, but on a deeply religious man's meditation on the teachings contained in the sacred texts of his faith.

St Thomas believed that God is supremely loving and good. As such, God invites each and every human being to share in and enjoy a new and utterly different kind of life beyond the grave. This life-after-death is beyond the scope of our human minds to even remotely imagine or express. Furthermore, as revealed in the post-resurrection stories concerning Jesus, it will *not* be an after-life lived as a disembodied soul.

The Righteous Entering Paradise, detail from *The Last Judgement* (1580–90).

In the afterlife:

◆ the soul of each person will receive a new and *glorified* body, which, like that of the risen Jesus, will be beyond the restrictions of space and time;

◆ each person will begin this new and eternal life with his/her individual identity intact, retaining all the characteristics and memories that make up each person's separate and unique personality.

This, St Thomas believed, is what God intends for each human being. It is a destiny in which *no other* creatures on Earth are invited to share.

Questions

1. What does it mean to claim that the soul of a human being is '*immortal*'? ➡

2. Why did St Thomas Aquinas claim that the human soul is immortal?

3. What were St Thomas' sources of inspiration for his account of life after death?

4. How did St Thomas describe the fate of the human soul in the afterlife?

Opposing views

For some people, any mention of human beings having souls or experiencing an afterlife is nothing more than a naïve and misplaced acceptance of utterly obsolete notions that have nothing to contribute to life in the twenty-first century. Those who subscribe to a materialist outlook demand that any claims regarding the soul and the hereafter be subjected to close scrutiny under laboratory conditions.

Theists respond to this by saying that:
◆ by adopting such a criterion, materialists *begin* by *ruling out* the possibility that such things exist;
◆ materialists demonstrate a complete *lack* of comprehension of what is involved in these topics.

Why?
If there *is* a spiritual aspect to a human being, then such a spiritual aspect, or *soul*, is *not*, by its very definition, a material thing. Therefore its existence could *never* be established by means of material tests. Accordingly, the claim that belief in the soul and an afterlife is wrong because they cannot be verified under laboratory conditions is clearly *open* to serious challenge.

Of course, none of this means that one can establish with certainty that there *is* a soul or an afterlife. However, it does show that such belief is neither irrational nor illogical. Indeed, recent advances in medical technology have led many people, including some who were previously quite sceptical, to wonder if indeed it may be meaningful to talk of the soul and an afterlife.

Near-death experiences

In recent times there has been an increasing interest among scientists in what are referred to as *near-death experiences* or *NDEs*. These are experiences described by some people who were deemed to have been *clinically dead*,* but who were subsequently *resuscitated*.

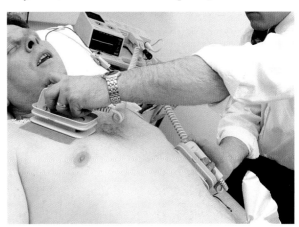

Male patient being defibrillated in hospital.

*Clinical Death
is said to occur when a person's:
◆ blood circulation and breathing have ceased due to cardiac arrest, i.e. where the heart stops beating in a regular rhythm;
◆ measurable brainwave activity ceases, usually within twenty to forty seconds.

It is largely due to recent improvements in medical technology that NDEs have become a matter for investigation at all. People who, in earlier times, would undoubtedly have died can now be restored to life. Two early pioneers in the field of NDEs were Dr Elizabeth Kubler-Ross, author of *On Death and Dying* (1969), and Dr Raymond Moody, author of *Life After Life* (1975). Each conducted separate investigations of the NDE phenomenon and made remarkably similar observations about it.

Both Kubler-Ross and Moody were intrigued by a common reaction to the NDE among the people they interviewed. Those who had been declared clinically dead but who were subsequently resuscitated often *complained* about being brought back to life because their experiences of a life beyond this life were so exquisite. As Dr Moody sifted through 150 case histories, he repeatedly encountered the same difficulty: all his interviewees stated that human language is simply inadequate as a means of describing what they had experienced. As one woman remarked:

This is a real problem for me because all the words I know are three dimensional. As I was going through my NDE, I kept thinking, 'Well, when I was studying geometry, they always told me there were only three dimensions and I always accepted that. But they were wrong. There are more.' And, of course, our world—the one we're living in now—is three dimensional, but the next one definitely isn't. And that's why it's so hard to tell you this. I have to describe it to you in words that are three dimensional. That's as close as I can get to it, but it's not really adequate. I can't really give you a complete picture.'

(Dr Raymond Moody, *Life After Life*.)

With the co-operation of those who claimed to have had a NDE, Dr Moody derived a common set of elements that define a NDE and proceeded to construct the following composite picture of a typical NDE, with each aspect in the order in which it would normally occur:

The individual may hear doctors or spectators pronounce him dead and experience a sensation of peace and quietness. There may then be a loud ringing or buzzing noise, and the individual simultaneously experiences himself moving rapidly down a long dark tunnel. Thereafter he finds himself outside his own physical body and often suspended above it. He realises that he still has a body, though of a different nature, and observes resuscitation attempts as an onlooker. He may be met by dead relatives, friends or guides who assist him and he feels the presence of a warm loving spirit. He enters a bright light or meets a being of light with whom he communicates non-verbally. This whole experience is accompanied by a sense of joy, love and peace.

The individual has a panoramic instantaneous playback of the major events of his life. Eventually he approaches some kind of a border, indicating a dividing line between earthly life and the next life, and realises that he must return to his earthly existence because the time for his death has not yet arrived.

Statistics reveal that NDEs are not a rare phenomenon. In 2001 British medical journal *The Lancet* published the findings of a thirteen-year study of the NDE phenomenon by a Dutch cardiologist, Dr Pim van Lommel. He stated that an estimated one in five people who were revived following a cardiac arrest reported memories of a NDE.[3]

---

[3] Regarding those cases where people did *not* recall an NDE after resuscitation, Dr Vivian Ellis, an obstetrician at Scripps Memorial Hospital, has suggested that this may be likened to the fact that some people can vividly recall their dreams while others have no memory of them at all.

Other research conducted by Kenneth Ring, Professor of Psychology at the University of Connecticut, indicates that there is no relationship between the occurrence of a NDE and age, sex, socio-economic group or religious background. Stories of NDEs come from all over the globe and they all share the core features identified by Dr Raymond Moody and described above.

These accounts of people's reputed progression to the afterlife and back again have convinced some people that they *do* offer us an optimistic glimpse of a life beyond this life. For some, these NDEs offer confirmation of life after death.

Others disagree, however. They remain cautiously sceptical about the evidential value of NDEs. As a result, a considerable debate has taken place regarding the nature and value of NDEs.

Questions

1. Explain the term '*Near-Death Experience*'.

2. When is *clinical death* said to occur?

3. What did Dr Kubler-Ross and Dr Moody both notice about many people who had been resuscitated following clinical death?

4. List the seven stages of a typical NDE.

5. How common are NDEs? Support your answer with evidence.

6. Is there any evidence to suggest that certain kinds of people are more likely to have an NDE than others? Explain your answer.

The debate on NDEs

Here we shall examine the various objections raised against NDEs and the responses offered by those who consider them to be a genuine phenomenon.

1. **Objection:**
   The large number of reported NDEs is entirely due to the recent publicity they have received since the publication of Kubler-Ross' and Moody's books.

Response:
If one looks back through history, one can find accounts of NDEs in *earlier* cultures.

For example:

◆ in his *Republic*, the fourth-century, Greek philosopher Plato mentioned the story of a soldier wounded in battle, who told of his journey from darkness to light accompanied by angelic beings;

◆ in his Ascent to Empyrean, the Dutch painter Hieronymus Bosch (d. 1516) depicted the

The Ascent of the Blessed, by Hieronymus Bosch.

being born, so they could not store such a memory and be able to recall it later in life.

3. **Objection:**

The *'tunnel experience'* is caused by an increased flow of carbon dioxide to the person's brain when the heart stops pumping oxygen. Research conducted in the 1950s revealed that people exposed to large doses of carbon dioxide gas had similar 'tunnel experiences'.

Response:

True, but their inhalation was not accompanied by experiences such as meeting a *'being of light'* or by *'life reviews'*. Further, those who suffer an acute imbalance in their supply of oxygen or carbon dioxide develop an *'acute confusional state'*, which is very different from a NDE. A person with the former condition becomes highly confused, thought processes fragment and he/she has little or no memory recall.

4. **Objection:**

Research indicates that if a NDE is induced artificially by using drugs such as LSD or Mescaline, it may lead to an *'out-of-body experience'*, together with flashes of light and fragmented or random memories.

Response:

True, but it will have neither the coherence nor the life-transforming effects of an authentic NDE. A major Dutch study conducted in 2001 declared that:

Transformational processes with life-changing insight and disappearance of fear of death are rarely reported after induced experiences.

5. **Objection:**

NDEs are merely hallucinations caused by people

deceased as having to pass through a tunnel towards a bright light.

2. **Objection:**

The *'tunnel experience'* is simply the memory of one's experience of being born (i.e. passing from the womb to the world outside) and is buried in one's unconscious. This memory is jolted back into the conscious mind by a major trauma, such as a cardiac arrest or a near-fatal accident.

Response:

This sounds plausible and would explain why people of different races and religious views have claimed similar NDEs. However, research strongly suggests that newborn babies are unable to understand and define their experience of being placed under great stress due to serious illness.

Response:

No. Research shows that NDEs are experienced exclusively by people declared *clinically dead*, and not by someone who is merely very ill.

6. **Objection:**

NDEs are the result of a shock to the brain, such as a temporal lobe seizure.

Response:

No. Any shock to the brain, be it physical, chemical or electrical, such as a seizure, produces *amnesia* at that moment. So the person may remember the events leading up to the shock and those that occurred after recovery, but the whole period in between is *forgotten*. Thus, a shock is *not* a sufficient explanation for a NDE memory.

7. **Objection:**

Only religious people who already believed in life after death experienced NDEs. Their *expectations* of such an experience caused them to have it. For example, consider how a Christian and a Hindu may both have a NDE in which they feel at peace, travel through a tunnel and see a light. However, if a figure is also present, in the Christian case it may be related to Christianity and in the Hindu case to Hinduism. These people merely experienced a hallucination boosted by 'picture images' of what they believe the next world is like.

Response:

No. People who were self-declared *atheists* have recounted their experiences of leaving their bodies, passing through a tunnel, meeting a being of light and having a life review. In his book *Life at Death*, Dr Kenneth Ring examined 102 cases of NDEs and, using three different methods of analysis, declared that religious belief seems to have *nothing to do* with what people claim to undergo in NDEs.

Question

1. Having reviewed the debate regarding NDEs, what is your view regarding their authenticity?
   Give reasons for your answer.

?

The impact of NDEs

Many of those who have claimed to have experienced a NDE have stated that they found it difficult, at least initially, to settle back into the mundane routine of ordinary life in this world. Perhaps this is not surprising given that they claim to have experienced

what Carl Gustav Jung described as something

… so unspeakably glorious that our imaginations do not suffice to form even an approximate idea of it.

The long-term effects on those reputed to have undergone a NDE are reported to be:

affected by this *hellish*-type of NDE. In many cases it led to the person having a complete change of heart and radically changing his/her lifestyle.

The implications of NDEs

Advocates of the NDE phenomenon claim that there is more than sufficient evidence to assert that NDEs really *do* occur. On this basis, they ask people to reflect on the consequences of this phenomenon to enhance their understanding of the human person.

Consider the following:

Case 1

Where '*clinical death*' is pronounced, the following three criteria are observed:

◆ the absence of spontaneous breathing;
◆ the lack of a heartbeat;

◆ a lack of any fear of death itself, although a retention of the desire to avoid a lingering, painful death;
◆ a greater appreciation of life as a gift to be cherished;
◆ a renewed interest in learning as a means of worthwhile self-development;
◆ a reduced interest in material possessions;
◆ a desire to live in greater harmony with God and one's fellow human beings.

Contrary to popular belief, however, *not* all those people who claim they experienced a NDE say that it was a pleasant experience. Researchers at Yale University Medical Centre have collected some fifty or so cases of *negative* NDEs. The people who claim to have had these experiences do not agree in every detail. They do recall the tunnel and out-of-body experience, but describe their destination in the afterlife either as a place of terrifying emptiness or a place of shocking torment. All admit to being profoundly

♦ within seconds of the above, the pupils of the eyes become fixed and dilated.

The third of these criteria indicates the loss of those areas of the brain believed to be responsible for our thought processes (*the cerebral cortex*), which is swiftly followed by the areas of the brain responsible for sustaining life (*the brain stem*). Thus in cases of people being declared 'clinically dead', their brains would not be expected to sustain thought processes at all. Yet as studies have shown, people have claimed to have had NDEs in exactly this situation. How could such lucid and well-structured thought processes, together with such clear and vivid memories, occur in people who have little or no brain function?

Case 2

Vicky Noratuk was an American woman whose NDE was examined in a BBC television documentary entitled *The Day I Died*, first broadcast in February 2003. After being involved in an automobile accident she was declared clinically dead, but was resuscitated. Afterwards she told her doctor about her NDE, which involved the usual elements of an out-of-body experience, life review and so on. She was even able to describe her hospital surroundings in detail. This was what puzzled researchers, because Vicky had been blind since birth. Her brain could not have provided her with the visual information she possessed, as she had no memories on which to draw.

Reflections

Some doctors and psychologists have concluded that the workings of the human brain alone are *not* enough to explain the phenomenon of NDEs. They assert that current theories about the mind and the brain need to be re-examined.

Many scientists currently equate mind (our mental life) with the electro-chemical activity of brain cells (neurons). Certainly studies have shown that a particular thought or feeling will cause certain sets of neurons in various parts of the brain to become physiologically active. However, this might only imply that such cells act as a *mediator* in expressing such thoughts and might *not* necessarily be their place of origin.

The suggestion now being made by some researchers into NDEs is that the human mind may not entirely be the product of matter. Our mental life may not be completely dependent on the workings of the brain. This has led some to claim that the NDE phenomenon points to a non-material (i.e. spiritual) dimension to the human person that survives the death of the physical body.

The vast majority of those who have had a NDE are convinced that human beings do survive bodily death. To *outside* observers of the NDE phenomenon who do not share their certainty, the question of whether or not there is life after death remains intriguingly *open*. Though, on balance, it would seem that it is more probable that there *is* a life after death.

Questions

1. Describe the reported long-term effects on those who are reputed to have undergone a NDE.

2. (a) What is a *hellish*-type of NDE?
   (b) Typically, what impact does it tend to have on the person who experiences it? ➡

3. Dr Susan Blackmore is a leading atheist and psychologist. She claims that all NDEs are explicable purely in terms of the brain's electro-chemical functions. Why have other doctors and psychologists drawn a *different* conclusion, i.e. that the workings of the brain are *not* enough to explain the phenomenon of NDEs?
Refer to both (a) clinical death cases and (b) the case of Vicky Noratuk in your answer.

4. Do you find the claim that NDEs offer a glimpse of the afterlife as comforting and reassuring, or not? Give reasons for your answer.

Reincarnation

The Hindu belief in *reincarnation* has become more popular recently in the Western world. This is the belief that:

After the death of the body, the soul (called atman) *survives and enters another body, animal or human, in a perpetual cycle of rebirth (called* samsara).

What determines the direction a soul will take on re-entry as a reincarnated life form? This depends on the *karma* (or merit) the soul has earned in its immediate previous existence.

According to the *Law of Karma*:

From good must come good, from evil must come evil.

Hindus believe that for each level of existence there is a specific level of religious duty (called *dharma*) that must be followed for the accumulation of *positive* karma. **For example:**

◆ the *dharma* of a dog would be loyalty and obedience to its master;

A Hindu cremation in Kathmandu, Nepal.

- for an elephant it would involve non-violence and service to its master;
- the human *dharma* would be to live a good life as a member of a particular social class (called a caste).

The soul is reborn into a higher or lower caste, or form of living thing, depending on the amount of karma—positive or negative—acquired by how well it performed its defined religious duty.

For example:

- an animal may rise to human rebirth over a period of time, or all at once if some heroic animal deed saved a human life;
- in contrast, if a human being acts selfishly and destructively, he/she can be reborn into a lower form of life, such as a dog or monkey.

Hindus believe that one can only escape the cycle of rebirth (*samsara*) by:

- storing up sufficient good merit(positive karma)

through generous and conscientious actions;
- freeing oneself from all attachments to material things;
- practising spiritual disciplines, such as *yoga*, to acquire the strength, commitment and insight to sustain this.

When a soul reaches this level of enlightenment, it is said to have achieved *nirvana*, i.e. release from *samsara*.

Hindus vary in their beliefs about what happens to the soul at this point:

- most believe that the soul is completely absorbed into the impersonal world-spirit and ceases to have any individual existence;
- some say that slight differences remain, so the soul can still be identified.

Even the latter view represents a very *different* view of the soul's fate after death from that held by the members of the Abrahamic faiths.

Questions

1. What is meant by *reincarnation*?

2. Explain *the Law of Karma*.

3. What is meant by *dharma*?

4. According to Hindu teaching, how can one escape the cycle of rebirth?

5. What is meant by *nirvana*?

6. What do Hindus believe happens to the soul after death?

Evidence for reincarnation

A small but growing number of people who are not members of an Eastern religion find the idea of reincarnation credible. They do so for two reasons:

(1.) The testimony provided by people who have undergone hypnotic regressions

In a number of well-documented cases, a person was

hypnotised and was able to talk at length and in detail about what it is claimed he/she did in a previous existence. Sometimes these individuals *appear* to have lived more than one previous life.

(2.) The experience of déjà-vu (French expression meaning 'already seen')

This is the feeling some people experience of having encountered some place or situation before, in what they believe to have been a previous life.

Probing the mind

Psychology is *the science that studies human behaviour and development.* One of its most important discoveries has been the realisation that the human mind (i.e. our capacity for thinking, feeling and choosing) has two distinct but *interacting* aspects: (1) the conscious and (2) the unconscious.

The following extract explains what is meant by the 'unconscious' and will provide the key to understanding why some people sincerely believe they have been reincarnated when there may be another, more plausible explanation.

Have you ever had the experience of not being able to remember something when you wanted to, and then suddenly remembering it later when it was no longer useful? It was there all the time; you just could not grasp it.

When a person is unaware of something it is said to be unconscious. When he becomes aware of it, then it becomes conscious. Unconsciousness means unawareness; consciousness means awareness. Of course, not all things buried in our minds are equally unconscious. Some things can be brought to consciousness quite easily, such as your address,

date of birth or a good friend's telephone number. Other things would be very difficult to bring to consciousness, maybe impossible under ordinary circumstances, such as childhood experiences before the age of two.

Impressions of sounds, sights, touches, smells and tastes pour into us all the time. We remain unconscious of most of them because they are unimportant. For instance, right now you are receiving impressions from your feet touching the floor, from your eyes seeing your hands and catching glimpses over the top of this book, from your ears hearing little background noises and so on. While you were concentrating on reading, all kinds of little sense impressions were unnoticed. They were unimportant. You became conscious of them only when your attention was drawn to them.

(Anthony Panzarella, *Growth in Christ.*)

Examining the evidence

A. Hypnotic regression

Case One

In 1952 an American woman named Virginia Tighe was placed under hypnosis and appeared to recall a previous existence in which she had lived as a nineteenth-century Belfast woman named *Bridie Murphy*. Her story convinced some people that they had found proof positive for reincarnation.

Careful investigation by psychologists revealed that Virginia Tighe was merely the *unwitting victim of her own unconscious memories, which she had recalled in a garbled/confused manner*. The investigators discovered that the Belfast house she described in great detail bore a very close resemblance to the house in Philadelphia where she had lived as a small child. Further, while living there she had a neighbour named Bridie Murphy with whom she used to spend a lot of time as a little girl. Bridie was an elderly woman who had emigrated to America, but was homesick for Ireland, and she loved to tell Virginia stories about her life there.

Case Two

In 1956 Canadian psychiatrist Dr H. Rosen revealed that when placed in a hypnotic trance, one of his patients had written down a full page in *Oscan* dialect, a long dead language once spoken in central Italy before it was conquered by the Romans, more than 2,500 years earlier.

Again, detailed investigation revealed that Rosen's patient was *not* recalling some knowledge that could only be derived from a previous existence. It was discovered that, many years before, the patient had been working in a library where he saw displayed in an open book the only written example of Oscan language known to exist. He possessed what could be called a '*photographic memory*', which accurately recorded this information, but which afterwards slipped from his consciousness into his unconsciousness. There it remained, until it was *recalled* when he was placed in a hypnotic trance by Dr Rosen.

B. The experience of déjà-vu

Case Three

In 1906 an Anglican clergyman named Forbes Phillips published an account of a strange experience he had while holidaying in the city of Rome. While there he had visited a number of the leading tourist attractions. When he visited three particular places—the Thermae of Caracalla, the Appian Way and the Tivoli—he had what he could only describe as a most peculiar feeling. He had never been there before, yet these locations seemed unusually familiar to him. It was as if he had *lived there before*, long ago.

Subsequent investigation revealed that when Rev. Phillips visited other tourist sites in Rome, he did not have the same experience, even though they belonged to the same era as the others. Psychiatrists believe that as an avid reader, Rev. Phillips had most likely read about those locations several years earlier, but that the actual sight of them brought *back* the buried memory of them into his consciousness.

Sometimes another reason for the feeling of *déjà-vu* is advanced: that some people have an as yet inexplicable facility for *pre-cognition*, i.e. being able to *anticipate* what he/she is about to experience. A person might have a dream in which he/she seems to get an advance warning of some event or impressions of the layout of some place he/she has never before visited, such as, for instance, a rival football team's stadium.

Some researchers believe that the phenomenon of *déjà-vu* may have its roots in the minuscule time lapse that occurs between our initial experience of some person, place or thing, and our subsequently becoming *aware* of what we are experiencing. In this reading of it we have not really recalled an earlier experience, merely misinterpreted our present experience and drawn the wrong conclusion!

Christianity and reincarnation

The Catholic philosopher Peter Kreeft identifies three reasons why Christians have always rejected the idea of reincarnation:

◆ it involves a very low opinion of the body, presenting it as a prison or punishment for the soul. This implies that God has put us on Earth to punish us, which contradicts the Christian belief in a loving and just God;

◆ reincarnation claims that we are really pure spirits imprisoned in our bodies and thereby denies the psychosomatic unity of the human person;

◆ the idea that we are reincarnated in order to learn lessons we failed to learn in a past earthly life runs contrary to both common sense and sound educational psychology. We cannot learn something if there is no continuity of memory. We can learn from our mistakes only if we *remember* them. People do *not* usually remember these past reincarnations.

Questions

1. Why, in your opinion, might reincarnation seem an attractive idea to some people who are not members of an Eastern religion? Explain your answer.

2. Explain the meaning of the following terms:
   (a) *consciousness* and (b) *unconsciousness*.

3. In your own words, explain the role of the *unconscious* in human life.

4. What is your evaluation of the evidence for reincarnation offered by
   (a) hypnotic regression and (b) the experience of *déjà-vu*?
   Give reasons for the opinions you express.

5. Read the following statement:

   Men only die once, and after that comes judgement.

   (Letter to the Hebrews 9:27)

   Explain Christian objections to the idea of reincarnation.

Section

2

The Evidence for the Life of Jesus of Nazareth

Introduction

Christianity has its origin in the story of a Jewish peasant named *Jesus of Nazareth*. He lived in the Roman province of Palestine some time between 6 BCE and 33 CE.

The name *Jesus* was a common one among Jewish males 2,000 years ago. It is a Latin version of the Greek name *Iesous*, which was itself a rendering of the Hebrew name *Yehosua* (*Joshua*), which means *God saves* or *God is salvation*. Though dismissed as an insignificant nobody by the rich and powerful of his era, today Jesus is *the* central figure in the belief and worship of his estimated 2 billion followers worldwide.

Doubts raised about Jesus

Since the nineteenth century a number of writers have sought to challenge the Christian belief that Jesus of Nazareth is the Son of God.

The Saviour, by Titian.

- Ernest Renan claimed that Jesus was little more than a well-intentioned fraud.
- Albert Schweitzer thought that Jesus was nothing more than a deluded visionary.

- Adolph von Harnack admired Jesus as a great moral teacher, but rejected any claim regarding his divinity.

One writer went even further than this. John Allegro claimed that Jesus of Nazareth had never even existed. He stated that Jesus was merely a fictional character, fabricated by a community of renegade Jews.

Confirming the existence of Jesus

Although they may disagree regarding his identity, there is broad agreement among historians that a person named Jesus of Nazareth did exist. This is because there are two separate streams of historical evidence that independently *confirm* his existence. These written sources are both Christian and non-Christian.

- *Non-Christian sources*
  A number of ancient authors refer to Jesus of Nazareth as a historical figure. These include the Jewish historian Josephus and the Roman writers Pliny the Younger, Seutonius and Tacitus. None of these writers could be accused of having a pro-Christian bias: some were openly hostile to Christianity; others were, at best, indifferent to it.

- *Christian sources*
  The earliest surviving Christian documents to mention Jesus are the epistles (i.e. letters) of St Paul. They contain very little biographical detail, however. The most important documentary evidence of Christian origin is offered by the four Gospels: each was produced by a different first-century author, traditionally identified as Mark, Matthew, Luke and John.

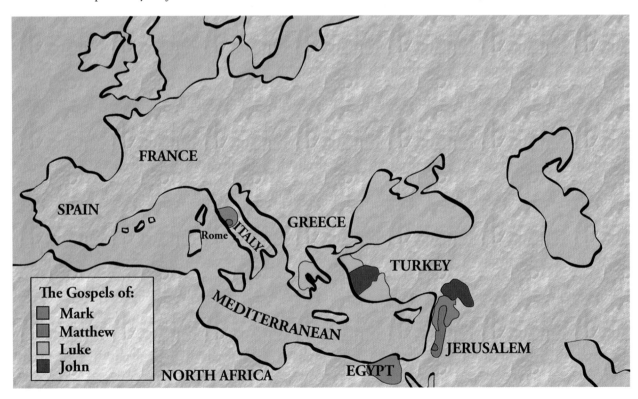

The Communities of the Gospels: historians' approximations of the areas in which each of the four New Testament Gospels was used.

Dating the Gospels

The most widely held opinion is that:

◆ Mark was composed between 60 and 70 CE;

◆ Matthew and Luke between 70 and 80 CE;

◆ John between 90 and 100 CE.

Some scholars dissent from this opinion and claim that all four Gospels were written *before* the destruction of the Temple in Jerusalem in 70 CE. Whatever the exact date, all scholars agree that the Gospels were written before the end of the first century CE.

Questions

1. What is the meaning of the name *Jesus*?

2. Consider the following statement:

   The bottom line for Christians is that they have no historical evidence that Jesus of Nazareth ever existed.

   (a) How might Christians respond to such a claim?
   (b) How might they defend the historical existence of Jesus?

The purpose of the Gospels

The four Gospels are *not* biographies in the modern sense of the word.

For example:

◆ they do not offer us a physical description of Jesus;

◆ they do not tell us much about his childhood.

In these matters they are quite similar in form to other ancient biographies written in the Roman world. If one reads any of the lives of the emperors, philosophers or heroes composed at that time, one will notice that they are all highly selective in their content and concentrate on the major events in their chosen subjects' lives. The primary focus of such books is to help the reader to understand the *meaning* of these remarkable people's lives.

In the case of the four Gospels, the authors (called 'evangelists') concentrate primarily on the most significant moments in the life of Jesus of Nazareth: his parables, miracles, suffering, death and resurrection. It must be admitted, however, that the evangelists did *not* set out to offer readers objective reports on the life of Jesus, but rather to persuade people to have faith in him. The evangelists clearly assume that Jesus is alive, is risen from the dead and that his resurrection vindicates him as the Son of God. Before one is tempted to simply reject the Gospels as nothing more than examples of religious propaganda, one should note that non-Christian writers such as Josephus and Tacitus *corroborate* the basic details of the story set out in the Gospels, namely that:

◆ Jesus of Nazareth was a real person who lived in Palestine during the procuratorship of Pontius Pilate;

◆ Jesus gained a reputation as a miracle-worker;

◆ Jesus offended his society's ruling class;

◆ Jesus was executed by crucifixion.

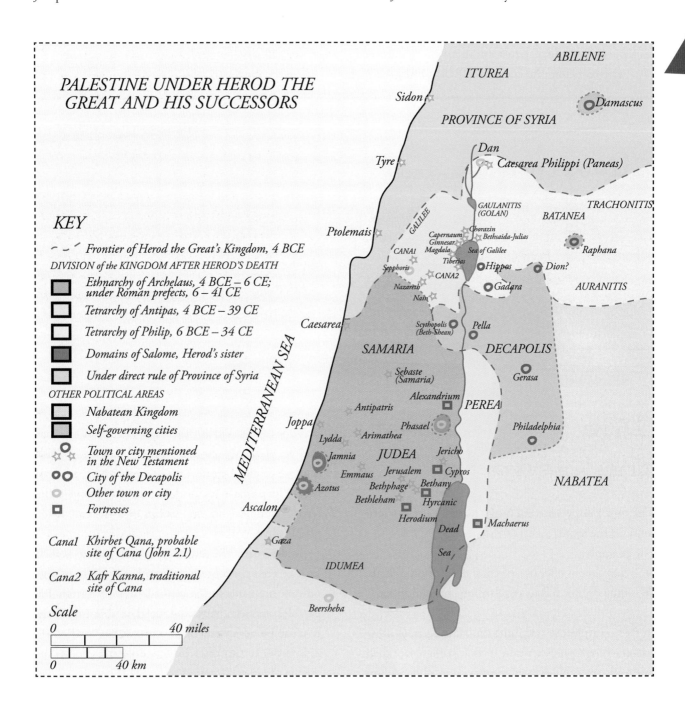

PALESTINE UNDER HEROD THE GREAT AND HIS SUCCESSORS

KEY

– – – ´ *Frontier of Herod the Great's Kingdom, 4 BCE*

DIVISION of the KINGDOM AFTER HEROD'S DEATH

▨ *Ethnarchy of Archelaus, 4 BCE – 6 CE; under Roman prefects, 6 – 41 CE*

☐ *Tetrarchy of Antipas, 4 BCE – 39 CE*

☐ *Tetrarchy of Philip, 6 BCE – 34 CE*

▨ *Domains of Salome, Herod's sister*

☐ *Under direct rule of Province of Syria*

OTHER POLITICAL AREAS

▨ *Nabatean Kingdom*

☐ *Self-governing cities*

☆○☆ *Town or city mentioned in the New Testament*

○○ *City of the Decapolis*

○ *Other town or city*

▢ *Fortresses*

Cana1 *Khirbet Qana, probable site of Cana (John 2.1)*

Cana2 *Kafr Kanna, traditional site of Cana*

Scale

0 — 40 miles

0 — 40 km

> Palestine was a tiny province of the mighty Roman Empire. It measured about 150 miles from north to south, and 60 miles from east to west. It was about the same size as the modern province of Munster in Ireland. Though small geographically, Palestine was of enormous strategic importance because it was the crossroads where the overland trade routes from Europe, Asia and Africa met.

The historical accuracy of the Gospels

There was no pressing need for written accounts of the life of Jesus of Nazareth in the first two decades of the Christian era. The early Christian communities included people who had known Jesus and had witnessed his deeds. It was as these eyewitnesses began to die that it became essential to record and preserve Jesus' story and teachings for future generations.

When the evangelists came to write their different accounts in the second half of the first century CE, they were able to consult both collections of Jesus' sayings, such as the 'Q' document, as well as the memories of those who had actually known him and witnessed the key events of his life. As ancient people did not have easy access to writing materials and books were scarce, first-century Jews had developed refined techniques for memorising long sermons, poems and prayers. Indeed, a good memory and a receptive ear were considered essential social skills in the ancient world. This enabled witnesses to recall accurately Jesus' words and actions, or, at least, to give the closest approximation possible.

Further, in keeping with the established practice of religious teachers in the ancient world, Jesus deliberately set out his teachings in the form of stories and proverbs to help his disciples to remember them and recall them accurately later. However, critics of the Gospels rightly point to the *different versions* of the same prayers or teachings recorded in them.

For example:

◆ Matthew 6:9–13 offers a longer version of the *Lord's Prayer* than Luke 11:2–4.
  ➡ A reasonable response here would be to say that Jesus himself may have given two different versions of the prayer on two separate occasions and each evangelist later recalled a different one. In any case, the two evangelists offer *complementary*, rather than contradictory, versions of the *Lord's Prayer*.

◆ Luke 16:18 forbids men to divorce their wives, but Mark 10:12 forbids *both* men and women from divorcing their spouses.
  ➡ This is an example of how the evangelist Mark added to the original words of Jesus to *clarify* his teaching. As Christianity expanded beyond Palestine, the evangelists had to explain the meaning of Jesus' teaching to a non-Jewish audience. Whereas a woman could not initiate divorce proceedings in Jewish society, she could do so in many *non-Jewish* societies. Mark therefore extended the prohibition on divorce to cover both women and men, so that his readers would not misunderstand Jesus' opposition to divorce, regardless of whether it is sought by the husband or the wife.

There is *no* evidence that the evangelists sought to mislead their readers. Their aim was to write *truthful* accounts; to have done anything else would have been an utter betrayal of everything Jesus stands for.

The reliability of the Gospel texts available today

Sadly, the original first-century Gospel manuscripts are unavailable to modern scholars. They probably either decayed with age and use, as all books do, or else were destroyed in one of the periods of religious persecution suffered by the early Christian communities within the Roman Empire.

The earliest complete manuscript copy of the original New Testament text is the *Codex Sinaiticus*, produced around 350 CE, some three centuries after the events described therein. However, the earliest existing copy of Julius Caesar's *Gallic Wars*, written in the first century BCE, was produced in the eighth century CE, some 900 years after the original text.

Fortunately, archaeologists have so far located 116 Christian papyri, dating from the second and third centuries CE. These include fragments of the four Gospels, the earliest of which is a section of the fourth Gospel (John 18:31–33), which is held in the Rylands University Library in Manchester, England, and dates from about 130 CE. This fragment was preserved in the dry sands of Egypt. Scholars have used it and a dozen other surviving fragments from the second and third centuries to confirm the accuracy and reliability of the complete fourth-century manuscript, on which Christians depend today. There are good grounds for accepting the Christian Church's claim that the Gospels have been transmitted *intact* down through the centuries and that the editions used today are *authentic* and *reliable*.

St John the Evangelist, by Pedro Berruguete. The evangelist, to whom the letters of John are traditionally ascribed, is accompanied here by his traditional symbol: an eagle.

Questions

1. What does it mean to say that:

   The four Gospels are not biographies in the modern sense of the word? ➡

2. What is the primary focus of such ancient literature as the four Gospels?

3. How might the four Gospels be defended against the charge that they are

   nothing more than examples of religious propaganda?

4. One Christian scholar has written of the Gospels that

   there seems to have been a reverence (in them) for the remembered speech and acts of Jesus.

   What evidence is there to support such a view?

5. Contemporary Christians are confident that they possess editions of the four Gospels that are faithful copies of the original first-century manuscripts. What reasons do they have for believing this?

Marriage and Children

Could Jesus have been married? Could he have had children?

Over the last sixty years there have been several authors who have claimed that there was a romantic relationship between Jesus and Mary Magdalene and that it resulted in a marriage and children. Certainly, Mary Magdalene was a close friend of Jesus and one of his inner circle. She stood with and comforted Jesus' mother at the foot of the cross and was the first person to whom Jesus appeared after his resurrection.

However, the overwhelming majority of scholars *reject* the claim that Jesus and Mary Magdalene married and had children. They do so for the following reasons:

◆ while it is reported that Jesus had a mother, an adoptive father, cousins and that several of his apostles were married, there is *no reference* made in the Gospels, nor in any other first-century text, to Jesus being married or having a child;

◆ there were both married and unmarried women

Mary Magdalene.

rabbis were unheard-of in first-century Palestine. Again, most scholars *reject* this line of argument. Consider:

◆ although celibacy was not part of mainstream Judaism, there was *no requirement* for a Jewish male to marry. The historian Josephus mentions how the Essenes did not marry (although this does not necessarily mean that Jesus was ever an Essene himself). John the Baptist was unmarried. Thus, contrary to some recent claims, bachelorhood (i.e. being a single male) was *not* considered an unnatural state for a man at that time;

◆ there are clear indications in the Gospels that although Jesus was sometimes referred to as a '*rabbi*', he did not hold any kind of officially sanctioned position recognised by the Jewish authorities. For instance, the chief priest and scribes asked Jesus:

> '*What authority have you for acting like this? Who gave you authority to do these things?*'
> (Mark 11:28)

There is also mention of the fact that Jesus had not been formally trained.

For example:
In response to Jesus' wisdom and insight, his listeners

> *were astonished and said, 'How did he learn to read? He has not been taught.'*

Indeed, on three occasions Jesus referred to himself as '*didasklos*', meaning *a teacher*,[4] rather than '*hrabbi*' (*rabbi*), meaning *my master*. There are good reasons for believing that Jesus was *not* a *rabbi* in the strict sense, otherwise his opponents would not have questioned both his authority and his credentials. If there was an expectation

among Jesus' disciples, but there is no evidence that he was in any way romantically involved with any of them. If he had been, it would have given rise to scandal and no doubt would have been exploited by his enemies because such behaviour would have been *totally unacceptable* within Jewish culture of that era;

◆ the writers of all four Gospels named women who travelled with Jesus. Often their husbands' names were mentioned to help identify them (see Matthew 27:55–56 or John 19:25). *None* of them named Mary Magdalene, or any other woman, as the wife of Jesus.

While admitting this as true, some writers have responded by asserting that as Jesus was a *rabbi*, he would have had to have been married because single

---

[4] See Matthew 10:24, Luke 6:40 and John 13:14.

that a *rabbi* should marry, it did *not* necessarily apply to Jesus.

Finally, some writers have appealed to a few lines in the so-called *Gospel of Philip* to support their claims that Jesus and Mary Magdalene shared some form of romantic relationship. This text is generally regarded as an unreliable source of information for the life of Jesus. The reasons for this are:

◆ the Gospel of Philip was not written until the *third* century, a time far removed from first-century Palestine;

◆ the author(s) of this text was not a Christian. It was written by a member of a secretive and elitist group known as *the Gnostics* (from the Greek, meaning 'knowledge'). They held ideas diametrically *opposed* to those of Jesus;

◆ the text has many gaps, but it seems to refer to Jesus as 'the companion' who kisses Mary Magdalene. The term 'companion' does *not* necessarily mean husband or sexual partner. Indeed, this meaning is unlikely because the Gnostics saw sex as wicked. It is more likely that, given what is known about Gnostic attitudes towards sex, this kiss referred to in the text is one of *fellowship*, without any element of sexual attraction.

A document such as the Gospel of Philip is only of value in that it provides insights into the mindset of the person who wrote it and the times in which he/she lived. It is of no value for anyone seeking to support the claim that Jesus married Mary Magdalene. It would seem, then, that there is *no evidence* to support the assertion that Jesus was married and/or had children.

Question

1. Read the following statement:

   Jesus as a married man makes infinitely more sense than the standard biblical view of Jesus as a celibate bachelor.

   Do you agree/disagree with this claim? Give reasons for your answer.

The Teachings of Jesus and their Impact

Jesus as teacher

Jesus of Nazareth is referred to as 'a teacher' forty-eight times in the Gospels. What does it *mean* to call him a teacher? What *kind* of teacher was Jesus?

Today when people speak of a teacher, they are usually referring to a person possessing recognised third-level educational qualifications who is employed by a school to offer instruction to its students. But in a broader sense, one can say that

a teacher is anyone who shows others how to do something.

Therefore anyone who helps someone to learn how to read, bake a cake or drive a car can be described as a teacher. *This* is the kind of teacher Jesus was. He had a lower-class upbringing in a small village and did not enjoy the benefit of a formal education, nor was he ever licensed to teach by the religious authorities of the time. Further, Jesus was an *itinerant* (i.e. wandering) teacher. One evangelist records him as saying:

'Foxes have lairs, birds have nests, but the Son of Man has nowhere to rest his head.'
(Matthew 8:20)

Jesus teaching in the synagogue.

Jesus was wholly dependent on the goodwill and generosity of others for his food and shelter. This gave him a very real appreciation for the daily struggles of ordinary people. Yet, despite his small-town upbringing, poverty and lack of formal education, the Gospels portray Jesus as an extraordinarily capable, open-minded and well-informed person. Consider:

◆ Jesus repeatedly demonstrated a clear understanding of the complex political and social issues of the day;

◆ he had a thorough grasp of the teachings of the different religious groups in Palestine and readily debated with them;

◆ he was fluent in Aramaic (the everyday language of people in Palestine), Hebrew (the language of religious scholarship) and Greek (the language of trade and diplomacy);

◆ he was a highly charismatic speaker who drew large crowds and held their attention with his profound insights and attractive style of communication;

◆ he was always willing to communicate and interact with those *marginalised* within his own religious community (e.g. prostitutes and tax-collectors) and those completely *outside* of it (e.g. Samaritans and Romans).

Jesus strongly emphasised certain ideas in his teaching, such as forgiveness of one's enemies and the renunciation of greed and selfishness, but he did *not* offer any radically new rules for human conduct. Indeed, all his teachings could already be found in the Jewish *Torah*, though he presented them in fresh and thought-provoking ways that challenged his listeners.

Christians believe that Jesus' true originality lies not so much in what he taught, but in *who he is*. Like the Old Testament prophets before him, Jesus called on people to repent and reform their lives. Unlike those prophets, Jesus *never* used such traditional formulae as:

'Thus says the Lord …'

Instead, Jesus spoke authoritatively in his own name:

'I tell you truly …'

He issued commandments and he forgave people's sins. These were things the Jews believed were reserved to *God alone*. During his public ministry, Jesus' followers concluded that he had to be the long-awaited messiah. After his resurrection, they came to believe that Jesus spoke with an utterly unique authority—that of God himself—and worshipped him. (This is a topic to which we shall return later.)

The Kingdom of God

The consensus among modern scholars is that the central message of Jesus' teaching concerned 'the kingdom of God'. One evangelist summed up Jesus' public ministry thus:

He went round the whole of Galilee, teaching in their synagogues and proclaiming the Good News of the Kingdom.
(Matthew 4:23)

Although the expression 'the kingdom of God' is mentioned about 100 times in the synoptic gospels, nowhere does Jesus define explicitly the precise nature of this kingdom. This suggests that he was talking about an idea that was, in some form, familiar to his Jewish listeners.

In the Old Testament, Yahweh/God is frequently referred to as '*the King*' who:

◆ created the world;

◆ renews its fertility annually;

◆ sustains his people's place in the world;

◆ protects them from the forces of evil.

In the early years of their religion's history the Jews understood Yahweh as exclusively *theirs*, i.e. the divine

The Sermon on the Mount, by Joos de Momper the Younger.

coming of God's kingdom as an historic, political event that would occur when:

◆ a descendant of King David would restore Israel as a powerful, independent state among the nations of the world;

◆ all hostilities between nations and oppression of peoples would end;

◆ God's justice and order would prevail across the world.

Some, such as the Zealots, wanted to hasten its arrival by force of arms. Jesus, on the other hand, offered people a very *different* vision of the kingdom of God. Consider the very language he used: despite his many references to the 'kingdom', Jesus is not recorded as referring to God himself as a king, nor does he use royal imagery in his remarks about *the kingdom of God*. Jesus makes it very clear that the kingdom of God is not a people, a place or a thing. In his teaching, it is *within* each person and can be found among them. As one evangelist writes:

> *Asked by the Pharisees when the kingdom of God was to come, Jesus gave them this answer, 'The coming of the kingdom of God does not admit of observation and there will be no one to say "Look here! Look there!" For, you must know, the kingdom of God is among you.'*
> (Luke 17:20–21)

The kingdom of God is a *relationship* between each individual human being and God, which people *express* through the lives they lead. The whole thrust of Jesus' teaching was that the kingdom of God is *both*:

◆ **a reality already present,**
but only activated properly by Jesus and his public ministry,

and

◆ **a future phenomenon,**
which will be brought to completion at some point in the future known only to God.

ruler of one people only. However, as the centuries passed they came to view Yahweh's kingship as *universal*, i.e. not just confined to ruling over the Jewish people. Although Yahweh's rule was not yet widely acknowledged by other peoples, the Jews hoped that one day all other people would come to accept Yahweh as the one true God and recognise his rule over all creation. This, they believed, would come about either by Yahweh's direct intervention or through his chosen/anointed one: the Messiah.

By the time of Jesus of Nazareth, the Jews had suffered so many serious setbacks as a conquered and oppressed people that they yearned deeply for the arrival of the Messiah. Most Jews envisaged the

In the Beatitudes (Matthew 5:1–12) and the Lord's Prayer (Matthew 6:9–13), Jesus told his listeners that in the kingdom of God:

◆ humanity's deepest needs are satisfied;
◆ sins are forgiven;
◆ the sick are made whole again;
◆ the weak are protected;
◆ evil is overcome;
◆ justice is dispensed;
◆ lasting peace and joy are experienced.

Further, whereas traditionally the kingdom of God had been understood as belonging *exclusively* to the Jewish people alone, Jesus declared that it was open to everyone—to Jew and non-Jew alike.

Entry into the kingdom of God

Throughout the Gospels Jesus invites people to enter into a partnership with him. He called people to be his co-workers in bringing the kingdom of God to fruition. But he made it very clear that most people would find this very difficult to do (Matthew 16:24–26).

First, people would have to humbly repent of their sins and ask God for forgiveness. Secondly, people would have to undergo a *metanoia*, i.e. freely choose to completely transform their whole lives, so that they become:

◆ open-hearted and receptive to Jesus' message;
◆ whole-heartedly committed to faithfully living each day according to that message.

Jesus fleshed out what this would demand of his disciples in '*the Sermon on the Mount*' (Matthew 5–7).[5] So that his Jewish listeners would not be confused, Jesus made it clear that his teaching in no way con-

tradicted the Mosaic Law. He said that his mission was to fulfil Mosaic Law and give it new meaning. In the section in Matthew 5:1–12 known as *the Beatitudes* (from the Jewish expression for '*how fortunate are those who …*'), Jesus sets out the kind of person a co-worker is called to be. Namely:

◆ selfless and loving;
◆ obedient to the will of God;
◆ passionate for justice;
◆ merciful and compassionate;
◆ deep-thinking;
◆ willing to endure suffering for what is right.

The parables of the kingdom

Much of Jesus' teaching about the kingdom of God was presented in the form of *parables*. The parable was a common art form in the story-telling culture of Palestine in the first century CE. Jesus' parables were vivid, memorable and intriguing stories. They involved incidents rooted in the everyday lives of his audience, so that people could readily identify with them and grasp their message.

These parables compared or linked the life experiences of Jesus' listeners to the kingdom of God. They were intended to help them understand:

◆ what is meant by the kingdom of God;
◆ how to find it;
◆ what it means to live as a citizen of it.

These parables were often *inconclusive*. Jesus sought to prompt his listeners to reflect on what he had said, to encourage them to figure out its meaning and then to make their own response to it. Contemporary Christians believe that Jesus' parables still contain life-transforming messages for us today. They are *not* just stories from long ago.

---

[5] This sermon is now thought to be more a summary of Jesus' teaching rather than an eyewitness' report of a particular sermon.

A list of the parables

Most scholars accept the following list:

- ◆ **Parables in all three synoptics:**
  A Divided House (Mark 3:23–26 and parallels)
  The Sower (Mark 4:2–9 and parallels)
  The Mustard Seed (Mark 4:30–32 and parallels)
  The Wicket Tenants (Mark 12:1–11 and parallels)
  The Fig Tree (Mark 13:28–29 and parallels)

- ◆ **Parables common to Matthew and Luke:**
  The Two Builders (Matthew 7:24–27; Luke 6:47–49)
  The Yeast (Matthew 13:33; Luke 13:20–21)
  The Lost Sheep (Matthew 18:12–14; Luke 15:4–7)
  The Wedding Banquet (Matthew 22:1–14; Luke 14:15–24)
  Faithful and Unfaithful Slaves (Matthew 24:45–51; Luke 12:42–46)
  The Talents or Pounds (Matthew 25:14–30; Luke 19:11–27)

- ◆ **A Parable only in Mark**
  The Growing Seed (Mark 4:26–29)

- ◆ **Parables only in Matthew**
  The Sower of Seeds (Matthew 13:24–30)
  The Hidden Treasure (Matthew 13:44)
  The Pearl (Matthew 13:45–46)
  The Great Net (Matthew 13:47–48)
  The Unforgiving Servant (Matthew 18:23–35)
  The Vineyard Labourers (Matthew 20:1–16)
  The Two Sons (Matthew 21:28–31)
  The Ten Bridesmaids (Matthew 25:1–13)
  The Judgment of the Nations (Matthew 25:31–46)

- ◆ **Parables only in Luke**
  The Creditor (Luke 7:41–43)
  The Good Samaritan (Luke 10:30–47)

The Unexpected Guest (Luke 11:5–8)
The Rich Fool (Luke 12:16–21)
The Barren Fig Tree (Luke 13:6–9)
Choosing a Seat (Luke 14:7–11)
The Lost Coin (Luke 15:8–10)
The Prodigal Son (Luke 15:11–32)
The Dishonest Manager (Luke 16:1–8)
The Rich Man and Lazarus (Luke 16:19–31)
The Widow and Unjust Judge (Luke 18:1–8)
The Pharisee and the Tax Collector (Luke 18:9–14)

◆ **Parables in John:**
The Good Shepherd (John 10:1–18)
The Vine and Branches (John 15:1–10)

Questions

1. What *kind* of teacher was Jesus? How would you describe him?

2. In what way could Jesus be considered '*original*'?

3. By the first century CE, how did most Jews understand the expression '*the kingdom of God*'?

4. In what way was the vision of the kingdom of God offered by Jesus different from that held by his fellow Jews?

5. What is the importance of '*metanoia*' in Jesus' teaching on the kingdom of God?

6. What kind of people does Jesus indicate in the Beatitudes that God desires as his co-workers in building up his kingdom?

7. What is the meaning and the purpose of Jesus' *parables*?

The Parable of the Good Samaritan

STORY

The Good Samaritan, by Vincent van Gogh.

There was a lawyer who, to disconcert Jesus, stood up and said to him, 'Master, what must I do to inherit eternal life?'

Jesus said to him, 'What is written in the Law? What do you read there?'

The lawyer replied, 'You must love the Lord your God with all your heart, with all your soul, with all your strength and your neighbour as yourself.'

Jesus said, 'You have answered right, do this and life is yours.'

ANALYSIS

This parable is told in response to the lawyer's question: '*Who is my neighbour?*'

The setting of the parable is the Jerusalem–Jericho road. It was a steep path that wound down from the peaks of Zion to the flatlands of the Jordan valley, through dry and desolate terrain. In the time of Jesus it was regarded as 'bandit country', where unwary travellers were in danger of being waylaid by thieves. His Jewish listeners would have readily sympathised with the unfortunate traveller's plight.

The traveller who falls victim to thieves is simply called 'a man'. By implication he is Jewish, but Jesus does not say whether he is rich or poor. His social status is not alluded to, only that he is a human being in need.

The priest and the Levite were both members of Judaism's religious establishment. Both had a duty to put their religious beliefs into practice by helping this man.

However, neither even stopped to check if he was still alive. They continued on their way. Did they fear a trap? Possibly. More likely they feared that if the man had already died, they would be rendered 'unclean' by touching his corpse. Their religion's strict purity laws held that such an act would harm their relationship with God.

Jesus seems to have been implying that an inflexible, legalistic interpretation of religious rules had, for some people, come to take precedence over their responsibility to help a fellow human being in dire need. No doubt to the amazement of most, if not all, of his listeners, Jesus made a *Samaritan* the hero of this story.

But the man was anxious to justify himself and asked Jesus, 'And who is my neighbour?'

Jesus replied:

'A man was once on his way down from Jerusalem to Jericho and fell into the hands of brigands; they took all he had, beat him and then made off, leaving him for dead. Now a priest happened to be travelling down the same road, but when he saw the man, he passed by on the other side. In the same way a Levite who came to the place saw him and passed by on the other side.

But a Samaritan traveller who came upon him was moved with compassion when he saw him. He went up and bandaged his wounds, pouring oil and wine on them. He then lifted him on to his own mount, carried him to an inn and looked after him.

Next day, the Samaritan took out two denarii and handed them to the innkeeper. *"Look after him"*, he said, *"and on my way back I will make good any extra expense you have."'*

Then Jesus asked, *'Which of these three, do you think, proved himself a neighbour to the man who fell into the brigands' hands?'*

The lawyer replied, *'The one who took pity on him.'*

Jesus said to him, *'Go, and do the same yourself.'*

Samaritans were *not* regarded as neighbours by Jews. They were viewed as *enemies*. The Samaritans were descendants of the Jews who had lived in the old northern kingdom of Israel, which broke away after the death of King Solomon and was conquered by Assyria in 722 BCE. The Samaritans were no longer considered Jews because they had intermarried with non-Jews. Further, they were considered to be *heretics* because they accepted only the first five books of the Tenakh, as revealed by God, and refused to worship in the temple in Jerusalem. Jesus would have shocked and challenged his Jewish audience by portraying a Samaritan as willing to demonstrate such deep compassion and kindness to one in need when his own fellow Jews had failed to do so. Typical of a master storyteller, Jesus ends by turning the question

'Who is my neighbour?'

back on the lawyer who had asked it in the first place. Jesus asks him to draw out the lesson of the story for himself.

There is no place for bigotry and selfishness in the kingdom of God, only for compassion and love.

Questions

1. Why would most, if not all, of Jesus' audience have found it very difficult to accept a Samaritan as being willing to save an injured and helpless Jew?

2. What point was Jesus making when he referred to the priest and the Levite refusing to do anything to help the injured man?

3. Does this parable justify the claim that Jesus was *'a master storyteller'*? Explain your answer.

4. How might Christians today apply the message of this parable? Consider such questions as inter-faith or inter-racial relations.

The Parable of the Prodigal Son

STORY

The tax-collectors and the sinners were all seeking Jesus' company to hear what he had to say, and the Pharisees and the scribes complained.

They said, 'This man welcomes sinners and eats with them.'

So Jesus spoke this parable to them:

'A man had two sons. The younger said to his father, "Father let me have the share of the estate that would come to me." So the father divided the property between them. A few days later the younger son got together everything he had and left for a distant country where he squandered his money on a life of debauchery.

When he had spent it all, that country experienced a severe famine, and now he began to feel the pinch, so he hired himself out to one of the local inhabitants who put him to work on his farm feeding the pigs. And he would willingly have filled his stomach with the husks the pigs were eating, but no one offered him anything. Then he came to his senses and said, "how many of my father's paid servants have more food than they want, and here I am dying of hunger! I will leave this place and go to my father and say: Father, I have sinned against heaven and against you; I no longer deserve to be called your son; treat me as one of your paid servants." So he left the place and went back to his father.

While he was still a long way off, his father saw him and was moved with pity. He ran to the boy, clasped him in his arms and kissed him tenderly. Then his son said, "Father, I have sinned against heaven and against you. I no longer deserve to be called your son."

ANALYSIS

Jesus' audience was composed of two groups: his society's *insiders* (the Pharisees and scribes) and its *outsiders* (prostitutes and tax-collectors). Jesus told this parable in response to the Pharisees' and scribes' criticism of him for declaring that the kingdom of God was open to *everyone*, even sinners.

The younger son's request would have been an extraordinary one to make in the culture of the time. His demand for his inheritance would have been understood as tantamount to wishing that his father was dead! The chief character of this parable is *not* the prodigal (wasteful) son, but *the father*. Indeed, some now refer to this story as 'the parable of the forgiving father'.

The father of this story is not any ordinary father. He is depicted as possessing unlimited love for both his children, each of whom is guilty in his own way:

- ◆ the younger son for selfishly squandering his inheritance;
- ◆ the elder son for being territorial, hard-hearted and self-righteous.

Both sons needed their father's forgiveness and he gave it freely, without hesitation.

This story would have shocked not only the Pharisees and scribes but most of Jesus' listeners. They would have thought that the best the prodigal son could have hoped for was to be forgiven and taken back as a hired servant; nothing more. Instead, Jesus stated that the father put a *robe* around his penitent son to symbolise his restoration as an honoured member of the family, and placed a

But the father said to his servants, "Quick! Bring out the best robe and put it on him; put a ring on his finger and sandals on his feet. Bring the calf we have been fattening, and kill it; we are going to have a feast, a celebration, because this son of mine was dead and has come back to life; he was lost and is found." And they began to celebrate.

Now the elder son was out in the fields, and on his way back, as he drew near the house, he could hear music and dancing. Calling one of the servants he asked what it was all about. "Your brother has come," replied the servant, "and your father has killed the calf we had fattened because he has got him back safe and sound." The elder son was angry then and refused to go in, and his father came out to plead with him; but he answered his father, "Look, all these years I have slaved for you and never once disobeyed your orders, yet you never offered me anything to celebrate with my friends. But for this son of yours, when he comes back after swallowing up your property— he and his women—you kill the calf we had been fattening."

The father said, "My son, you are with me always and all I have is yours. But it is only right we should celebrate and rejoice, because your brother here was dead and has come to life; he was lost and is found.'"

ring on his son's finger and *sandals* on his feet to affirm that his son was a free man and not his servant.

When the younger son came to his senses and returned home, he got far more than a mere 'welcome home' party. His father knew that his son had finally turned his life around, was ready to ask for and accept forgiveness and start his life anew.

The Return of the Prodigal Son, by Rembrandt.

Because of this, his father restored his prodigal son to his former position as a *hereditary* son, meaning he would one day receive half of what his older brother had come to expect as his *full* remaining inheritance.

Jesus made the point that God sees each and every human being as an *equal* member of his kingdom. His love, fairness and forgiveness have a depth and a quality that goes far beyond what human beings can ever hope to comprehend. God's love and mercy is unlimited and inexhaustible. It is never too late to recognise it and accept it.

Questions

1. Why did Jesus tell this parable?

2. Is it true to say that *both* sons needed their father's forgiveness? Explain your answer.

3. Why would this story have shocked the Pharisees and scribes who had listened to it? ➡️

4. What point was Jesus trying to make about God's mercy and forgiveness?

5. Read the following statement:

'Parables force us to ask ourselves if we are giving priority to the important dimensions of life.'

How might one apply the parable of the prodigal son to such matters as:
(a) the value of material possessions;
(b) a lifestyle devoted to putting one's own pleasure before everything else;
(c) the importance of family;
(d) relations between siblings;
(e) human love compared to God's love.

The Miracles of Jesus

Meaning

In common usage the word 'miracle' is used to express wonder and amazement.

For example:

◆ *'the mobile phone is a miracle of modern communications'*;

◆ *it's a miracle that anyone survived that car crash.*

When used in a strictly religious sense, the term *'miracle'* refers to:

an unusual and unexpected creative action, performed either directly by God or indirectly by God through human beings, that provokes wonder and manifests the presence, power and goodness of God in human history by bringing about changes in people or in things.

Importance

It is sometimes claimed that religious faith is not based on miracles, but there are very strong grounds for saying that it *is.*

Consider the following:

◆ all three monotheistic faiths—Judaism, Christianity and Islam—view the very existence of the universe

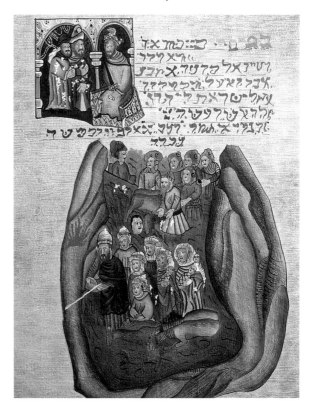

Moses leading the Children of Israel through the Red Sea (fifteenth century).

as miraculous. They state that it exists only because it was created *ex nihilo* (out of nothing) by God;

- *in Judaism*, Moses is believed to have been given the power to perform miracles when he was demanding that the Egyptian pharaoh free the Hebrew slaves;
- *in Christianity* the miracles of the Incarnation and the Resurrection of Jesus are of central importance;
- *in Islam* the dictation of the Qur'an to Muhammad is regarded as miraculous because he was said to have been illiterate.

The question of miracles cannot be ignored when discussing religion.

Credibility in a scientific age

Some contemporary writers—religious as well as non-religious—dismiss the whole notion of miracles as an outdated expression of a more gullible and superstitious era. They suggest that belief in miracles should be consigned to the dustbin of history, along-

Lab researcher examining sample tissue.

side such *discredited* notions as the Earth being flat and the sun orbits the Earth. They claim that advances in scientific knowledge have demonstrated that the whole idea of miracles is *nonsense*.

Others argue that this is *not* the case. Contrary to what is often claimed, they say modern science is *not* necessarily hostile to the idea of miracles. True, one must begin by admitting that the whole notion of miracles is a very difficult one to accept for many scientifically minded people. Scientists, whatever their specific area—physics, chemistry or biology—investigate the world around them in order to formulate scientific laws. But one must ask:

What are scientific laws?

Let us begin by distinguishing between the two very different ways in which the word 'law' is used. They frequently get confused in people's minds. Consider:

1. **Law as prescriptive**

   The word 'law' can be used in a *prescriptive* sense, as in *the law of the state*, meaning instructions given to the citizens of a country regarding how they *should* behave.

   For example:
   They should not commit murder or steal from one another.

   Such laws can be broken, however, as in the case of homicide and theft.

2. **Law as descriptive**

   The word 'law' can be used in a *descriptive* sense, as in the case of *the natural sciences*, where laws describe how things *normally* happen in the world.

   For example:
   How blood clots or how coral reefs are formed.

Scientific laws do *not* prescribe what must happen but rather, on the basis of past observation, they *predict* what can reasonably be expected to happen in the future. Nothing more.

The idea that scientific laws describe the natural world with absolute certainty is still quite widespread, but it is mistaken.

When formulating an explanation for an event, scientists think in terms of degrees of *probability* (likelihood) rather than certainty. They seek to find the best explanation for something, then work on the basis of this *until* some new evidence comes to light that challenges this accepted explanation. This may lead them to reconsider, change their minds and try to formulate a new scientific law that describes more accurately how the world works.

So, scientific laws indicate only what one can reasonably expect to happen. They say *nothing* about the possibility of miracles occurring, other than that they are *not* what one would normally expect to occur. Jews, Christians and Muslims accept that miracles do not often occur in the ordinary course of events in this world. However, they claim that there is no reason to rule out the possibility that God could choose to act in such an extraordinary way. Science *cannot* rule out the possibility that miracles have occurred in the past, or might happen in the future.

Questions

1. Explain the term '*miracle*'.

2. What are the grounds for claiming that *religious faith is based on miracles*?

3. What are *scientific laws*?

4. Is modern science *necessarily* hostile to the possibility of miracles? Explain your answer.

Miracle-workers in the ancient world

Scholars have revealed that Jesus of Nazareth was not the only person of that era who was said to have performed miracles. They have identified three others:

◆ Appolonius of Tyana;
◆ Honi ha Me'aggel;
◆ Hanina ben Dosa.

Let us consider each in turn.

Appolonius of Tyana was a wandering teacher of Greek origin who spent most of his life in what is now Turkey during the first century CE. The only remaining record of his deeds is a historical novel written by Philostratus for the Empress Julia Domna. As a historical source, the novel is of little value. It was written over a century after Appolonius' death and the author had no access to eyewitness accounts. The novel itself seems to have been largely intended as an anti-Christian tract. Indeed, the 'miracles' attributed to Appolonius in the novel are *very different* from those attributed to Jesus. One 'miracle story' recounts how a plague besetting the city of Ephesus was brought to an end by stoning a beggar to death. In contrast, Jesus restored people to health and even to life again. He never took a life.

Honi ha Me'aggel ('the Circle Drawer') was a Jewish holy man said to have lived in the century before Jesus was born. Only one miracle is attributed to him, in the Babylonian Talmud (*Taanit* 23a). It involves God answering his prayer for rain to fall after a prolonged drought.

Hanina ben Dosa was a Jewish holy man who began his ministry about twenty years after the execution of Jesus. Six miracles he is said to have performed are recorded in the Talmud, which was compiled about three centuries after his death. Like Jesus, Hanina attracted criticism for certain things he said and did. Unlike Jesus, he died in peace of old age.

Hanina is said to have been able to make it start raining and then cease raining. On one occasion he healed himself after being bitten by a poisonous snake. On another, he healed the son of a famous Pharisee, Gamaliel, who had been ill with a high fever.

The miracles of Jesus

Authentic miracle-workers were *rare* in the ancient world. It is claimed that when Jesus worked miracles,

> … *all were astounded and praised God saying, 'We have never seen anything like this'.*
> (Mark 2:12)

According to the Gospels, Jesus performed at least thirty-five miracles. These can be grouped under four different headings:

- healing of the sick;
- mastery over nature;
- casting out demons;
- restoration of the dead to life.

Clearly, the miracles attributed to Jesus were of a *higher calibre* than those attributed to either Appolonius, Honi ha Me'aggel or Hanina ben Dosa. Further, Jesus' miracles have a *messianic dimension* that is missing in the miracles attributed to others.

The Gospels tell how John the Baptist sent messengers to ask Jesus if he really was the long-awaited Messiah (i.e. *anointed one of God*). Jesus answers them as follows:

> *Go back and tell John what you have seen and heard: the blind see, the lame walk, lepers are cleansed, the deaf hear, the dead are raised to life, the Good News is proclaimed to the poor and happy is the man who does not lose faith in me.*
> (Luke 7:22–23)

The five miracles listed, together with the proclamation of the Good News to the poor, were strongly linked in the minds of many Jews at that time with the coming of the prophesied Messiah.

The evidence for Christian claims about Jesus

Christians claim that there are sound reasons for believing that Jesus really *did* perform these miracles:

- the Gospels' accounts of these miracles were

Jesus turning water into wine at the wedding feast of Cana.

based on eyewitness reports available to the evangelists;

◆ even Jesus' most forthright opponents—the Pharisees—did *not* deny that he could work miracles, although they claimed he had been given the power to do so by the devil, not by God;

◆ the Jewish historian Josephus, who wrote in the latter half of the first century CE, referred to Jesus as '*a doer of wonderful deeds*';

◆ Celsus, a fierce critic of Christianity who lived in the second century CE, *never* once disputed the claim that Jesus had actually performed miracles.

Christians point to the clear consensus among ancient writers, both Christian and non-Christian, that *Jesus was a miracle-worker* and hold that there *is* a factual basis for the miracle stories recorded in the Gospels.

Questions

1. List the four kinds of miracle attributed to Jesus.

2. Compare the miracles said to have been performed by Jesus with those attributed to other reputed miracle-workers of that era.
How do his miracles differ from theirs?

3. Christians believe that there are 'sound reasons' to support their claim that Jesus really performed miracles.
(a) What are these 'sound reasons'?
(b) Do you agree or disagree that they offer 'sound reasons'?
Explain your answer.

Jesus and the Centurion, by Veronese (Paolo Caliari).

Case Study 1:

The miracles of healing

In the time of Jesus most Jews believed that there was a very real link between sickness and sin. They thought that as God is the source of life and health, any person who became ill or suffered a disability did so because he/she had done something to deserve God's anger and disapproval. The consequences of contracting a serious illness, like leprosy, were disastrous. Such people were considered *impure* and were cut off from participating in the religious life of their community. This in turn led to their social exclusion because it was assumed that, as God had rejected them by making them ill, everyone else should reject them, too. As a result such people were usually reduced to begging and survived on the margins of society.

In light of the above, it is little wonder that a person like Jesus, who was reputed to work miracles, attracted large crowds. Most of his fellow Jews believed that only if a person were restored to health could he/she be said to have regained God's approval and thus be re-admitted into society.

Thanks to modern psychiatric medicine, it is now believed that *some* illnesses, such as *paralysis*, can be attributed to a person suffering from a profoundly unhappy mental state. It seems that a terrible tragedy or bitter experience can affect a person's mind so badly that it exacts a high physical toll, causing the body, in a sense, to 'shut down' certain of its functions. In such a case it is *not* possible to cure the person's physical ailment without healing his/her psychological problems first.

It may well be that some, or even many, of the

people Jesus healed endured just such an illness. Whereas today such people would be prescribed a lengthy course of counselling together with medication—with no guarantee of success—Jesus just sat and talked with them, almost radiating what Christians believe to have been his unique love and goodness. He could pinpoint the source of such people's mental distress and *immediately* free them of their crippling burdens. As the deep-rooted psychological causes of their unhappiness suddenly faded away, so too did the paralysis that had blighted their lives.

This may not sound spectacular at first, but it is a miracle nonetheless. In a very real sense, Jesus restored people to health and thereby gave them back their lives as accepted members of their community.

Not all illnesses are *psychosomatic*, however, i.e. caused by a person's mental state having a detrimental effect on his/her bodily health. Jesus is reported to have healed people of a wide variety of ailments, ranging from internal haemorrhaging to leprosy. Such illnesses are caused by a specific set of *physical*, rather than psychological, factors. Jesus is reputed to have cured people of these and *other* illnesses he encountered. Therefore the healing miracles of Jesus *cannot* be explained away easily.

Questions

1. What was the prevailing attitude towards illness in Jewish society in the time of Jesus?

2. Why would Jesus' reputation as a miracle-worker have drawn large numbers of sick people to him, seeking a cure?

3. (a) What is a *psychosomatic* illness?
   (b) How might Jesus have continually succeeded in healing those who suffered from such an illness?
   (c) Could such a healing still be regarded as *miraculous*? Explain your answer.

4. Can all the healing miracles of Jesus be put down to curing only those people who suffered from psychosomatic illnesses?
   Give reasons for your answer.

Case Study 2:

The restoration of life to Jairus' daughter

Let us begin by reading the Gospel account:

There came a man named Jairus, who was an official of the synagogue. He fell at Jesus's feet and pleaded with him to come to his house, because he had only one child, a daughter about twelve years old, who was dying …

Then someone arrived from the house of the synagogue official to say, 'Your daughter has died. Do not trouble the Master any further.'

But Jesus had heard this, and he spoke to the

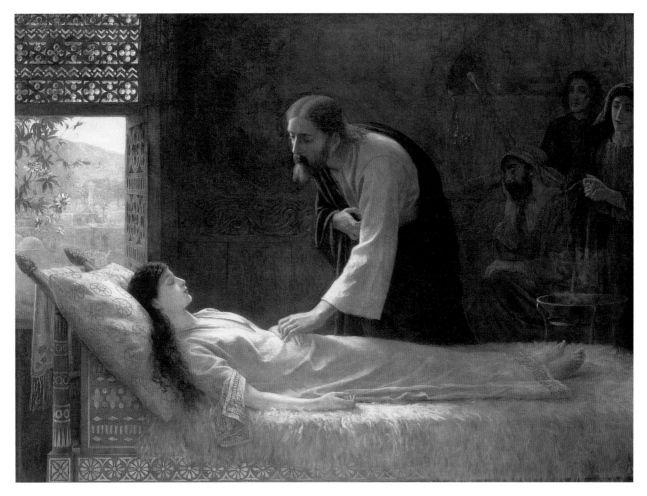

The Raising of Jairus' Daughter (1889), by Edwin Longsden Long.

man. 'Do not be afraid, only have faith and she will be safe.'

When Jesus came to the house he allowed no one to go in with him except Peter, John and James, and the child's father and mother. They were all weeping and mourning for her, but Jesus said, 'Stop crying; she is not dead, but asleep.' But they laughed at him, knowing she was dead.

But taking the child by the hand Jesus called to her, 'Little child, I tell you, get up'. And her spirit returned and she got up at once. Then he told them to give her something to eat. Her parents were astonished, but he ordered them not to tell anyone what had happened.

(Luke 8:41–42 and 49–56)

Many people today are *sceptical* of such stories. Perhaps they might respond to this story by claiming that:

◆ Jairus' daughter was not really dead at all, but was in a *coma*, i.e. a state of unconsciousness and general unresponsiveness distinguishable from sleep in that the person does *not* respond to external stimuli (e.g. shouting and pinching) or to internal stimuli (e.g. a full bladder);

◆ the evangelists and the witnesses who told them this story might have made an understandable mistake. All they may have witnessed was a purely *coincidental* recovery from a coma, which happened by chance after Jesus had arrived.

Could it be that the story of Jairus' daughter only

appeared to be a miracle? Possibly. But there are difficulties in advancing such an explanation.

Consider the following:

◆ coma results from damage to those areas of the brain involved in conscious activity or the maintenance of consciousness. This damage may be due to a head injury, encephalitis (inflammation of the brain) or meningitis (inflammation of the brain's protective coverings);

◆ none of these is a trivial condition. Even *today* they require urgent and serious medical intervention in order to treat them successfully, and there is no guarantee of success. If Jesus *instantly* healed a child suffering from such a serious medical condition, it was no mean feat;

◆ even in less severe forms of coma, the comatose person may respond to stimulation by making a sound or moving slightly. However, Jairus' daughter was *unable* to do so, otherwise those present would have noticed it;

◆ sometimes, even in a deeply comatose state, a person can still show *some* automatic responses, such as breathing unaided, coughing, blinking or showing roving eye movement. These indicate that the person's lower brain stem, which controls these responses, is still functioning. However, Jairus' daughter is not said to have displayed any of these responses. This would indicate that she had suffered a total loss of brain stem function. To all intents and purposes, therefore, she had most likely died *before* Jesus arrived at her home.

Christians believe that a strong case can be made that Jairus' daughter really *was* dead and that *Jesus restored her to life and full health*. The evangelists make it clear that the restoration of this child to life was not a one-off event. On other occasions Jesus is said to have restored life and health to the widow of Nain's son (Luke 7:1–17) and to Lazarus (John 11:1–44).

Questions

1. What is a *coma*?

2. How might a modern sceptic explain the story of Jairus' daughter?

3. What arguments do Christians put forward to support the claim that the child really *was* dead and that *Jesus restored her to life and full health*?

The purpose of Jesus' miracles

The Gospels indicate that Jesus worked miracles neither as a gimmick to win people over nor as a means to provide them with some 'magic short-cut' to faith in him. Indeed, on many occasions Jesus explicitly told those whom he had healed *not* to tell anyone else what he had done for them. Initially it was probably Jesus' miracles, more than his teachings, that attracted the large crowds who assembled to hear his message.

Why, then, did he perform miracles?

Clues to answering this question can be found in the Gospels. In the *synoptic* Gospels the miracles of Jesus are referred to as '*dunameis*', meaning *acts of power*.

The Resurrection of Lazarus, by Jean-Baptiste Corneille.

They were performed for two reasons:

◆ as a compassionate response to and reward for the deep faith some people already had in him; and

◆ to strengthen and confirm their faith in him.

In *John*'s Gospel, the miracles of Jesus are called '*semeia*', meaning *signs*. They were so called because they formed an integral part of his teaching about the kingdom of God. They were believed to reveal that:

◆ God the Father is the *creator* who is present and active in the world in ways that surpass all human understanding;

◆ Jesus was fulfilling his roles as *Messiah* and *redeemer*. He had come into the world to liberate people from the power of sin and death. His miracles pointed to a world in the future in which no one will ever again experience illness and death.

Questions

1. Why might Jesus have told people he had cured *not* to announce publicly that he had done so?

2. What was the *purpose* of the miracles performed by Jesus?

3. Review the evidence for and against Jesus as a miracle-worker. Which side do you find the most convincing? Give reasons for your answer.

4. Read the following statement:

   There is a paradox related to miracles. If you truly have faith in God, you do not need a miracle as proof of anything. If you do not have faith in God, no seemingly miraculous event will persuade you that faith makes sense.

   (a) What do you think this means?
   (b) What does it tell you about the nature of religious faith?

The Condemnation of Jesus

Introduction

The Gospels tell us that Jesus of Nazareth was arrested by a force of temple guards in the Garden of Gethsemane on what Christians refer to as 'Holy Thursday' night. Both the location and timing of his arrest are significant.

Jesus was a popular religious figure. Any attempt to arrest him by day in a public area, such as the temple, would quite likely have provoked the kind of riot the Jewish authorities were anxious to prevent. By arresting him at a quiet location just outside the city of Jerusalem, under cover of darkness, they could avoid any public demonstration.

The fact that none of Jesus' disciples was arrested with him is significant. It would indicate that the Jewish authorities were quite aware that Jesus was *not* planning to lead an armed rebellion against Roman rule over Palestine.

So why, then, did they arrest Jesus in the first place?

Reaction to Jesus

The pretext for Jesus' arrest was his behaviour in

Jerusalem in the days immediately leading up to the annual Jewish feast of Passover (what Christians since have referred to as Holy Week). Perhaps as many as 300,000 Jewish pilgrims could have converged on the city at that time of year for seven days of prayer, ritual purification and sacrifice in the temple. When Jesus entered Jerusalem (on what Christians call Palm Sunday), he was greeted by cheering crowds who threw down their cloaks

Christ's Entry into Jerusalem, by Duccio di Buoninsegna.

and palm branches before him. Although the whole event passed off peacefully, it would most likely have greatly worried the Sanhedrin's leaders.

The Sanhedrin was the seventy-strong ruling council and religious court of the Jewish faith. It

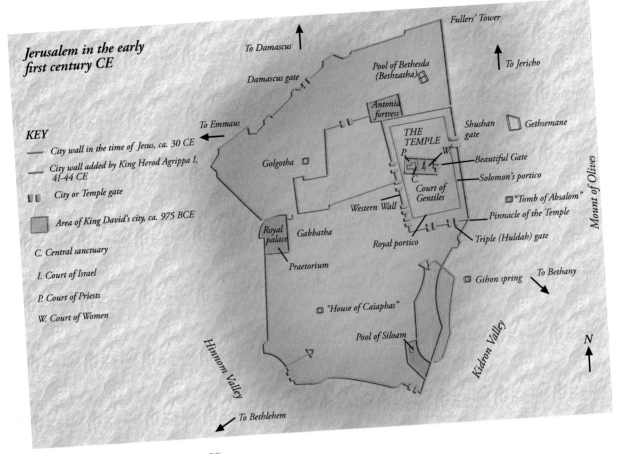

Jerusalem in the early first century CE.

(Map labels)
Jerusalem in the early first century CE

To Damascus

Damascus gate

Fullers' Tower

Pool of Bethesda (Bethzatha)

To Jericho

To Emmaus

Antonia fortress

Shushan gate

Gethsemane

KEY
— City wall in the time of Jesus, ca. 30 CE
— City wall added by King Herod Agrippa I, 41–44 CE
⊔⊔ City or Temple gate
▢ Area of King David's city, ca. 975 BCE
C. Central sanctuary
I. Court of Israel
P. Court of Priests
W. Court of Women

THE TEMPLE
P. I. W.
C.
Court of Gentiles

Golgotha

Beautiful Gate

Solomon's portico

"Tomb of Absalom"

Mount of Olives

Western Wall

Pinnacle of the Temple

Royal palace

Gabbatha

Triple (Huldah) gate

Royal portico

Praetorium

Gihon spring

To Bethany

"House of Caiaphas"

Kidron Valley

Hinnom Valley

Pool of Siloam

N

To Bethlehem

was headed by a high priest elected from among its members, whose appointment had to be approved by the Roman *praefectus*. The Romans expected the Sanhedrin to maintain public order in Jerusalem. Passover was a particularly sensitive event on the Jewish calendar because most Jews believed that it would be the occasion when the long-awaited Messiah (saviour) would finally reveal himself to them.

The Jews were a people with a proud history who yearned to regain their lost independence, which to them meant far more than the achievement of national liberation. Jewish national identity was intimately bound up with their religious beliefs. Whereas the Romans were liberal polytheists, Jews were devout monotheists. They despised the Romans as idolatrous and most Jews accepted their prophets' declaration that God would send a Messiah to lead them to freedom and restore their nation to new heights of greatness among the other nations of the world. Leading figures in the Sanhedrin may have become fearful

that Jesus was about to declare himself to be the long-awaited Messiah, or be put forward as such by others with their own agendas, such as the militant separatist Zealots.

The Sanhedrin was probably well-informed about Jesus' statements and activities up to this point. It knew that he had gained a sizeable following in his native Galilee. More worrying from its point of view was that Jesus had challenged those religious authorities he had encountered so far. The Gospels record a number of tense confrontations between Jesus and the Pharisees in Galilee, and later with the Sadducees in Judaea. These two groups differed on many things, but they both agreed that they could not allow someone like Jesus to openly challenge the versions of Judaism they each advanced. For this reason the leading Pharisees and Sadducees decided to arrest Jesus and find a way to have him put to death.

The date for this event is not easy to establish: historians place it somewhere between 29 and 33 CE.

Questions

1. Why was Jesus arrested at night and in the Garden of Gethsemane?

2. Jesus alone was arrested. In what way is this significant?

3. Explain the role of the Sanhedrin in Palestine at that time.

4. With which groups had Jesus clashed over the interpretation of Judaism before his arrival in Jerusalem?

What Jesus stood for

As discussed in Chapter 9, Jesus offered people a truly radical vision of what human life can and should be, which he referred to as *the kingdom of God*. He taught that it would liberate people from sin and from all forms of oppression, give them justice and fulfil their hopes. By proclaiming and living out his message, Jesus inevitably clashed with the ruling religious elite of Judaism. They either actively encouraged or tacitly permitted four forms of oppression that Jesus opposed vigorously:

◆ *ritualism;*

◆ *patriarchalism;*

◆ *legalism;*

◆ *exclusivism.*

Before examining each of these abuses and the alternative vision proposed by Jesus, one needs to bear in mind the following points:

◆ although the Romans might also have had their reasons for getting rid of Jesus, his main quarrel was with the leaders of his *own* people. It is *not* anti-Semitic to point this out. Jesus was a devout and loyal Jew; his message was rooted firmly in the rich and ancient teachings of Judaism. He did not seek the destruction of his own people, but instead sought to fulfil all that their sacred texts had prophesied;

◆ Jesus would *not* have stopped at condemning abuses within the religion of his own time. There is every reason to think that he would have applied the same standards to every *other* religion, too, including that which has since called itself 'Christian'.

With these points in mind, let us consider the four important issues on which Jesus disagreed profoundly with the religious authorities of his day.

Ritualism

Ritualism refers to the performance of religious acts with little or no inner conviction due to a lack of any sincere love for God. Jesus warned people about the danger of over-emphasising the *external* aspects of religion, i.e. dietary laws, ritual purifications, sacrifices and so on. He called on people to look first to their *inner* purity because the essence of religion is

> ... *to love God with one's entire heart, entire mind and entire effort and love one's neighbour as oneself.*
> (Mark 12:32–33)

The Cleansing of the Temple, by Giotto. Whatever Jesus' precise motives, there was certainly much popular resentment against the wealth and splendour of the Temple, which had been lavishly rebuilt by Herod the Great, partly as a monument to his dynasty. The scale of the undertaking was such that it was finally completed only six years or so before its destruction in 70 CE.

By teaching this message Jesus was challenging the entire system of worship promoted by the temple priests in Jerusalem.

Jesus greatly angered the temple priests with regard to the issue of *forgiveness of sins*. The priests insisted that any sinner (e.g. a tax-collector) who wanted to be re-admitted into the Jewish community had first to earn forgiveness by following a lengthy process of purification rituals. Only *after* he had completed these could he be considered worthy of forgiveness.

Jesus rejected this approach as being too concerned with judging people on the basis of outward appearances. In contrast, he began by directly forgiving the person who wanted to repent and told him to '*go and sin no more*'.

Jesus went even further when he ejected the money-changers from the temple compound. By doing this, he directly challenged the entire system of temple worship and all the vested interests surrounding it. He was not the only one to have objected to the

financial corruption within the temple: many Pharisees shared his criticism of it. But *only* Jesus acted defiantly against it.

The temple priests were humiliated by this very public exposure of corrupt practices that they had either refused to prevent or in which they had, in some way, been willing participants. They were no longer prepared to allow Jesus to challenge their authority in such a public fashion.

Legalism

Legalism, like ritualism, is a constant danger in *any* religion. It involves a blind, unquestioning obedience to, and rigorous, inflexible application of, the letter of religious laws to human life situations. Legalism usually promotes a shallow, self-righteous attitude that reduces religion to the level of a heartless set of rules and regulations, devoid of any real love for either God or other people.

It is quite likely that legalism unintentionally crept into Jewish religious practices as a reaction to their repeated conquest by foreign powers. Rigorous adherence to their religious laws allowed the Jews to successfully preserve their distinctive identity as a people. Unfortunately, by the time of Jesus an attitude had developed among many religious figures—such as the temple priests and many (though not all) of the Pharisees—that placed too great an emphasis on observable *outward* behaviour as an indication of a person's zeal for serving God faithfully. This led to an oppressive system of rule-keeping, which threatened to suck the very life out of the rich and vibrant religion of Judaism.

The Gospels give numerous instances where Jesus challenged such legalism as having no place in the kingdom of God. On one notable occasion he healed a sick man on the Sabbath day, much to the anger of the Pharisees, who debated whether to stone him to death for doing so. Jesus wanted people to know that, in the kingdom of God, life and health come *before* the rigid observation of religious regulations (see Matthew 12:9–19).

Patriarchalism

As still remains the case in so many ways today, women in the time of Jesus lived in *patriarchal* societies, i.e. where society was structured to ensure that men controlled and dominated women's lives.

Jesus shocked both his own male followers and his opponents by:

◆ including women among his disciples—it was considered a source of scandal for women to travel with a *rabbi*;

Christ with Martha and Mary, by Claude Saint-Paul II.

◆ emphasising equality of respect for women;

◆ encouraging women to join men in the pursuit of knowledge and in areas of activity outside what their society would condone;

◆ taking an uncompromising stand against the unjust treatment of women (see John 8:1–11 and Luke 13:10–17).

The society of that era reduced women to the status of second-class citizens, but Jesus treated women as his *equals*. Indeed, the *first* person with whom Jesus conversed after his resurrection was a woman: Mary Magdalene (see John 20:15–17). By his words and actions Jesus made it clear that discrimination on the basis of gender has no place in the kingdom of God.

Exclusivism

The Jewish people were profoundly grateful to have been made God's '*chosen people*'. Some, however, took all of this too far. They became too proud and refused to associate with a whole range of people, both within their own community (e.g. prostitutes and tax-collectors) and without (e.g. Samaritans and Romans).

Unlike other important religious figures, such as Hanina ben Dosa, Jesus went out of his way to reach out to and mix with those Jews who, because of their lifestyles, had been marginalised or even ostracised by many of their fellow Jews, who believed themselves to be decent and God-fearing. When challenged about this, Jesus is said to have responded that he had '*not come to call the just but sinners*' (Mark 2:17). He wanted to extend to such people an invitation to enter the kingdom of God, too. Nonetheless, Jesus undoubtedly offended many of his fellow Jews even more by broadening the contemporary Jewish definition of 'neighbour' to include anyone, irrespective of his/her religious, tribal or ethnic identity.

For example:

- the Roman centurion in Luke 7:1–10;
- the Samaritan woman at the well in John 4:1–30.

These were the very people, he said, for whom the kingdom of God was coming. Indeed, Jesus went to great lengths to help people understand that in the kingdom of God, all the barriers that divide human beings—race, gender, religion and social class—are torn down.

Christ and the Woman of Samaria at the Well, by Philippe de Champaigne. When Jesus asked a Samaritan woman to give him a drink, she was initially wary (John 4:9), as relations between Jews and Samaritans were often hostile. According to John 4:7–29, Jesus revealed himself to her as a prophet and as the Messiah, declaring that Samaritans would share in the 'living water'—the gift of divine spirit that Jesus brought. Samaria was an early destination for the missionary apostles, and Philip is said to have had great success there (Acts 8:5–8).

Questions

1. (a) What is *ritualism*?
   (b) How did Jesus oppose it?

2. In what ways did Jesus' stance on the forgiveness of sins anger the temple priests?

3. *Jesus challenged the entire system of temple worship.* What evidence is there to support such a statement?

4. (a) What is *legalism*?
   (b) How might legalism have crept into Jewish belief and practice by the first century CE?
   (c) How did Jesus oppose legalism during his public ministry?

5. (a) What is *patriarchalism*?
   (b) How did Jesus oppose the patriarchalism of his own era?

6. (a) Identify some forms of patriarchalism in contemporary Irish society.
   (b) What steps, in your opinion, should be taken to combat them?

7. (a) What is *exclusivism*?
   (b) How did Jesus differ from the other important religious figures of his day with regard to the treatment of society's outcasts?

8. (a) In what ways did Jesus broaden his religion's definition of the term 'neighbour'?
   (b) What point was he making by doing so?

The role of the Sanhedrin

Judaism's ruling council—the Sanhedrin—was dominated by the Sadducees, namely the nobles and temple priests. It was clear to them that Jesus posed a direct challenge to the whole established religious and social order that was the very basis of their power. Recent scholarship has revealed just how fragile the Sadducees' grip on power was at that time.

They were only a small minority within the Jewish community and held a belief system significantly *different* from their fellow Jews.

For example:

◆ the Sadducees did not believe that a messiah would be sent by God;

◆ the Sadducees rejected belief in life after death.

The Sadducees' chief rivals within the Sanhedrin were the Pharisees. The latter had gained widespread popularity and respect for openly criticising the financial

Christ instructing Nicodemus, by Jacob Jordaens.

Jesus could neither be persuaded to co-operate with the Sanhedrin nor be intimidated into silence. If Jesus was not prepared to stop, then it was necessary to silence him, once and for all.

Of course, to take such action against a popular figure at a time when Jerusalem was teeming with enthusiastic pilgrims risked triggering a wave of unrest. Caiaphas may have been confident that he could depend on the assistance of the Roman military to dispose of Jesus swiftly and safely, without threatening public order.

The interrogation of Jesus

After his arrest, Jesus was brought under guard to the temple complex. There he was interrogated either by a group of priests or by the whole of the Sanhedrin. The Gospels of Mark and Matthew suggest that Jesus was put on trial by a religious court, but John's account indicates that it was more an inquiry to determine the grounds upon which the Sanhedrin would refer Jesus' case to the Roman *praefectus*.

It seems that Jesus' interrogators began by accusing him of predicting the destruction of the temple and of threatening to disrupt public order. Jesus offered no reply to such charges and the priests could find no one to substantiate them. The chief priest, Caiaphas, went on to accuse Jesus of claiming to be the Messiah. Although each of the Gospels has Jesus offering a slightly different response to this assertion, they all indicate that what he said was interpreted as a '*yes*'.

Technically, it was *not* against Jewish law to claim to be the Messiah. According to Luke, however, Caiaphas followed his earlier question by asking Jesus if he also claimed to be *the Son of God*. According to

corruption that the Sadducees had either permitted or promoted within the temple's precincts. In addition to being branded as corrupt, the Sadducees were widely regarded as being little more than the hired lackeys of Palestine's Roman overlords. Indeed, the man who occupied the key post of high priest and leader of the Sanhedrin was appointed to the position by the Roman *praefectus* (governor). Any high priest who failed to play his part in maintaining the smooth and orderly functioning of Palestine would lose the confidence of the *praefectus* and be swiftly dismissed.

The Gospels tell us that Joseph Caiaphas, an experienced administrator, was the high priest who ordered Jesus' arrest. He no doubt did so because he realised the threat Jesus posed to the established religious and social order of Palestine, without which neither he nor the Sadducees would have any authority or power. It was no doubt clear to Caiaphas that

The Arrest of Christ, by Duccio di Buoninsegna.

John's Gospel, when Jesus had previously referred to himself as '*the Son of God*', he had openly declared himself *equal* to God (see John 5:18). Caiaphas was no doubt well-informed about this. So when Jesus responded to his question by saying,

'*You say that I am*',

Caiaphas immediately accused him of committing blasphemy.

For Jews, the term '*blasphemy*' referred to

anything causing serious offence to the dignity of

God, such as misusing the divine name or claiming divinity for oneself.

The chief priest and the other members of the Sanhedrin who were present declared that Jesus should be put to death, as was prescribed by Mosaic Law for any person deemed to be a false prophet (see Deuteronomy 18:20). Whatever conclusion the Sanhedrin might reach regarding Jesus, they had *no* authority to impose the death sentence on Jesus and carry it out. That right was reserved *exclusively* to the Roman *praefectus*, Pontius Pilate.

Questions

1. (a) How strong was the Sadducees' grip on power?
    (b) How were the Sadducees regarded by most of their fellow Jews?

2. Why did the high priest, Caiaphas, order the arrest of Jesus?

3. (a) What is *blasphemy*?
(b) On what grounds was Jesus accused of committing blasphemy?
(c) What was the penalty under the Mosaic Law for committing blasphemy?

4. Why did the Sanhedrin decide to then bring Jesus before the Roman *praefectus*, Pontius Pilate?

Pontius Pilate

It is believed that Pontius Pilate was *praefectus* of Judaea and Samaria from 25 until 36 CE. For most of this time he lived at the coastal city of Caesarea, where his luxurious villa was cooled by the sea breeze. He visited Jerusalem only during major festivals, to ensure that public order was maintained. At all other times he *avoided* the hot and dusty city.

Ancient sources offer us two substantially different portraits of Pilate. The Gospels present him as someone who wanted to apply the law fairly, but who was weak in the face of the Sanhedrin's determination and reluctantly condemned Jesus to death. The Jewish historian Josephus and the Roman author Tacitus paint a very different picture of Pilate. They describe him as an arrogant, cruel and unnecessarily violent bully—so much so, in fact, that in 36 CE Pilate was ordered to return to Rome and defend himself against complaints made about him for acting with excessive cruelty towards the Samaritans.

All of this has led some scholars to doubt whether such a man as Pilate would have spent any time at all agonising over the fate of a Jewish holy man who had angered the Sanhedrin. After all, Pilate needed the Sanhedrin's co-operation to keep the peace. It is claimed that Pilate would have simply categorised Jesus as a troublemaker, dispensed with a lengthy trial and swiftly sentenced him to death without a moment's hesitation.

Perhaps it happened this way; perhaps *not*. Recent scholarship has unearthed a fascinating insight into how Rome maintained its control over its far-flung territories through the use of an extensive network of spies and informants. Pilate would have received regular reports on anything of interest. Surely, then, stories of a man reputed to work miracles would have reached his ear? With his curiosity aroused and forced, reluctantly, to stay in Jerusalem for the Passover festival, Pilate may have been more inclined than usual to make time to hear Jesus' case.

The trial of Jesus

According to the Gospels, Jesus' trial before Pontius Pilate followed the standard Roman judicial procedures of that time:

◆ the setting was an open, paved area just outside the Roman *praetorium* (military headquarters);

◆ it began with Jesus' *accusers* (a delegation of Sanhedrin members) laying formal charges against him;

◆ the *defendant* (person on trial) was questioned

Pilate questions Jesus: Pilate's question, 'Are you the King of the Jews?' is the central focus of the Gospel accounts.

and allowed an opportunity to respond;
◆ after considering the evidence offered, the *praefectus* rendered his verdict.

The Sanhedrin's delegation knew that Pilate had no interest in hearing that Jesus had been accused of blasphemy. The Roman *praefectus* would have dismissed this as merely an internal Jewish religious dispute. So instead they phrased their accusation against Jesus in strictly *political* terms, telling Pilate that Jesus had claimed to be *the king of the Jews*. This was a very serious charge to make. Anyone proven to have made such a claim would be regarded as having committed an act of rebellion against the empire and of encouraging others to do likewise. The punishment for such a crime was always death.

When Pilate asked Jesus directly if he were a king,

Jesus replied,

> *Yes, I am a king.*
> (John 18:37)

Jesus then clarified his answer by stating:

> *My kingdom is not of this world. If my kingdom were of this world, my followers would have fought to prevent my capture. But my kingdom is not of this kind.*
> (John 18:36)

By making this statement, Jesus made it abundantly clear that he was *not* some Jewish rebel seeking the end of Rome's occupation of Palestine.

The Gospels indicate that Pilate arrived at the same conclusion: he saw *no* evidence to support the Sanhedrin's accusation. Jesus had done nothing to merit the death penalty. Indeed, Pilate seems to have decided that he should let Jesus go free. Pilate was well aware that releasing Jesus straight away would anger and embarrass the Sanhedrin, so he ordered that Jesus be flogged before setting him free, in order to appease them.

The verdict

To Pilate's surprise, the Sanhedrin delegation persisted in its demand for Jesus' condemnation and execution. Perhaps partly out of his annoyance at their questioning of his judgment, Pilate still refused to do so. Then, according to John's Gospel, the temple priests reached for what today would be termed '*the nuclear option*': they threatened to lodge an official complaint about Pilate's handling of the incident with the Emperor Tiberius, in Rome. They would accuse Pilate of:

(a) neglecting his duty as *praefectus* to preserve the peace by failing to eliminate someone whom the Sanhedrin had warned had sought to undermine Roman rule in Palestine;

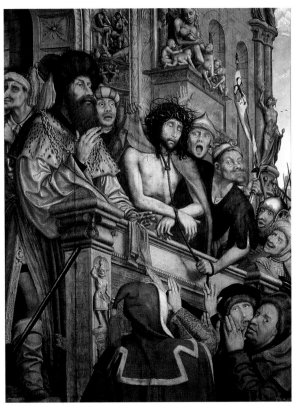

Ecce Homo ('Behold the Man') by Quentin Massys or Metsys.

(b) displaying disloyalty to the emperor by failing to execute a man who had admitted to being a 'king', no matter what he had claimed to mean by saying this (see John 19:12).

The threat of an appeal to the emperor seems to have unnerved Pilate. He knew that the Emperor Tiberius was a deeply suspicious man, who might just take the accusations seriously. If so, Pilate might be fortunate if the only thing he lost was his job. Then again, the Sanhedrin might be bluffing. But he may well have asked himself: '*Why take such a risk?*'

Pilate's whole career had been motivated largely by self-interest. The life of one man, even if he was *innocent*, was probably of little concern to him. Why should he risk alienating the Sanhedrin when its co-operation on other matters was so often useful to him? Pilate decided to give in to their demand. He declared Jesus guilty of *treason* and condemned him to death.

Questions

1. What did Josephus and Tacitus say about Pontius Pilate?

2. Why might Pilate have been more inclined than usual to consider the case of Jesus?

3. (a) What charge did the Sanhedrin delegation make against Jesus?
   (b) Why did they choose to avoid accusing him of blasphemy when they brought him before Pilate?

4. (a) What conclusion did Pilate reach after questioning Jesus?
   (b) Why, do you think, did he reach this conclusion?

5. What did the Sanhedrin delegation threaten to do if Pilate continued to resist their demand to condemn Jesus?

6. (a) How did Pilate respond to the Sanhedrin's threat?
   (b) Why, do you think, did he do so?

The Death and Burial of Jesus

Introduction

In recent decades a few authors have claimed that Jesus of Nazareth did *not* die on a cross. Some have based their assertion on statements contained in the so-called *Gospel of Barnabus*, namely that Judas Iscariot was crucified in place of Jesus. However, this document is regarded by scholars, almost unanimously, as a medieval *forgery*. So as a source about the life and death of Jesus, the Gospel of Barnabus is *worthless*.

If we consult *authentic* texts by *non*-Christian authors of the first and second centuries CE, such as the Jewish historian Josephus and the Roman historian Tacitus, they *all agree* on this point: Jesus of Nazareth was executed on the orders of the Roman *praefectus*, Pontius Pilate. Indeed, it is the opinion of most classical scholars that the death by crucifixion of Jesus is one of the *most well attested events* in ancient history.

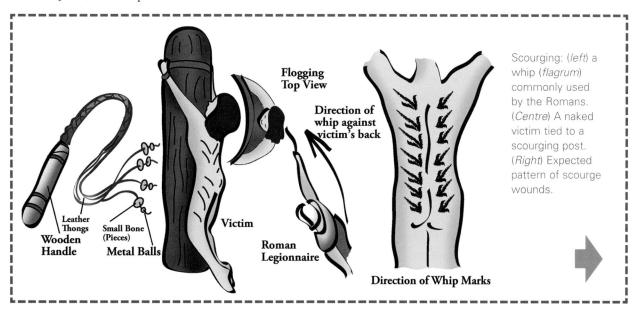

Flogging Top View

Direction of whip against victim's back

Leather Thongs

Wooden Handle

Small Bone (Pieces)

Metal Balls

Victim

Roman Legionnaire

Direction of Whip Marks

Scourging: (*left*) a whip (*flagrum*) commonly used by the Romans. (*Centre*) A naked victim tied to a scourging post. (*Right*) Expected pattern of scourge wounds.

5 to 6 ft (1.5 to 1.8 m)
75 to 125 lb (34 to 57 kg)

Patibulum

Stipes

Sedile

Stipes

**8 to 15 ft
(2.4 to 4.5 m)**

Crucifixion: (*left*) victim carrying the *patibulum* (crossbar) to the site of the stipes (upright posts). (*Right*) The low Tau cross (*crux Commissa*) often used by the Romans at the time of Jesus.

Crucifixion was a barbaric form of the death penalty that the Romans had adopted from their old foes, the Carthaginians. It was a method of execution reserved for enemies of the Empire. According to Josephus, it was normal practice for a condemned man to be scourged (flogged) before crucifixion so as to weaken him and shorten his agony. After enduring scourging, the prisoner was forced to carry the 6 ft long wooden crossbeam (not the whole cross) to his place of execution, where stood a 15 ft high permanent post onto which the crossbeam was fastened. The prisoner was stripped, then secured to the cross by nails through the wrists and feet. Usually he was also tied to the cross to prevent his body tearing free later.

According to the Roman author Cicero, the mere threat of crucifixion was often enough to keep subject peoples and slaves in line. It was such a public, painful, slow and humiliating way to die that the idea of it terrified people. It was intended to act as a clear warning to anyone who might be tempted to challenge the imperial might of Rome.

Questions

1. What documentary evidence is there to support the belief that Jesus of Nazareth died on a cross?

2. Why did the Romans use crucifixion as a punishment for non-Romans who broke their laws or challenged their rule?

Dead or comatose?

It has been suggested that when he was taken down from the cross, Jesus could have been in a drug-induced coma rather than dead. Certainly people in first-century Palestine knew about pain-killing drugs. The most widely used was derived from the *mandrake*, a plant with purple flowers and a strange, forked root. The root could be shredded and made into a solution. A dry sponge was immersed completely in this liquid, until it became thoroughly saturated. After this the sponge was soaked in water, which caused it to give off fumes that could be inhaled by the person suffering pain. These fumes acted as a powerful anaesthetic, which usually rendered a person unconscious and therefore unaware of the pain. This drug could also give an anaesthetised body the *appearance* of death because:

◆ a person's breathing decreased to the point of being almost undetectable;
◆ he/she experienced paralysis of the limbs.

The Gospels record that the Roman soldiers at Golgotha offered Jesus a drink from a sponge soaked with vinegar. This may have been intended to revive Jesus and thus prolong his agony, or there may have been a painkiller mixed into this liquid—if not mandrake, then perhaps myrrh. Mark and Matthew say that Jesus tasted the sponge, but refused to drink from it. Luke does not say whether he drank it or not. John writes that when Jesus was close to death he said, '*I thirst*', and a sponge soaked in vinegar was offered to him. He drank some and then died.

It is possible that the vinegar solution was laced with a painkiller. The consensus among medical experts, however, is that it is *extraordinarily unlikely* the someone could have administered an anaesthetic of just the right dosage required to render Jesus unconscious, but allowing him to be revived safely later. Even in the twenty-first century, calculating the exact amount of anaesthetic needed to sedate a patient is not an easy matter. It requires considerable skill and judgment to prevent a patient being harmed in some way. When one considers the relative lack of sophistication in medicine in Palestine 2,000 years ago, the likelihood of Jesus being drugged and revived afterwards is, to say the very least, *remote*. Indeed, given the excruciating pain he was suffering, the level of dosage required to alleviate his pain would have been of such potency as to have surely proven *fatal* to him.

Furthermore, given the awful extent of his injuries, Jesus would have required several months to recuperate. It would have been impossible for him to have recovered sufficiently by Easter Sunday morning. Jesus would have been an invalid, wracked with severe pain, unable to walk or hold a conversation and in need of constant medical care. Yet the evangelists make it clear that those disciples who claimed to have encountered Jesus after his resurrection said that he was *free of any pain* and *able to move with complete freedom*.

Questions

1. Why might someone claim that Jesus had been in a drug-induced coma rather than dead when placed in the tomb?

2. What reasons are offered for accepting the claim that Jesus did indeed die on the cross?

Crucifixion, by Andrea Mantegna.

Cause of Death

The Gospels make no attempt to hide the fact that Jesus suffered an appalling death. However, even before he came to be crucified, Jesus was *already* in a gravely weakened state:

◆ while he had prayed in the Garden of Gethsemane,

In his anguish his sweat fell to the ground like great drops of blood.
(Luke 22:44)

This may have been a very rare condition called *haematidrosis*, in which blood is expressed from the sweat glands. It is an indicator that Jesus was under extreme stress. After this point an intolerable level of stress was brought to bear on his mind and body:

◆ he was severely beaten by the temple guards after his arrest;

◆ he was scourged on Pilate's orders. A Roman scourging was a horrific experience; the harrowing flagellation scene in the film *The Passion of the Christ* conveys how truly awful it was. Sometimes a scourging was in itself enough to kill a person;

◆ after this, Jesus was forced to carry the instrument of his execution a distance of three-quarters of a mile to a small outcrop of rock just outside the city walls named *Golgotha* (*'place of the skull'*).

Jerusalem was a hilly city. The strain this journey would have placed upon a man who was exhausted, dehydrated and had suffered significant blood loss cannot be underestimated. Little wonder that the Roman guards forced a bystander, Simon of Cyrene, to help Jesus carry the crossbeam: they may have feared that Jesus would die on the way.

Immediately upon his arrival at Golgotha, Jesus was crucified. Sometimes a victim could take days to die, and crucifixion was intended to be a slow and torturous form of execution. A crucified man was left to suffocate gradually. His chest muscles became ever weaker under the pressure of gravity caused by his body weight, until he could no longer breathe. Sometimes a crucified prisoner could last for days on a cross. Jesus died after about six hours, which was relatively quickly. Why?

Some medical experts have concluded that Jesus died from a form of *acute shock* before suffocation had set in fully. The serious injuries he had sustained both before and during his crucifixion placed his body under such uncontrollable pain that it simply ceased to function. Other experts believe that his death was due to a *pulmonary embolism*, i.e. an obstruction of the pulmonary artery leading from the heart to the lungs by a blood clot caused by the multiple traumas he had endured. All agree that he *died* on the cross, whatever the precise cause.

The Church of the Holy Sepulchre

The Church of the Holy Sepulchre is located in the Christian quarter of Jerusalem's Old City. It encloses the traditional sites of both the crucifixion and the tomb of Jesus. There is archaeological evidence that Christians have prayed at this site since the mid-first century CE.

The church is run jointly by six different Christian denominations from within the Catholic and Orthodox traditions. In order to prevent disputes over who should own the building's keys, it was decided long ago to entrust them to two Muslim families. Their descendants still retain custody of the keys to this day.

Questions

1. Why do many scholars believe that Jesus was already in a gravely weakened state *before* he was crucified?

2. What are the two most likely causes proposed by medical experts for Jesus' death?

Ensuring Jesus' death

Jesus had made powerful enemies who had strong motives for ensuring his death.
Consider:
◆ though he had been coerced into acting against

Jesus, as *praefectus* Pilate would not have wanted anyone to survive crucifixion because this would have undermined an occupied nation's fear of Roman power;
◆ the Sanhedrin would not have permitted someone who had so openly challenged the very basis of their authority and taught what they considered blasphemy to survive and resume his ministry.

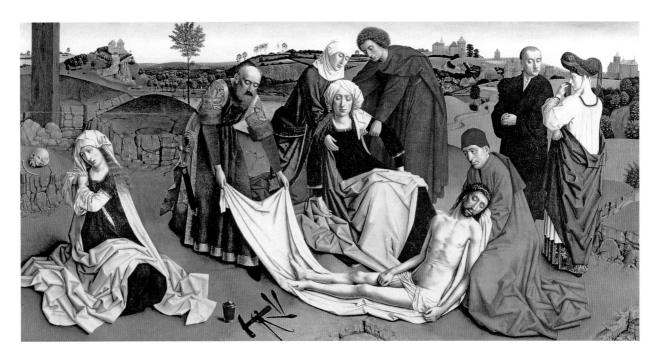

The Deposition (Descent from the Cross), by Petrus Christus. Joseph of Arimathea (*left*) helps lay out the body of Jesus as Mary Magdalene (*far left*) and the Virgin Mary (*centre*) lament. St John the Evangelist is traditionally depicted, as he is here, supporting Jesus' mother.

Accordingly, before Jesus' body was removed for burial, both the Roman *praefectus* and the Jewish Sanhedrin would have sought a guarantee that he was dead.

Neither had any reason for concern, however, as Roman executioners of that era were highly accomplished specialists in killing, widely noted for their efficiency and thoroughness. Under Roman law the soldiers tasked with carrying out an execution had to sign a document certifying that the prisoner had died. These soldiers knew that if they failed to ensure a prisoner's death and then falsified this document, it would, once discovered, result in their *own* executions.

According to one evangelist (John 19:31–37) the Roman guards believed Jesus had died, but in order to remove any doubt one of them thrust a lance up into his side before his body was taken down from the cross for burial. Most medical opinion holds that Jesus was most certainly dead before this was done. This action removed any chance that he could have survived. The wound described caused a dark blood clot to seep from the torn flesh, followed by a watery serum. This would indicate that the lance had perforated one of his lungs and possibly his heart, too.

The burial

Jesus was crucified and died on a Friday. For Jews, this was the day of preparation for the Sabbath, which began at sundown on Friday and continued until sundown on Saturday. According to Jewish law (Deuteronomy 21:22–23), the body of an executed man was not permitted to remain on public display overnight. It was believed that as the executed person was in some way cursed by God, leaving his body exposed overnight would somehow defile (contaminate) the land by showing disrespect to God. As Jesus died some time around mid-afternoon, his body had to be buried quickly because Jewish law forbade such activity after sunset.

A prominent and wealthy member of the Sanhedrin, Joseph of Arimathea, who had been a secret disciple of Jesus, is said to have gone to Pilate and secured permission to bury Jesus that day. With the help of some workmen, Joseph had Jesus' body taken down from the cross and brought to a previously unused tomb nearby.

The Tomb of Jesus

The tomb was hewn out of solid rock. There was an outer chamber in which the body was prepared for burial, and an inner chamber in which the body was placed in a niche for storage. Jesus' body would have been wrapped up inside a long linen shroud (i.e. burial cloth) containing about 70 lb of spices. These spices preserved the body, alleviated its decaying odour and acted as a sort of adhesive for the shroud itself.

Once the body was wrapped, completely and tightly, a piece of cloth similar to the shroud but much smaller would have been placed over Jesus' head. Then a large, circular stone, weighing about 1 tonne, would have been rolled along a groove to seal off the entrance to the tomb.

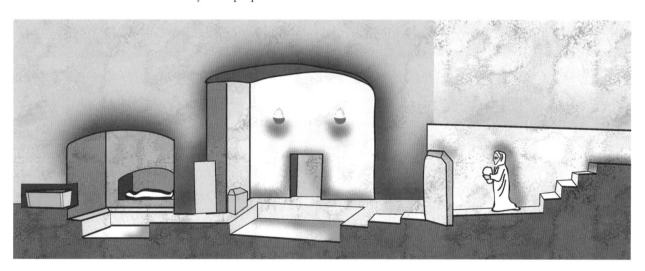

Side view of tomb.

Questions

1. Why would both Pilate and the Sanhedrin have sought to ensure that Jesus had indeed died on the cross before allowing his body to be taken down for burial?

2. Why would the Roman execution squad have wanted to ensure that Jesus was dead?

3. How did Jesus' executioners *guarantee* that he was dead?

4. Why did Jesus' body have to be taken down from the cross and buried in a hurry on Good Friday?

5. Where was Jesus buried?

The Shroud of Turin

For centuries a linen cloth known as *the Shroud of Turin* (because it has been preserved in the Cathedral of St John the Baptist in Turin, Italy) has been venerated by Christians as the actual shroud in which Jesus' body was wrapped when placed in the tomb on Good Friday.

This shroud, which is roughly 14 ft long and 3.5 ft wide, bears the faint image of a man who was crucified and then laid out for burial. When Secondo Pia took and examined the first ever photographs of the shroud in 1898, he made an extraordinary discovery: the photographic negatives revealed all kinds of fascinating detail, which until then had been completely hidden from the naked eye.

A detailed forensic analysis of these photographic negatives on both the front and the back of the shroud revealed that this was the burial cloth of a crucified man who was between 5 ft 11" and 6 ft 1" tall. The wounds on his body correspond to the wounds that the Gospels claim were inflicted on Jesus.

For example:

◆ there are wounds most likely caused by sharp thorns driven into the head;

◆ there is a lance wound in the victim's right side, as described in John's account;

◆ there are over 100 marks on the chest and dorsal area consistent with a Roman scourging;

◆ there are wounds in each wrist consistent with Roman methods of crucifixion;

◆ the man's right shoulder was dislocated—a common occurrence during crucifixion.

In 1988 the Catholic Church allowed radiocarbon-dating tests to be conducted on a fragment of the shroud. The tiny piece of cloth was divided between

Photographic negative showing details of the Shroud of Turin.

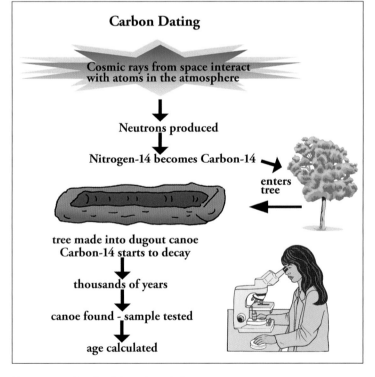

The process involved in carbon-dating.

laboratories in Oxford, Tucson and Zurich. All three laboratories agreed that the shroud dated from the period 1260–1390 CE and not from the first century CE. This appeared to settle the question of the shroud's date and provenance once and for all. It was widely regarded as a medieval forgery of some kind.

Contrary to expectations, this verdict has not settled the issue of the shroud's origins and authenticity. The 1988 results were later challenged by other scholars, who offered four main lines of criticism.

First objection

Linen, for an as yet unknown reason, generally gives a much more recent carbon date than other substances of an identical age. It has been discovered that if one carbon dates the linen wrapped around a mummified corpse, the corpse will have a much older dating than the linen in which it was wrapped. This fact was not known at the time the tests were done, so was not taken into account by the laboratories involved.

Second objection

Fungi and bacteria grow on ancient linen fibres. As a result, the linen shroud itself would have had a layer of bacterial contamination on it. Some scholars think this layer would have resisted removal by the dating process used; it would have to be removed to facilitate access to the original linen base before tests could be conducted, to ensure accuracy.

Third objection

The samples tested in 1988 came from a part of the shroud since known to have been touched repeatedly by ungloved human hands over the centuries when it was on public display to pilgrims. Every person who touched it left traces of his/her DNA, which contaminated it heavily. This was not taken into account in the 1988 tests.

Fourth objection

The shroud was almost destroyed by fire in 1532. Fire is known to introduce new contaminants to cloth and this, too, may have affected the carbon-14 dating of the shroud.

The Shroud of Turin is a puzzling artefact. Various suggestions have been offered to explain it, such as:

- although there are no brush strokes, the shroud may be a painting produced by daubing pigments;
- its image is a scorch produced by draping a linen cloth over a hot statue;
- it is a kind of 'vapourgram' in which gases given off by a decomposing body leave an imprint;
- the corpse's electromagnetic field interacted with the linen cloth to produce the image of a crucified man.

Scholars have tested each of these proposed explanations and declared them unsuccessful. The Shroud of Turin contains a three-dimensional image of a crucified man of such detail and quality that no known technique could produce it today, let alone during the Middle Ages. Further, the shroud contains details (for example, nailing through the wrists) unknown in medieval times. In addition, pollen traces found on the shroud have been traced to the environs of Jerusalem where the plant that produced them flowered around the time of Passover—the time when Jesus was executed.

Clearly, the radiocarbon tests need to be repeated. Nonetheless most Christian writers remain highly cautious about the shroud and advise against jumping to unwarranted conclusions. All one can reasonably say is that it is the shroud of a scourged and crucified man bearing the wounds of Christ, as described in the Gospels. It is unlikely that anyone is going to be able to prove beyond doubt that this is the shroud in which Jesus was wrapped. It therefore remains a fascinating historical artefact, one that sharply divides scholarly opinion as to whether it is genuine or a fraud.

Questions

1. Where is the shroud kept?

2. Why have generations of Christians venerated it?

3. What did Secondo Pia discover about it?

4. Why is it claimed that the wounds displayed on the figure in the shroud correspond to those described in the Gospels?

5. What did the Catholic Church permit in relation to the shroud in 1988?

6. Why was the shroud widely regarded as a medieval forgery thereafter?

7. State the four objections since raised by scholars to the tests conducted on fragments of the shroud in 1988?

8. What does the shroud contain?

9. Why do some scholars believe that it may be authentic?

10. Without further radiocarbon tests that take into account information that has come to light since 1988, what can one reasonably say about the Shroud of Turin?

11. Do you think that if the shroud is one day proven to be either genuine or a fraud that it would have any major impact on people's attitude towards Christianity? Explain your answer.

The Resurrection of Jesus

Introduction

The belief that Jesus of Nazareth rose from the dead on Easter Sunday morning is at the very heart of Christianity. There would be no Christian Church without it.

Consider:

Resurrection is not simply one aspect of Christianity. We cannot remove that piece of the Christian jigsaw labelled '*resurrection*' and leave anything which is recognisable as the Christian Faith. We destroy the entire picture. For Jesus himself, his cross and his resurrection from the dead are the three foundation stones on which Christianity rests.

People sometimes say, 'I'm not bothered about questions like: did Jesus rise from the dead? We've got his marvellous teaching. Surely that's what *really* counts?' This 'let's-concentrate-on-his-teaching' approach is attractive. But it misses the point. *For without his resurrection, it is extremely unlikely that we would have his teaching—or anything else in the New Testament. As Archbishop Michael Ramsey put it: 'No resurrection: no Christianity.'*

The Resurrection, by Andrea Mantegna.

> In the early Church there was no preaching of Jesus *except* as risen Lord. Nor could there be. For without the apostles' conviction that they had encountered Jesus alive again after his death, there would have been no preaching at all.
>
> There would have been deep mourning for a lost friend. There would have been great admiration for a dead hero. No doubt his profound teaching would have been remembered and cherished by his small, loyal circle of followers. But within a few generations he would have been *forgotten*.
>
> Of course, movements do grow and develop after the founder's death; we have ample evidence of this. It happens when the founder's followers are in a *buoyant* frame of mind – for everything depends on their 'get-up-and-go'. After Jesus' death, his disciples had just about enough get-up-and-go to restart their fishing business!
>
> (John Young, *The Case Against Christ*.)

The Gospel Stories

Each of the four evangelists offers his own account of what happened on what later came to be known as 'Easter Sunday'.

See:

> Mark 16:1–20;
> Matthew 28:1–20;
> Luke 24:1–48;
> John 20:1–29.

None of these accounts offers a description of the actual resurrection event itself. No one seems to have witnessed it. Instead, they report on what is said to have happened *afterwards*. The four Gospel accounts do *not* agree in every detail, however, which has led some writers to doubt their trustworthiness.

Christian scholars claim that differences in detail should not be a cause for concern.

Consider:

◆ whether one lives in the first century or in the twenty-first century, no two people ever see or remember an event in exactly the same way;

◆ differences in detail, though on inspection minor, serve only to underline the trustworthiness of these Gospel accounts. It means that despite the temptation to do so, no one tried to tidy up these texts by removing any inconsistencies. They were not harmonised. Variations in detail recorded by each evangelist were left untouched. The early Christians seem to have had too much respect both for these key sources and for the intelligence of open-minded readers to tamper with them.

What, then, can one say happened on Easter Sunday?

A careful reading of the four texts reveals that they all *agree* on a number of crucial points:

A. The Empty Tomb:

◆ shortly after dawn on Easter Sunday morning some of Jesus' female disciples went to his tomb to embalm his body properly;

◆ when they arrived at his tomb they were shocked and confused to find that it had been opened and his corpse was missing;

◆ those who made this discovery were either told by an angel (*per* the Synoptic Gospels: Mark, Matthew and Luke) or came to realise themselves (John) that Jesus had risen from the dead.

B. The Post-Resurrection Visitations:

◆ the disciples were still in a state of shock and deeply depressed by the death of Jesus. They did not initially believe the women's story;

◆ Jesus suddenly came among the disciples, greeting his astonished followers with reassuring words, such as '*Peace be with you*' (John 20:21);

◆ at first, the disciples were amazed and frightened when they saw the risen Jesus—a natural reaction in the circumstances. This quickly faded, however, and they all experienced a remarkable inner peace;

◆ the disciples recognised Jesus as living, not dead. But they were aware that he was *not* alive in exactly the same way as before his death. This they struggled to understand;

◆ Jesus told them to spread the news of his death and resurrection. He gave them a mission to 'Go, therefore, make disciples of all nations' (Matthew 28:19).

N.B.

Christian theologians state that …

Both the empty tomb and the post-resurrection visitations of Jesus are necessary because each supports the value of the other as evidence for belief in the historical truth of Jesus' resurrection.

Consider:

◆ the empty tomb, while *not* proof of the resurrection, is *a necessary precondition* for it. If the tomb was not empty, then the appearances of Jesus could be written off as mere hallucinations or the fanciful imaginings of grief-stricken people who refused to accept the death of their leader;

◆ without the appearances, the empty tomb could have been explained away as a simple act of grave-robbing by Jesus' followers, who perpetrated a hoax and hoped that some people would be gullible enough to fall for it.

Questions

1. Explain the following statement:

   '*No resurrection: no Christianity*'.

2. Why do Christian scholars state that differences in detail between the four Gospel accounts of the resurrection should *not* be a cause for concern?

3. On what points do the four Gospel accounts of the resurrection *agree*?

4. Why do Christians believe that *both* the empty tomb and the post-resurrection visitations of Jesus are *needed* to support the value of each other?

The Disciples Peter and John Running to the Sepulchre on the Morning of the Resurrection, by Eugene Burnard.

The possibility of a hoax

Some writers have claimed that Jesus' followers committed *a hoax*, i.e. played a trick intended to *deceive* people. It has been alleged that some of Jesus' disciples stole his corpse from the tomb and then invented the story of his resurrection.[6]

Christian scholars reject this accusation as untrue for the following reasons:

A. The impact of Jesus' death on his disciples

The Gospel accounts portray the execution of Jesus as having a shattering effect on the morale of his disciples. It is written that they fled in panic and abandoned him to a terrible, lonely death. This reaction is quite consistent with what is now known about the religious politics of that era. If the person one

believed to be the long-awaited messiah had been captured and put to death, then one had proof positive that he was a *fraud* and that one had backed the *wrong* person. Invariably in such cases the movement that surrounded a failed messianic pretender would either be wiped out by the authorities or dissolved rapidly of its members' own volition as they sought to avoid sharing the same fate as their former leader.

For Jesus' followers, his ignominious death would have been understood as undeniable confirmation that he was merely another in a long line of failed contenders for the title of 'messiah'. They would have had *no* expectation of ever encountering him again. Psychologically, the disciples would have been crushed not only by Jesus' death but also by the death of all the hopes they had built around the expectation of his success.

It is likely that the first thing they would have wanted to do was to quickly put some distance between

[6] This accusation was first made by members of the Sanhedrin and is recorded in Matthew 28:13.

themselves and Jesus. The story of Peter's public denial that he had ever even known Jesus (John 18:15–27) was probably an early attempt to begin the process of disassociating themselves from him. It shows an unflattering, but all too recognisably human, response by someone who has lost confidence in his leader and is gripped by fear and confusion. For this reason most scholars believe it to be an authentic account of Peter's immediate reaction and to offer an important insight into the mindset of Jesus' followers at the time of his death and its immediate aftermath.

There is every reason to think that the disciples would have wanted to avoid being seen anywhere near the tomb of Jesus. They had left the whole matter of his burial to Joseph of Arimathea. They did not enjoy the latter's reputation and membership of the Sanhedrin as protection against arrest and execution. The disciples would have no more wanted to steal Jesus' corpse from the tomb than bury it there in the first place. They would have been too traumatised, frightened and grief-stricken by all that had happened.

True, some of Jesus' female disciples were permitted to go to the tomb on Easter Sunday morning, but this was merely an act of respect by devoted friends. They went only to complete the process of embalming the corpse, which had commenced on Good Friday but had been interrupted by the Sabbath. Once this had been completed, they would no doubt have acted in the same way as the other disciples, namely to do nothing to bring the attention of the authorities on themselves and to return home quietly to the comparative safety of Galilee to pick up the threads of their former lives.

The disciples would—as would be the case for any people who have had their expectations smashed—have wanted to put the whole Jesus affair behind them. They would have had neither the desire to perpetrate a hoax, such as claiming Jesus had risen from the dead, nor would they have had anything to gain by doing so.

B. The choice of women as the first witnesses to the risen Jesus

In the first century CE women in Palestine had a very low social status. Consider the following statement:

Happy is he whose children are male, and alas for him whose children are female.
(B. Kiddushin 82b)

Noli me Tangere, by Emmanuel Lambardos. The olive tree growing over the empty tomb symbolises the victory of life over death. The blooming meadow in which the kneeling Magdalene encounters Christ represents the Garden of Paradise. Wrapped in its gleaming *chiton*, the body of the risen Christ, transfigured by the light of the Resurrection, bears the very luminous signs of the Passion: the wound in his side; the holes from the nails in the palms of his hands and on his feet. Christ shows his left hand to Mary Magdalene, while in his right hand he holds the list of human sins that he has redeemed by his death.

The beautiful and grieving Mary Magdalene, wrapped in her red cloak, recognises Jesus Christ, but the Lord quickly takes leave of her with the words, 'Do not hold me, for I have not yet ascended to the Father' (John 20:17).

As a result of this attitude the testimony of women carried very little weight in the law courts and in other areas of public life; only evidence offered by men was deemed to be worthy of consideration. Given this social bias, it is quite remarkable that the Gospel accounts of the events surrounding the resurrection of Jesus put women forward as their *principal* witnesses. It is Jesus' female disciples who are said to have been the first to hear the announcement of his resurrection by angels, while Mary Magdalene is reported to have been the first person to encounter the risen Jesus (John 20:11–18).

In the light of prevailing social attitudes, a story dependent on the testimony of women would *not* have found a receptive audience. Indeed, their story would have been more readily accepted as evidence *against* the claim that Jesus had risen. It should be remembered that initially the women were not believed even by Jesus' male disciples (Luke 24:10–11).

If Jesus' disciples had wanted to perpetrate a hoax, it seems highly *unlikely* that they would ever have chosen women as the first witnesses to the risen Jesus. Their testimony carried too little weight in such a male-dominated society.

C. The novel idea of Jesus' resurrection from the dead

Any attempt by Jesus' followers to pull off a hoax regarding his resurrection would have run into two major difficulties.

First, there was considerable disagreement within Jewish society about the whole idea of life after death. Essentially there were two schools of thought:

- the Sadducees rejected the possibility of any life beyond the grave;
- the Pharisees, and many ordinary Jews, did believe in life after death.

The Sadducees, who dominated the nation's ruling elite, were *not* open to persuasion by hoax or by any other means.

Secondly, there was very little in the Jewish sacred texts that would have prepared either the disciples or any other Jewish persons to expect the resurrection of a particular individual. This is because those who did believe in life after death accepted the version of it as set out in the Old Testament book of Daniel 12:1–4. They expected that:

- the resurrection would occur only when the end of this world had come;
- it would be a communal experience, i.e. everyone who had lived a good life would be raised up to a new life together.

The claim that one particular individual—Jesus of Nazareth—had risen from the dead before the end of the world would have been utterly unprecedented. It would have profoundly challenged the ideas of most Jewish people, including Jesus' *own* followers.

The Gospels portray Jesus' disciples as reluctant to accept his resurrection. In a way, one might say that they are presented as having the conclusion that he had risen *thrust upon them*. Consider the story of the two disciples travelling on Easter Sunday from Jerusalem to Emmaus, who encounter the risen Jesus. They are saddened and confused by what has occurred. Jesus tells them that all of this was

Ordained so that the messiah should enter into his glory.
(Luke 24:26)

Jesus then explains to them the meaning of all of the Old Testament prophecies regarding the Messiah. He indicates that his resurrection is part of God's plan. It is clear, however, that the whole idea of Jesus' resurrection was a novel one and did *not* fit neatly into the religious preconceptions of the Jewish people. If the disciples of Jesus had set out to deliberately perpetrate a hoax, they could hardly have chosen a more difficult idea for many of their fellow Jews to accept.

Unless, of course, what they claimed had actually happened.

D. The transformation of the disciples

Within days of Jesus' death and burial an extraordinary change came over his disciples. Initially they had been a pathetic, directionless group huddled away in locked rooms, demoralised and distraught by their leader's death and terrified of suffering the same fate. Then, a dramatic change came over them. Where before they had been afraid, they gained courage; instead of hiding, they went out into the streets preaching to crowds of people; instead of mourning a lost leader, they proclaimed him as risen from the dead. Such actions and words placed their lives in great danger. In the years that followed all but one of the apostles (John) would meet a violent death for preaching Jesus' message. Something happened in the aftermath of Jesus' death and burial, something that *transformed* the disciples. What could have had such a dramatic effect on them?

Psychologists have observed that dispirited people under great stress are *not* creative. People suffering the kind of demoralising blow Jesus' disciples had endured would neither have been capable of swiftly reorganising themselves nor of reinvigorating themselves with the kind of joyful certainty described in the *Acts of the Apostles*. These disciples would have required some extraordinary experience to transform them from frightened defeatists into courageous missionaries. Christians believe that this experience was provided by their encounter with the risen Jesus, which was why they were prepared to suffer and die for their beliefs.

Ecstasy of Mary Magdalene, by Peter-Paul Rubens.

The idea that they would have been willing to die for a hoax is very difficult to support. As one writer puts it:

> *The whip, the dungeon and the sword would soon have loosened their tongues. People will suffer and die for their convictions, but not for their inventions.*
> (John Young, *The Case Against Christ.*)

Questions

1. Why do Christian scholars reject the claim that the apostles stole the body of Jesus from the tomb in order to perpetrate a massive hoax? ➡

2. Why is the choice of women as the first witnesses to the risen Jesus significant to those who defend the historical truth of the resurrection?

3. Explain the prevailing Jewish beliefs about life after death in the first century CE.

4. The four Gospels portray the disciples as reluctant to accept the resurrection of Jesus. Why might this have been the case, given their beliefs about life after death?

5. What is meant by '*the transformation*' of Jesus' disciples, which occurred *after* his death and burial?

6. Why do Christians interpret this transformation as *evidence* for the truth of Jesus' resurrection?

Visitations or hallucinations?

Some writers who deny the resurrection of Jesus accept that his disciples sincerely believed that Jesus had risen from the dead and appeared to them. Nonetheless they go on to argue that the disciples were suffering from *hallucinations*, i.e.

> *apparent or alleged perceptions of a person or object not actually present.*

It is known from the testimony of many bereaved people that those who have lost loved ones sometimes believe they can experience their presence again. This can be either:

◆ *aural*, i.e. hearing his/her voice calling out; or
◆ *visual*, i.e. glimpsing his/her likeness in the street or walking up a stairs.

Some psychologists believe that these sorts of hallucinations stem from sudden, overwhelming memories flooding into the conscious mind. Indeed, for some people such experiences can be so strong that they believe they can hold a two-way conversation with their deceased loved one. Understandably, a person who is very stressed and grieving deeply can sometimes believe that he/she is seeing the one thing he/she most desires.

Certainly the disciples of Jesus would have missed him intensely and would have longed to see and hear him again. Could the post-resurrection visitations of Jesus be dismissed as grief-induced hallucinations?

Christian writers say '*no*' for the following reasons:

First, the post-resurrection visitations of Jesus have an unusual feature that clearly distinguishes them from grief-induced hallucinations. In most of the Gospel accounts the disciples did *not* recognise Jesus immediately.

Consider the following story, concerning the experience of Mary Magdalene:

> Meanwhile Mary stayed outside the tomb, weeping. Then, still weeping, she stooped to

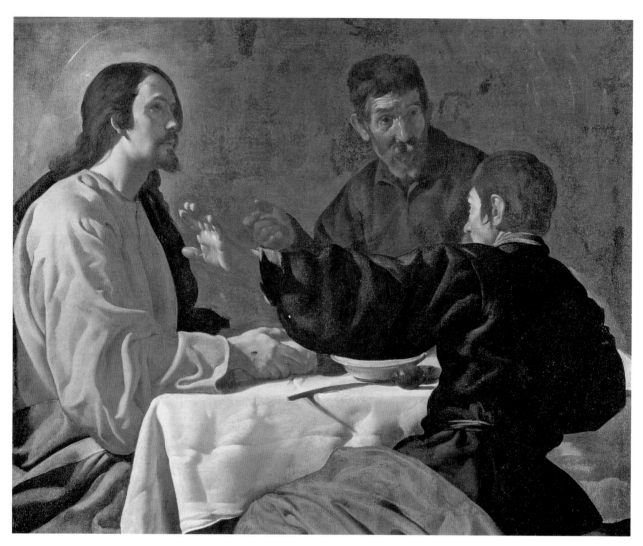

Supper at Emmaus, by Diego Rodriguez de Silva Velásquez.

look inside, and saw two angels in white sitting where the body of Jesus had been, one at the head, the other at the feet. They said, 'Woman, why are you weeping?' 'They have taken my Lord away,' she replied, 'and I don't know where they have put him.' As she said this she turned round and saw Jesus standing there, though she did not recognise him. Jesus said, 'Woman, why are you weeping? Who are you looking for?' Supposing him to be the gardener, she said, 'Sir, if you have taken him away, tell me where you have put him, and I will go and remove him.' Jesus said, 'Mary!' She knew him then and said to him in Hebrew, '*Rabbuni!*' – which means Master.

(John 20:11–16)

Notice that at first, Mary did not recognise Jesus. It was only when Jesus spoke to her, calling out her name, that she realised it was *him*.

This is very important. The defining characteristic of a grief-induced hallucination is *recognition*. The person having the hallucination is overwhelmed by the *imagined* presence of his/her deceased loved one, whom he/she *recognises instantly*. The disciples did *not* experience the risen Jesus in this way at all.

Secondly, hallucinations are experienced by individuals. For example, if several people in a group took mind-altering drugs, they would hallucinate together. However, each would experience a *different* hallucination from the other, because hallucinations arise from the subconscious mind, and each person's subconscious is as *uniquely individual* as his/her fingerprints. For these reasons the post-resurrection visitations of the risen Jesus *cannot* be dismissed as mere hallucination, grief-induced or otherwise.

Questions

1. What are *hallucinations*?

2. What are the two kinds of hallucination?

3. Why might a bereaved person sometimes believe that he/she can experience the presence of a deceased loved one?

4. Why do Christian writers *reject* the claim that the post-resurrection visitations of Jesus to his disciples were merely grief-induced hallucinations?

Visitations or ghostly apparitions?

Some writers have claimed that what the disciples experienced were ghostly apparitions. In common with most of their fellow Jews, the disciples of Jesus believed in the existence of ghosts.

A *ghost* may be defined as *the supposed apparition of a dead person or dead animal.*

Some people today are quite willing to believe in the existence of ghosts, while others reject the idea out of hand. Paranormal investigators have revealed *most* reported sightings of ghosts to be either deliberate frauds, mistaken interpretations of natural events or the over-heated imaginings of psychologically disturbed persons. However, *some* alleged ghost sightings are considered to be genuine because in a few authenticated cases there was:

◆ *more* than one *reliable* witness present;

◆ *more* than one sighting by other *credible* witnesses.

In other words, in these instances the ghostly apparitions seemed to be present independently of any human observer.

Some important features of these genuine ghostly apparitions are:
◆ they are *intangible* (i.e. not solid);
◆ they are *unable to communicate* in any way with the living;
◆ there is *no interaction whatsoever* between the apparition and the person(s) who witnessed it.

Christian parapsychologists such as Herbert Thurston and E.F. O'Doherty claim that there is no reason to believe that the existence of ghosts offers any evidence for life after death. They claim that research indicates that such unusual, strange occurrences are purely *natural* phenomena and therefore are matters for scientific exploration and explanation. They have no supernatural dimension and are of no religious significance.

Christ and St Peter, by Sir Anthony van Dyck.

At first glance, the stories of Jesus' various visitations might seem to lend credence to claims that what the disciples witnessed were just 'ghostly apparitions'.

For example:

- Jesus is reported as appearing in two places at the same time (Mark 16:9–12);
- Jesus could walk through a closed door (John 20:19–20);
- Jesus could vanish at will (Luke 24:31).

A careful reading of the Gospel accounts makes it clear that Jesus' visitations were *not* some kind of ghostly appearances.

Consider the following passages:

1. *They were still talking about all this when he himself stood among them and said to them, 'Peace be with you!' In a state of alarm and fright, they thought they were seeing a ghost. But he said, 'Why are you so agitated, and why are these doubts rising in your hearts? Look at my hands and feet; yes, it is I indeed. Touch me and see for yourselves; a ghost has no flesh and bones, as you can see I have.' And as he said this he showed them his hands and feet. Their joy was so great that they still could not believe it, and they stood there dumbfounded; so he said to them, 'Have you anything here to eat?' And they offered him a piece of grilled fish, which he took and ate before their eyes.*
(Luke 24:36–43)

2. *Thomas, called the Twin, who was one of the Twelve, was not with them when Jesus came. When the disciples said, 'We have seen the Lord', he answered, 'Unless I see the holes that the nails made in his hands and can put my finger into the holes they made, and unless I can put my hand into his side, I refuse to believe'. Eight days later the disciples were in the house again and Thomas was with them. The doors were closed, but Jesus came in and stood among them. 'Peace be with you,' he said. Then he spoke to Thomas, 'Put your finger here; look, here are my hands. Give me your hand; put it into my side. Doubt no longer but believe.' Thomas replied, 'My Lord and my god!'*
(John 20:24–29)

Notice the points made by the evangelists in the accounts above:

- Jesus was not only *visible* (seen) but also *tangible* (solid);
- he *interacted* with his disciples. He spoke to them and they responded to him. He ate the food they gave him. He even allowed one of them to touch his wounds.

These accounts assert that Jesus was *really*, physically present. His disciples did *not* experience ghostly apparitions.

But how could this be? How would it have been possible for the risen Jesus to do things that are impossible for a human being to do? Remember, the evangelists record how *initially* the disciples did *not* immediately recognise the person they encountered as Jesus, risen from the dead. Although it *really* was Jesus who came to them, the disciples found it very difficult to express that Jesus was now *different* from the person they had known *before* his death. The risen Jesus was living a *completely new* kind of life, which strained the evangelists' powers of expression to their limits.

Consider:

♦ Jesus had *not* been restored to his former mortal life. The disciples had witnessed the restoration to life of Lazarus and Jairus' daughter, but unlike them, the risen Jesus was no longer restricted by the laws of space and time that limit our human freedom of action. Uniquely, Jesus could pass through solid objects, bi-locate, become tangible or disappear at will;

♦ through his resurrection, Jesus had been transformed and glorified. His body was no longer subject to change, illness or death.

Questions

1. What is meant by '*a ghost*'?

2. Identify the important features of those few events regarded as *genuinely* ghostly apparitions.

3. What elements of Jesus' post-resurrection experiences might, *at first glance*, lend credence to the claim that they were merely 'ghostly apparitions'?

4. What points made by the evangelists in their accounts of the post-resurrection visitations of Jesus would *support* the claim that the disciples really *did* experience the risen Jesus and *not* some ghostly figure?

5. Explain the meaning of the following statement:

   The risen Jesus was living a completely new kind of life.

The importance of the resurrection

Christianity teaches that the story of Jesus did not end with his resurrection. Christians believe that:

♦ Jesus is not merely a historical figure. He *lives* today. He is the Son of God, the second person of the Holy Trinity;

♦ Jesus' resurrection is not simply a historical event, not something over and done. It is an *ongoing* story of *salvation* and *redemption* that includes all human beings since the resurrection.

Jesus offers people *salvation*, i.e. a way out of the

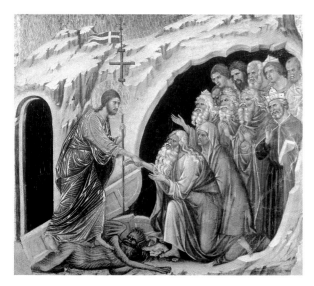

Christ's Descent into Hell, by Duccio di Buoninsegna.

creative power of God's love can confront and overcome the power of evil.

Jesus promised that God will provide his *grace* (i.e. his freely given, strengthening love) to enable people to do good and avoid evil. Thus, Christians are confident that life is not pointless, that it is *worth* the struggles involved in living, that death is not the end but rather a new *beginning* and that it is worthwhile making sacrifices and doing good.

By rising from the dead Jesus also offered people *redemption*, i.e. an opportunity to restore their relationship with God to what it was originally intended to be. Only then can people experience the fullness of life in this world, free from fear and full of hope that, after death, they will enjoy eternal peace and happiness in the presence of God.

Neither salvation nor redemption are forced upon human beings; Jesus extends an *invitation*. It is up to each person to decide how to respond to it.

suffering, confusion and alienation that are part of everyone's life. Human beings are incapable of achieving salvation on their own. Through his resurrection, Jesus demonstrated unequivocally that the

Questions

1. What do Christians mean when they say that *the story of Jesus did not end with his resurrection*?

2. What is meant by *salvation*?

3. What do Christians believe Jesus demonstrated by his resurrection?

4. What is *grace*?

5. What are the effects of grace on the life of a Christian?

6. What is meant by *redemption*?

7. Why are the salvation and the redemption achieved by Jesus described as *an invitation*?

The Identity of Jesus

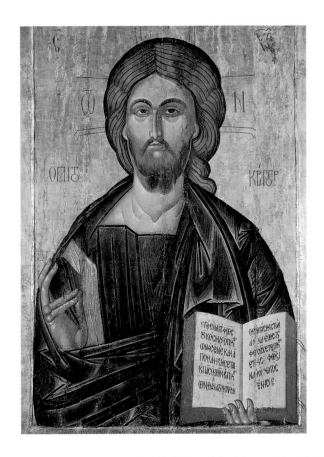

Christ Pantokrator, c. 1670, Workshop of the Moscow Kremlin Armory. The halo with super-imposed cross, bearing the words 'He that is' (Oø N) surrounds the face in a mystical aura that shimmers when the icon is lit by the flickering light of an oil lamp or candles. The choice of the text cited in the open book (Matthew 25:34–36: 'Come, O blessed of my father …') reminds us that on Judgment Day, Christ will recognise us according to the love we have had for our neighbours.

Introduction

The heart of Christianity is not a theory (i.e. a set of ideas), but *a person*: *Jesus of Nazareth*. Considered from a purely historical point of view, Jesus was a remarkable individual:

◆ he was an inspiring preacher who imparted a radical message;

◆ he set new standards for compassion and love in human relationships;

◆ he courageously confronted corruption and injustice and denounced hypocrisy and indifference wherever he encountered it;

◆ he treated everyone he met with equal respect, irrespective of their race, gender, religion or social status.

A few other people have *shared* these same qualities, such as Siddhartha Gautama and Muhammad.

While acknowledging the greatness of such figures, Christians view their own religion's founder in a way that is utterly unique among the major world religions. Consider:

- Buddhists regard their founder, Siddhartha Gautama—whose title 'the Buddha' means 'the Enlightened One'—as a holy and wise teacher. They do *not* see him as a saviour;
- Muslims revere Muhammad as 'the Prophet of Allah'. They believe him to have been the final and greatest prophet of God. They do *not* worship Muhammmad. They worship *only* Allah.

In sharp contrast to Buddhists and Muslims, Christians regard the founder of their faith—Jesus of Nazareth—as the *saviour* of the world and *worship* him. The Buddha and the Prophet Muhammad claimed to be *messengers* of the truth. Their followers believe that they each possessed deep insights into the truth and it is these insights that they have sought to live by and pass on faithfully from one generation to the next.

Christians, on the other hand, claim that Jesus *is the very source of all truth itself.* They believe that he is *God made man*, the Son of God and second person of the Holy Trinity.

In this chapter we shall explore how Christians came to understand Jesus in such terms. As we shall see, the early Christians did *not* reach such conclusions immediately. This understanding was the fruition of many years of prayer and reflection on Jesus' words and actions.

Questions

1. How do Buddhists view the Buddha?

2. How do Muslims view Muhammad?

3. How is the Christian understanding of their founder, Jesus of Nazareth, different from the above?

Prophet

From the outset of his public ministry, those who encountered Jesus asked the question:

Who is this man?

Initially, Jesus' disciples seem to have regarded him as

… a prophet mighty in deed and word.
(Luke 24:19)

They thought that he was yet another holy man sent by God to deliver a message to the Jews—one of a long line of such figures, stretching back to Moses (see Matthew 16:14). It was only in the latter stages of Jesus' public ministry that many of his disciples began to think of him as *more* than a prophet. They began to believe that he was the promised *Messiah*.

Messiah

In Luke's account of the two disciples who encountered the risen Jesus on the road to Emmaus (Luke 24:13–35), one of them, Cleopas, makes clear their deep disappointment at Jesus' death by saying:

We had hoped that he was the one to redeem Israel.
(Luke 24:21)

At the time of Jesus' trial and execution, there was a widespread expectation among many Jews that the arrival of the *Messiah* was imminent.

The word *messiah* means '*the anointed/chosen one*', whom the Jewish prophets had promised would be sent by God.

By the time Jesus began his public ministry the popular notion of this highly anticipated messiah was of a kind of superhuman warrior of noble birth, one appointed by God to free the Jews from foreign domination and then to rule over them with justice and integrity.

Jesus' strong words about the kingdom of God, coupled with the miracles he performed, led some of his contemporaries to think of him as the promised Messiah. Although Jesus did not deny that he was the Messiah, he repeatedly instructed those who wanted to openly proclaim him as such *not* to do so—at least not until he considered the time to be right. It was only when brought before the Sanhedrin that Jesus accepted the title 'Messiah' or, in its more familiar Greek form, '*Christ*'.

The High Priest put a second question to him, 'Are you the Christ,' he said, 'the Son of the Blessed One?'
Jesus answered, 'I am; and you will see the Son of Man seated at the right hand of the Power and coming with the clouds of heaven.'
(Mark 14:61–62)

The high priest and his fellow Sadducees did not

The Transfiguration, by Duccio di Buoninsegna. Jesus stands between the greatest prophets of Israel's past—Elijah and Moses—whom he both succeeds and transcends. The disciples Peter, John and James look on in awe.

believe in the idea of a messiah, so they would have *dismissed* out of hand anyone claiming to be this figure. For them, Jesus was someone who threatened their power and their privileged lifestyles. As such, he was a problem that needed to be *eliminated*.

To many who *did* believe in the promise of a messiah, Jesus was probably a puzzling figure because he was not what most Jews had been led to expect. Jesus was a Galilean carpenter's adopted son. In contemporary social terms, Jesus was a *nobody*. He was neither a warrior of noble birth nor a member of a priestly family. And still the poor, the sick and outcasts were drawn to him in great numbers because of what he said and did.

Nonetheless in the immediate aftermath of his execution, Jesus' disciples lost all faith in him. Their morale was utterly shattered. Undoubtedly, to them it would have seemed that their worst fears had been justified. For all he had said and done, Jesus was apparently just one more in a long line of failed pretenders to the title of 'Messiah'.

It was only *after* the resurrection that the disciples

began to comprehend the full meaning of all Jesus had said and done. He offered them, and they accepted, a radically *different* kind of messiah. The kingdom he had come to establish was not a political kingdom of this world. As was explained earlier in Chapter 9, it was far more than this.

Questions

1. What is a *prophet*?

2. Explain the term '*messiah*'.

3. What was a widespread popular notion of the messiah in the time of Jesus of Nazareth?

4. What was Jesus' reaction to those who wanted to publicly proclaim him as the messiah?
   Why do you think this was the case?

5. In what way might Jesus, as Messiah, have been a puzzling figure to many of his fellow Jews?

6. What event caused the disciples to re-evaluate their whole notion of Jesus as the Messiah?
   Why, do you think, this happened?

The authority of Jesus

In the days following the resurrection, the disciples became increasingly aware of the uniqueness and significance of Jesus. His life, death and resurrection utterly mystified them. It took them some time to work out his identity.

The disciples began by reflecting on all he had said and done. They remembered that, like any other human being, during his earthly life Jesus had been hungry, tired and thirsty. Jesus had experienced the full range of human emotions, from joy to sorrow. He had shared jokes with them and wept at the news of the death of his friend, Lazarus. Jesus had enjoyed the company of others, from intellectuals to children, from religious figures to social outcasts. He had treated all with equal compassion and respect. Yet this same Jesus had said and done extraordinary things.

Consider:

♦ in the Parable of the Sheep and the Goat (Matthew 25:31–46), Jesus told his listeners that it was he who would judge the world at the end of time. The Jews believed that God alone was the supreme judge of all. So how could Jesus of Nazareth claim this role?

♦ when the Pharisees challenged Jesus for permitting his men to pick corn on the Sabbath, Jesus

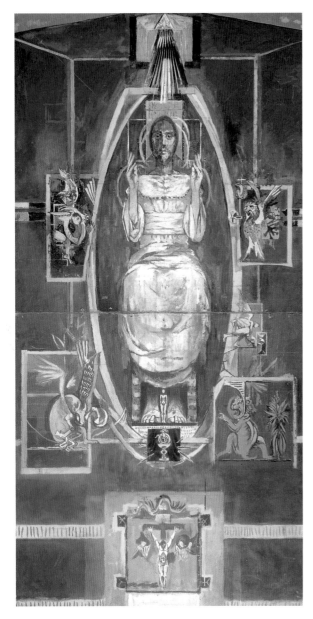

Christ in Glory, by Graham Sutherland.

- Jesus claimed to have the power to forgive sins. The Pharisees objected by saying

  Who can forgive sins but God alone?
  (Luke 5:21)

In response, Jesus worked a miracle by healing a paralytic to demonstrate that *he* had the authority to forgive sins;

- in *the Sermon on the Mount* (Matthew 5–7), Jesus placed his own set of commandments on the *same* level as those believed to have been given by God to Moses on Mount Sinai (Exodus 20:1–21). To do so was to explicitly claim the *same* authority as God;

- in some of his references to the kingdom of God, Jesus referred to it as *my kingdom* (see Luke 22:30 and John 18:36);

- in the Synoptic accounts of the Last Supper, Jesus is described as instituting a *new covenant.* The word 'covenant' is an important biblical term. It refers to an agreement entered into by two unequal partners, in this case God and humanity. The Old Testament presents God as always faithful to his people. But he also requires faithfulness *from* them. The Jewish people had failed, as a nation, to remain faithful to God. The prophet Jeremiah had declared that a new covenant was needed and that God would one day offer it to them. At the Last Supper, Jesus indicated by his words and actions that this moment had finally arrived and that *he,* Jesus, was the central figure in establishing a new, more glorious covenant;

- finally, to the amazement of his disciples, Jesus had risen from the dead to a new and glorified life.

The disciples of Jesus decided that, although he was a human being, Jesus was also clearly *more* than a human being.

responded by claiming to be greater than the Temple itself (Matthew 12:1–6);

- when Jesus caused controversy by curing a man of illness on the Sabbath, his opponents condemned him for breaking the strict religious laws of the day. Jesus responded by saying that he was

  … master even of the Sabbath.
  (Mark 2:28);

The Incarnation

Jesus' first disciples were devout Jews. As such they were all strict monotheists. Each day they would have recited the Shema:

> Hear, O Israel, the Lord our God is one Lord.
> (Deuteronomy 6:4)

Their understanding of the traditional Jewish God underwent a remarkable *transformation* once they reflected on the words and actions of Jesus. They came to recognise that:

◆ Jesus had a completely unique relationship with God.

> The Father and I are one.
> (John 10:29);

◆ Jesus had an authority equal to that of God;
◆ Jesus had a unique mission from God;
◆ Jesus was able to do things that were proper only for God to do.

All this led them to conclude that Jesus of Nazareth was *the Son of God*. Not a son of God—an expression used to describe good and virtuous figures in Jewish history—but *the* Son of God. They worshipped Jesus and did everything in his name. The implications of this belief and practice took many years to be revealed. In time, Christians referred to Jesus as *the Incarnation*, meaning:

> God in the flesh, i.e. in human form.

Contrary to some recent claims, the early Christians believed that Jesus was *both* God *and* man. It simply took some time to express the idea adequately, in a way that avoided confusion.

By the fourth century Christians agreed that *Jesus*

An Allegory of the Incarnation, by Giambattista Tiepolo.

was the eternal, only begotten Son of God, both fully human and fully divine. From Jesus' own words Christians developed their own distinctive view of God: *the Trinity.*

The Trinity

Christians are monotheists, but they hold beliefs about God that are *very different* from those expounded by their Jewish and Muslim brethren.

Christians believe in the doctrine (i.e. teaching) of the Trinity, which states that:

◆ while there is only one God, this God is *triune*, i.e. three-in-one;
◆ in this one God there are three distinct, divine persons—Father, Son and Holy Spirit—who

equally and eternally possess the same divine nature, united in perfect love;

◆ Jesus—the Second Person of the Trinity—is at once fully human and fully divine.

Christians believe that the Trinity represents the way in which God is both perfectly *transcendent* and perfectly *immanent*.

◀ *The Trinity*. Although the word 'Trinity' is not found in the Bible, it is a central doctrine of Christianity: Father, Son and Holy Spirit, three persons as one Godhead. The term evolved in the fourth century CE, after a long series of Christian debates. This Greek Orthodox icon depicts God's encompassing relationship of love (the Father), communication (the Holy Spirit in the form of a dove) and self-giving (Jesus).

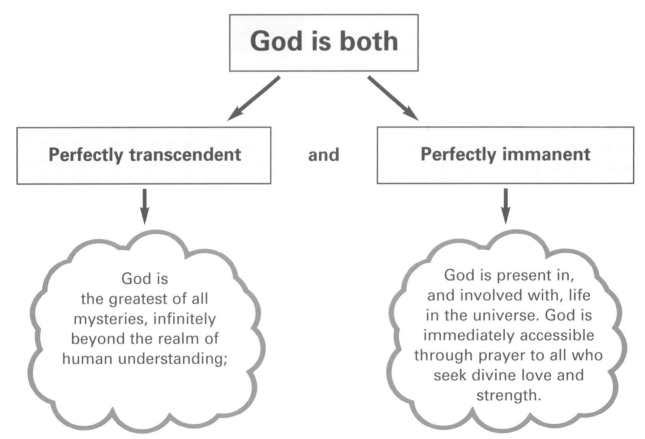

God is both

Perfectly transcendent

and

Perfectly immanent

God is the greatest of all mysteries, infinitely beyond the realm of human understanding;

God is present in, and involved with, life in the universe. God is immediately accessible through prayer to all who seek divine love and strength.

Questions

1. Why were the early Christians convinced that Jesus was a human being?

2. Identify any three things that led Jesus' disciples to conclude that Jesus was human, but also *more* than human.

3. What factors led the disciples to believe that Jesus was *the* Son of God?

4. Explain the term *Incarnation*.

5. What is meant by *the Trinity*?

Addendum:
The *Da Vinci Code* Controversy

The *Da Vinci Code* has been a commercial phenomenon since it was first published in 2003. It is a murder mystery that has topped international bestseller lists for several years, selling over 40 million copies worldwide. Though the book itself is a work of fiction, its author, Dan Brown, claims that it is built on a genuine historical foundation that the reader *must* accept as *factual* and *not* fictitious. Brown presents Christianity as nothing less than a gigantic fraud that has been perpetrated on humanity for the last 2,000 years, involving a vast conspiracy that is only *now* being exposed.

Brown's book has been sharply criticised by both Christian and non-Christian commentators. Reputable scholars have stated that his book grossly *misrepresents*, either purposefully or otherwise, many historical events, persons and institutions.

Consider the following:

According to Dan Brown	According to reputable scholars
• The '*Holy Grail*' was the womb of Mary Magdalene.	• *No*. The '*Holy Grail*' was a medieval term for the cup used by Jesus of Nazareth at the Last Supper.
• Jesus and Mary Magdalene married and Mary was pregnant at the time of the crucifixion. She later gave birth to a daughter, Sarah, whose descendants are still alive, thus preserving the bloodline of Christ.	• *No*. There is *not* the slightest shred of evidence, either archaeological or documentary, to support such a claim.

• Jesus wanted Mary Magdalene to lead the early Christians, *not* the apostle Peter.	• *No.* There is *not* the slightest shred of evidence to support such a claim. The Gospels make it clear that Jesus chose Peter.
• No one believed that Jesus was divine until the Council of Nicea in AD 325. Before that, Jesus was merely regarded as a '*mortal prophet*'.	• *No.* Christians worshipped Jesus as God made man long *before* the Council of Nicea. Brown ignores the Gospel of John (first century) and the Apostles' Creed (second century).
• The Roman emperor Constantine had the New Testament rewritten so as to remove all references to the humanity of Jesus.	• *No.* Constantine did *not* do this. A reader of the New Testament will see that it is *full* of references to the humanity of Jesus. The evangelists record how Jesus experienced hunger, fatigue, sadness and fear. They relate how Jesus bled and died in agony on the cross.
• The Dead Sea Scrolls were discovered in the 1950s.	• *No.* They were found *in 1947*.
• The Dead Sea Scrolls were among '*the earliest Christian records*'.	• *No.* They were written entirely by Jews. They contain *no* references whatsoever to Christianity.
• The Nag Hammadi Documents (discovered in Egypt in 1945) emphasise that Jesus was merely a good man who was in no way divine.	• *No.* Quite the contrary. These documents present Jesus as a divine being who took on human likeness, but was never truly human.
• The Nag Hammadi Documents recount the story of the Holy Grail.	• *No.* They do *not* mention it.
• The 'Q' document is Jesus' own written account of his teaching. This document is hidden away in the Vatican.	• *No.* The 'Q' document was *not* a text written by Jesus himself. It is a hypothetical document containing sayings of Jesus, believed to have been compiled after his death, which was consulted by the evangelists Luke and Matthew.

Both Catholic and non-Catholic scholars agree on this point. There is *no* evidence to support the claim that a secret document written by Jesus is hidden in the Vatican's archives.

- The Catholic Church is a fraudulent institution that uses monks drawn from a secret religious organisation called Opus Dei to murder anyone attempting to reveal the truth about Christianity to the masses.

- *No*. The Catholic Church was founded by Jesus Christ to continue his work. Over the centuries some of its members have done great harm and betrayed everything Jesus stands for, but so many more have played an enormous role in making the world a better place to live. Brown condemns all for the sins of a few.

  Opus Dei is *not* a religious order. It does *not* have any monks, assassins or otherwise. It is a Catholic organisation consisting mostly of laypeople who dedicate themselves to serving God in their daily lives, be it in the workplace or in the home. Only 2 per cent of its membership are priests.

The Last Supper, by Leonardo da Vinci.

According to Dan Brown:

◆ the artist Leonardo da Vinci was at one time the Grand Master of an ancient secret society called the Priory of Sion;

◆ the latter had a two-fold task: to defend the descendants of Jesus and Mary Magdalene and to preserve the 'real story' of their lives;

◆ *The Last Supper* painted by da Vinci contains clues as to the real relationship between Jesus and Mary;

◆ da Vinci placed the figure of Mary sitting next to Jesus at the Last Supper to indicate both her closeness to Jesus and her pre-eminence over his other disciples.

According to reputable scholars:

◆ the figure Brown refers to is not Mary Magdalene but St John the Evangelist;

◆ John's youthful, beardless complexion is typical of artistic depictions of young men at that time;

◆ the Priory of Sion is a modern hoax conjured up by a Frenchman named Pierre Plantard in the 1950s. It did not exist in the time of Leonardo da Vinci.

Questions

1. There is a story told about the German philosopher Hegel: when told by one of his students that his theories were contradicted by the facts, he replied: '*So much the worse for the facts.*'
Could Dan Brown be said to *share* the outlook attributed to Hegel in this story? Give reasons for your answer.

2. Read the following statement:

The misrepresentation of Christian beliefs in The Da Vinci Code is so aggressive and continual that we can only conclude that it is the result either of wilful ignorance or purposeful malice.
(C.E. Olsen and S. Miesel, *The Da Vinci Hoax*, Ignatius Press, 2004.)

Do you think this is a fair comment on Dan Brown's book?
Give reasons for your answer.

Section

C

The World's Religions

Predictions

In the nineteenth century writers such as Auguste Comte and Ernest Renan confidently predicted that:

◆ the existing major world religions would either die out altogether or decline to the point that they survived only as tiny groups on the margins of mainstream society;

◆ no new religions would emerge.

They made these claims because they believed that human history consisted of three stages:

The 1st Stage beginning at the dawn of human history.

In this stage human beings engaged in primitive, superstitious practices centred initially on nature worship and later developing into polytheism.

The 2nd Stage beginning in the so-called 'Axial Period', dating from 900 BCE to 500 BCE.

In this stage a major shift occurred in a number of eastern and near-eastern civilisations and there emerged more sophisticated religious explanations, such as

Auguste Comte.

monotheism, and a rich variety of religious literature, myth and ritual.

The 3rd Stage beginning with the eighteenth-century European intellectual movement known as 'the Enlightenment'.

In this stage science was thought to have completely debunked and replaced religion as the source of truth about the human condition. It was anticipated that religious beliefs would die out among rationally minded people, just as primitive superstitions had earlier. Thus, places of worship would still be admired for their architectural beauty and might, perhaps, function as museums, but would no longer be used for religious rituals. The few people who insisted on practising religious faith would be tolerated by the majority and viewed as eccentric advocates of an outdated world view. They would exist on the fringes of mainstream society and exert no influence.

The current situation

While it is clearly the case that much of Northern Europe is becoming less and less religious, elsewhere in the world this is not the case. As the sociologist Peter Berger has shown, there has been—and continues to be—a spectacular growth in traditional forms of religion throughout the Americas, Africa and Asia in the period since Comte and Renan made their predictions. Indeed, this same period has also witnessed the emergence of a number of new religions, such as Mormonism and Jehovah's Witness.

It would seem that the world's religions are still regarded by the greater majority of humanity as being capable of addressing our most important human needs. There is little reason to doubt that the world's religions will remain as central an element of modern society in the future as they have in the past.

Questions

1. What did nineteenth-century writers such as Comte and Renan predict about the future of the major world religions?

2. Why did they make this prediction?

3. What has the work of sociologists, such as Peter Berger, revealed about the accuracy of this prediction? Explain your answer.

On being a world religion

The title '*world religion*' is generally used to indicate the world-class status and global influence of particular faith communities. Those commonly acknowledged as such include:

♦ Hinduism;
♦ Buddhism;
♦ Judaism;
♦ Christianity;
♦ Islam.

To qualify as a *world* religion, each of the above has had to demonstrate that:

Norman Rockwell's painting *Do onto Others*, which is prominently displayed in the United Nations building in New York City.

- it contains a belief system of such richness and complexity that it is capable of supporting a civilisation;
- it offers an account of life that can sustain people in all social classes, can deal with the real complexities of human relationships, is able to absorb new ideas and discoveries and is capable of entering into dialogue with other traditions.

Differences

It is sometimes remarked that

All religions are basically the same.

This is said because they are observed to have the following elements in common:
- they offer insights into the meaning and purpose of human life;
- they present opportunities for people to participate in communal worship through set rituals that both celebrate and reinforce their beliefs;
- they advance moral codes intended to guide people to do good and avoid doing evil in the many personal choices they have to make.

Even a cursory study of the world's religions quickly reveals that there are major *differences* between them. Each religion fulfils the tasks listed above in its *own* unique and distinctive way. While they can, and do, co-operate on matters of common concern, such as the defence of human rights and the protection of the environment, the major world religions *disagree* profoundly with one another on many fundamental issues.

Each of the major world religions offers its own answers to life's most profound questions. As we shall see, in many cases their conclusions are clearly *incompatible*.

For Example:
The crucifixion of Jesus

Christians believe that Jesus Christ is *God incarnate*. He died on a cross, was buried, but subsequently rose from the dead. Muslims reject this completely. They acknowledge Jesus as a prophet, but *not* as the Son of God and do not accept that Jesus was ever crucified. The Qur'an (Sura 4:156) states that a '*substitute*' was crucified in his place.

It is important to understand *why* Muhammad and the first Muslims held such a view. They believed that Jesus was a great and holy prophet. They could not accept that Allah would allow one of his favoured servants to suffer such a humiliating death. Thus, the Qur'an's statement about a '*substitute*' is primarily concerned with upholding the Islamic understanding of Allah, rather than making any assertions about what happened at Calvary on Good Friday. At base, though, Christian and Muslim views on this topic are poles apart and that is unlikely ever to change.

Questions

1. What are the criteria that must be fulfilled for a faith community to be considered a *world* religion?

2. Read the following statement:

   All religions are basically the same since they all more or less denounce selfishness, and promote the Golden Rule.

   How would you respond to this statement? Give reasons for your answer.

The eastern religions

Hinduism

Hinduism is the oldest of the world's religions. It is thought to have originated in the Indus river valley about 2500 BCE. There are presently about 900 million Hindus, most of whom live in India, although Hinduism also has a significant presence in Indonesia and South Africa. Unlike all of the other major religions, Hinduism did *not* spring forth from the life of any single, inspirational religious figure. Although it does have its sacred texts—the *Vedas*—these do not hold any authority within Hinduism comparable to the Bible in Christianity or the Qur'an in Islam.

Hinduism is diverse, having such a vast array of structures, rituals, festivals and caste systems associated with it that it is often referred to as 'a fellowship of faiths'. Unlike the Abrahamic faiths, it does *not* envisage God as a specific entity, but rather as an impersonal cosmic force of life known as *Brahman*. Each of Hinduism's 330 million gods are said to emanate from Brahman. A Hindu is free to worship his/her favourite god or gods, but the most widely worshipped are

Young Hindu woman offering prayers.

Brahma (the creator), *Vishnu* (the preserver) and *Shiva* (the destroyer).

Within Hinduism each human being is believed to consist of a body and a soul. However, the soul is actually a fragment of Brahman that has somehow become separated from its source and imprisoned within a human body. The only way the soul can find release is to undergo repeated *reincarnation*, i.e. a cycle of birth, death and rebirth. Each Hindu must strive to accumulate sufficient *karma* (spiritual progress) so that he/she eventually achieves *nirvana*, i.e. a state of spiritual perfection that permits the re-absorption of the soul into Brahman.

Unlike the Abrahamic faiths, Hinduism does *not* teach that there is any final judgment of humanity before God. It emphasises *dharma*, i.e. the need to act in accordance with one's responsibilities under the caste system. It claims that through the cycle of death and rebirth a person effectively reaps in one life what he/she has sown in a previous life.

Many Hindus make a pilgrimage to the River Ganges for the public ritual of *Kumbh Mela*, during which they bathe in what they believe to be the river's spiritually purifying waters.

Buddhism

Today there are more than 350 million Buddhists, mostly concentrated in India, Southeast Asia and China. Buddhism's teachings resemble those of Hinduism in some ways, although there are important *differences between them*. To begin with, unlike Hinduism, Buddhism sprang forth from the life of one individual: Siddhartha Gautama, a Hindu prince who was born in what is now Nepal during the sixth century BCE.

As a young man, Siddhartha Gautama was very preoccupied with questions concerning the meaning of life, suffering and death. At the age of twenty-nine he decided to abandon the lavish lifestyle into which he had been born and go in search of answers to these questions, a search that utterly consumed his waking hours. For several years he travelled widely, consulting the leading Hindu gurus (wise men) of

Gold Buddha at Sop Ruak, Golden Triangle, northern Thailand.

his day. None of their answers satisfied him. He then meditated for long periods, seeking answers based on all he had experienced. Eventually, on his thirty-fifth birthday, he achieved what he believed to be the solution to the mysteries of the universe and reached what Buddhists call *bodhi*, or 'enlightenment'. From that point on Siddhartha Gautama was referred to as '*the Buddha*', meaning '*the Enlightened One*'.

The Buddha appears to have ignored the question of whether or not there is a Supreme Being. He preferred to devote his energy to advocating a spiritual strategy that he believed would best help people to cope with the day-to-day challenges of earthly life. After the Buddha's death, however, his followers split on the issue of divinity, with some of them choosing to deify the Buddha and developing complex systems for worshipping him.

The Buddha's teachings are known as the *dhamma*. Fundamental to these are '*the Four Noble Truths*', namely:

- everything in this worldly life involves suffering;
- suffering is caused by selfish desire;
- there is a way to release oneself from suffering;
- that way is '*the Eightfold Path*'.

The Eightfold Path involves the pursuit of mental discipline and moral purity leading to the overcoming of attachment to worldly possessions. This may require several *reincarnations* to be achieved.

Buddhists believe that by following the Eightfold Path they can:

- eliminate desire;
- achieve compassion for all living things;
- experience utter serenity and joy.

Once they have done so, they can attain the deathless state of perfect enlightenment known as '*nirvana*'.

As in Hinduism, Buddhists reject any notion of a

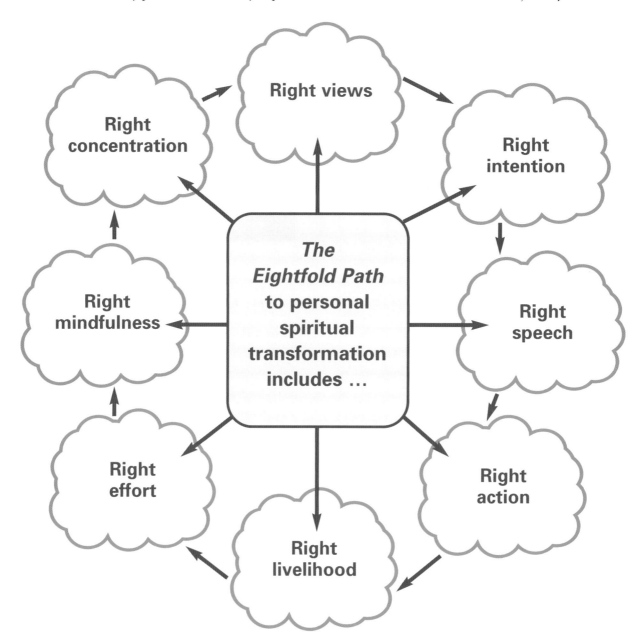

final judgment before God. Instead, they hold that only full enlightenment can end the cycle of death and rebirth and liberate human beings from the suffering experienced in this world. For both Buddhists and Hindus, the individual soul ceases to exist once it attains enlightenment by becoming a part of Brahman. After that reunion, nothing relating to life in this world either exists or matters for the soul.

Questions

1. Explain each of the following terms in Hinduism:
   (a) *Brahman*;
   (b) *reincarnation*;
   (c) *karma*;
   (d) *nirvana*;
   (e) *dharma*;
   (f) *Kumbh Mela*.

2. Why is Siddhartha Gautama known as '*the Buddha*'?

3. How does Buddhism *differ* from Hinduism in terms of:
   (a) its foundation; and
   (b) the question of God's existence?

4. What are the '*Four Noble Truths*'?

5. What does the '*Eightfold Path*' involve?

6. What is the purpose of following the Eightfold Path?

7. How do both Hindus and Buddhists view the notion of a *final judgment* of the individual before God?

The Abrahamic religions

Now we shall examine the three religions that trace themselves back to Abraham, the first patriarch of the Hebrew people.

Judaism

In purely numerical terms, Judaism, with some 18 million adherents worldwide, is the smallest of the major world religions. Only in Israel do the Jews form a national majority, although there are large Jewish communities in the United States of America, Britain and France. Since their religion was founded by Abraham around 1700 BCE, the Jews have endured an extraordinary history of undeserved persecution and homelessness. Despite this, the Jews as a people have made a contribution to the advance of human civilisation that is out of all proportion to their numbers.

The cornerstone of Judaism is the Shema:

Jewish family praying before Seder dinner during the festival of Passover. Outside Palestine, Passover is celebrated for eight days. The Seder meal consists of food that symbolises the flight of the Israelites from Egypt, led by Moses.

Hear O Israel: the Lord Our God is One Lord.

Everything centres on the supreme, just, loving creator God, who made a *covenant* (i.e. sacred agreement) with Abraham and Moses that all subsequent generations of Jews are expected to honour. A Jew does so by faithfully observing God's laws, as enshrined in the Ten Commandments.

The Jewish view of the human predicament is that suffering is the result of *sin* (i.e. wilful wrong-doing) and that all human beings are sinners in need of a *messiah* (saviour). Jews anticipate the arrival of a messiah who will bring peace and justice to the world. Until the messiah's arrival, obedience to *God's* laws is the only way to salvation. This obedience will bring righteousness in *this* life and allow one to achieve eternal life with God in Heaven in the *next*.

Christianity

Although it began in a small corner of the Middle East some 2,000 years ago, Christianity is now the world's largest and most widespread religion, with approximately two billion members. Like Buddhism, Christianity was also propelled by the personal charisma of its founder: Jesus of Nazareth.

Jesus was a Jew. Christianity sprang forth from, and incorporated many elements of, Judaism in both its doctrines and its rituals. Like Judaism, Christianity is *monotheistic* (i.e. professing belief in a single, supreme divine being). However, Christianity has a unique understanding of God as a *Holy Trinity*. Christians claim that Jesus is the incarnate Son of God, the Second Person of the Trinity. They do so on the basis of what is disclosed in the Gospel accounts of his teaching, miracles, death and resurrection.

Jesus is not simply to be worshipped but to be followed. He provided the true exemplar for Christian living. In his life on Earth, Jesus befriended those rejected by 'respectable' society, healed the sick, defended the weak, opposed legalism and exposed hypocrisy. By his rising from the dead he demonstrated that God's love is stronger than death and that not even the tragedies of this world can defeat God's plan for creation.

Woman praying with Rosary beads.

Jesus promised that all those who faithfully follow his example will one day share in the resurrected life, where they will each experience eternal love, peace, joy and wisdom in the presence of God. The grand, life-affirming message of Jesus has encouraged Christians to:

◆ found countless hospitals, hospices, schools and universities;

◆ produce some of the greatest masterpieces of art, architecture, music and literature;

◆ sponsor vast networks to provide relief to those in need and work for reconciliation and peace.

Islam

There are some 1.3 billion members of Islam, who are referred to as *Muslims*. Islam is the world's second largest religion. As the majority of the population in the Middle East is Muslim, there has been a tendency by some commentators to identify Islam with Arabic society. Although it is true that Islam began in what is now Saudi Arabia in the seventh century CE, it has since spread far beyond the Arab world. Today, most Muslims are not Arabs. There are major Muslim populations across Northern Africa, Eastern Africa, Central Asia and Southeast Asia.

Islam was founded by an extraordinarily dynamic and inspirational political and religious figure named Muhammad. Muslims proclaim Muhammad to have been the greatest and final prophet of *Allah* (the Arabic word for '*God*'). Allah is said to be the one and only, the God of absolute unity who is eternal, omnipotent and omniscient, yet utterly loving, just and compassionate. Muslims completely reject the Christian belief in the incarnation because they consider any attempts by us to associate humanity with God to be a gross insult to God's total 'otherness' and unequalled greatness.

Islam's sacred text is the Qur'an, thought to have been transmitted to humanity through the prophet Muhammad. It contains what Muslims believe to be the *final* revelation of the true path humans must follow to God. It calls on people to practice complete submission to the

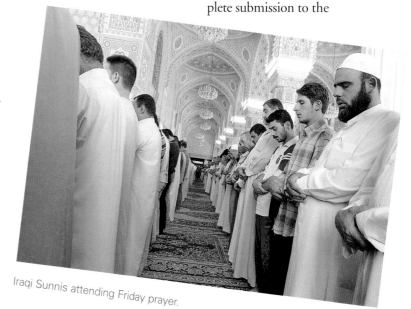

Iraqi Sunnis attending Friday prayer.

revealed will of Allah. It is because of this that this religion is called 'Islam'—an Arabic word meaning 'submission' and 'peace'—as the Qur'an teaches that it is only by submission to Allah that one can find the path to inner peace.

Following the way of submission involves abiding by the Five Pillars of Islam. These are:

1. **Shahadah**   Recognising Allah as the one and only true God and Muhammad as his prophet (i.e. holy messenger).

2. **Salat**   Engaging in ritual prayer five times a day and attendance at the mosque on Friday.

3. **Zakat**   Giving alms to the poor.

4. **Saum**   Fasting during the holy month of Ramadan.

5. **Hajj**   Making a pilgrimage to the Kaaba (House of Allah) in Makkah at least once in one's lifetime.

As with Christianity, Islam teaches that God holds each person responsible for his/her actions. Those who are obedient to the will of Allah will be rewarded in heaven; those who disobey Allah will suffer unending punishment in hell.

N.B.

The diversity within the world's religions

Not only are there profound differences in belief and practice between the world's religions, there are also significant differences on certain matters within each of them. There is no major world religion of which one can confidently state that 'everyone believes that ...' There is nothing like complete agreement in any of them on issues such as:

◆ the interpretation of sacred texts;

◆ leadership and organisational structures;

◆ the forms of worship;

◆ the status and role of women.

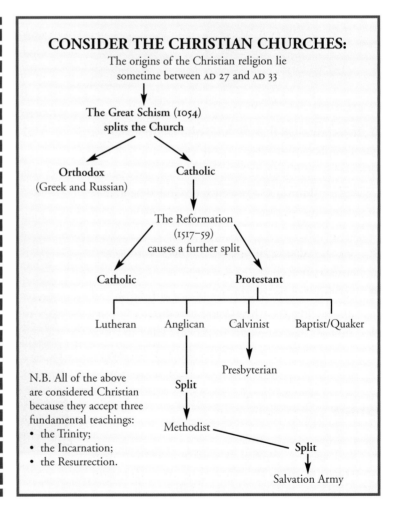

CONSIDER THE CHRISTIAN CHURCHES:

The origins of the Christian religion lie sometime between AD 27 and AD 33

The Great Schism (1054) splits the Church

Orthodox (Greek and Russian)   Catholic

The Reformation (1517–59) causes a further split

Catholic   Protestant

Lutheran   Anglican   Calvinist   Baptist/Quaker

Presbyterian

Split

Methodist

Split

Salvation Army

N.B. All of the above are considered Christian because they accept three fundamental teachings:
• the Trinity;
• the Incarnation;
• the Resurrection.

Questions

1. Explain each of the following terms in Judaism:
  (a) *the Shema*;
  (b) *covenant*;
  (c) *sin*;
  (d) *messiah*.

2. What do Christians believe about Jesus of Nazareth?

3. What is the Christian view of the afterlife?

4. Explain each of the following terms in Islam:
  (a) *Allah*;
  (b) *Qur'an*;
  (c) *Islam*.

5. Explain each of *the Five Pillars* of Islam.

6. On what issues are there often disagreements *within* the world's religions?

Inter-religious dialogue

Some people are dismayed by the obvious disagreements between the world's major religions.
Consider:

◆ for the Abrahamic religions, God is a person, while for Hindus, God is an impersonal life force;

◆ for Hindus the world has always existed, while for the Abrahamic religions it was created from nothing by God;

◆ for Buddhists and Hindus we must undergo repeated reincarnations, while for the Abrahamic religions we have only one life in which to determine our eternal destiny.

Some well-intentioned writers have sought to devise some forms of belief that would somehow eliminate these differences. None has met with either acceptance

or success. This is, perhaps, hardly surprising. Universal agreement on any topic, including religion, is clearly an unattainable goal given the vast array of cultural, political and social systems to which people subscribe. Pluralism is a fact of life in our world. But this does *not* imply that there is no point in the world's religions communicating with one another. On the contrary, there is every reason for them to do so.

In recent decades there has been a growing and encouraging trend towards *inter-religious dialogue*. Spiritual leaders drawn from the different religions have come together in the hope of gaining both a clearer understanding of the issues that divide them and a better appreciation of what they hold in common. There is *no* need for the member of any religion to fear that such discussions may lead to a dilution or diminution of those religions involved. There is much to discuss, and those who disagree do not have to consider each other to be enemies. Indeed, most religions teach their members to respect others, to value freedom of conscience and to demonstrate their love and compassion towards others. It is a mark of a mature religious faith to be able to disagree with someone and yet maintain a friendship with him/her.

No one pretends that such dialogue is easy, but mutual understanding should no longer be considered a luxury. Given the gravity of the many crises facing humanity, dialogue between the world's religions is an absolute *necessity*.

In a document entitled *Toward a Global Ethic* (1993), thinkers drawn from all the major religions set out what they believe to be the four key areas of common concern for all people of faith.
These are:

(1) The fostering of a culture of non-violence and respect for human life.

(2) The development of a just economic order.

(3) The encouragement of tolerance and truthfulness.

(4) The pursuit of equal rights and partnership between men and women.

These thinkers claim that these four aims provide a realistic and workable basis for mutual co-operation between the different religions. They admit that living up to these principles will prove challenging, but say they are essential for the future progress of the human race.

Questions

1. Identify three areas of *disagreement* between the world's religions.

2. Why does this diversity of belief and practice occur?

3. Do you believe that it is possible for these differences to be, one day, *eliminated* altogether? Explain your answer.

4. How should the members of the different religions approach inter-faith dialogue in order for it to be productive?

5. (a) Identify issues of *common* concern for all the world's religions.
   (b) How might they assist each other in confronting and resolving them?

Pope Benedict XVI meets with Jewish leaders in Germany.

Why Christianity?

Christians believe that they have received a unique and special revelation that is expressed in their creeds and lived out according to a particular set of moral values. However, the *magisterium* (i.e. teaching authority) of the Catholic Church calls on all Catholics to build '*bonds of friendship*' with non-Christians of good character. It acknowledges the authentic search for God in every valid religion and admits that Catholics can learn from other religions, e.g. from the love of simplicity in Islam, or from the love of nature in the Eastern religions. Catholics are advised *to reject nothing of those things that are true and holy in other religions*, while still witnessing to their own Christian faith and way of life.

Most Christian denominations today hold similar views. They acknowledge that non-Christians are also striving for the common good of humanity. This raises an important question: why choose to be a Christian and not, say, a Jew or a Muslim?

In his book, *An Approach to Christianity*, Christopher Butler offers this answer:

◆ he begins by pointing out that a person's actions and words can reveal a great deal about his/her character;

◆ the most complete act of revealing one's true nature to another person is when one says or does something which shows just how much one really loves that person;

◆ a person's words and actions reveal the true nature and extent of his/her love;

◆ by what he said and did Jesus revealed the love of God in a way and to a depth never before experienced;

- in Jesus of Nazareth, God became a human being and lived among the people of first-century Palestine;
- by his death on a cross and his rising to new life, Jesus redeemed human beings from the power of sin and death;
- people will *not* find anything like this in any other religion;
- God has *most fully* revealed the truth about his nature and the depth of his love for human beings through the life, death and resurrection of his Son, Jesus Christ.

This answer is intended to be neither chauvinistic nor triumphalist. As the Anglican Archbishop of Canterbury, Dr Rowan Williams, has commented:

There is a confidence that arises from being utterly convinced that the Christian creed and the Christian vision have in them a life and a richness that can embrace and transfigure all the complexities of life. This confidence can rightly sit alongside a patient willingness to learn from others in the ordinary encounters of life together in our varied society.
(Inaugural Press Conference, 2002)

A Christian's confidence in the truth of the Gospel message carries with it a humble respect for those who earnestly hold a different creed. However, the Christian Church still has a strong *missionary* mandate. Christians are obligated to preach the message of Jesus to non-Christian people, under the proviso that any decision in matters of faith must be free and without any hint of coercion.

The Catholic Church teaches that those people who, through no fault of their own, do not come to know Jesus Christ, but who seek God with a sincere heart and try to do God's work, will be welcomed into eternal joy and peace by God.

Questions

1. Read the following statement by the great Hindu holy man Mahatma Gandhi:

   Reverence for other faiths need not blind us to their faults. We must be keenly alive to the defects of our own faith also ... Looking at all religions with an equal eye, we would not hesitate, but think it our duty to blend into our faith every acceptable feature of other faiths.

   How might a Christian apply these words to his/her relations with non-Christians?

2. What reasons does Christopher Butler offer for being a Christian rather than a member of another religion?

3. What does the Catholic Church, and many other Christian denominations, teach about non-Christians and eternal salvation?

Religious Faith in Contemporary Ireland

Introduction

Until quite recently, if you walked down the streets of almost any city or town in Ireland, you would have expected to see churches, both Catholic and Protestant. When people thought about religious diversity, it was largely limited to Catholicism and Protestantism because even though minority religions, such as Judaism, have long played a significant role in Irish society, Christianity has been the dominant religious tradition on the island of Ireland for the last 1,500 years.

In the twenty-first century, this situation has begun to change:

- recent census figures reveal a significant increase in the number of non-Christians living in Ireland as a result of both immigration and a number of former Christians opting for other religions;
- the beliefs and practices of non-Christian religions have become part of the mosaic of Irish society, with Hindu terms such as 'karma' and 'reincarnation' entering into people's vocabulary and Buddhist meditation techniques being adopted in programmes of stress management.

At the same time as it is becoming more religiously *diverse*, Ireland is also becoming a more *secularised* society.

> ## N.B.
> Membership of a religion may be measured according to:
> - participation in religious activity;
> - commitment to religious beliefs and norms;
> - acceptance by co-believers;
> - formal registration of membership.

Secularism

Secularism is both a philosophy of life and a movement of thought:

- it is a *philosophy of life* that limits itself to the here and now—it is derived from the Latin word *saeculum*, meaning 'this present age'—often to the exclusion of humanity's relationship with God in this life and the next;

The Religions of Contemporary Ireland

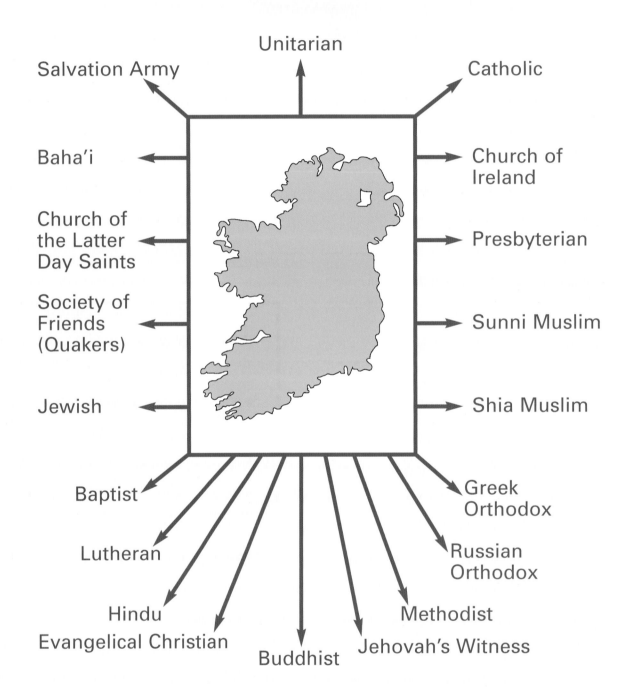

Unitarian

Salvation Army

Catholic

Baha'i

Church of Ireland

Church of the Latter Day Saints

Presbyterian

Society of Friends (Quakers)

Sunni Muslim

Jewish

Shia Muslim

Baptist

Greek Orthodox

Lutheran

Russian Orthodox

Hindu

Methodist

Evangelical Christian

Jehovah's Witness

Buddhist

George Jacob Holyoak, the British writer who coined the term 'secularism'.

◆ it is a *movement of thought* that seeks to reduce or to remove the influence of religions in areas such as education, health and social services.

Those who advocate secularism say they are simply seeking to create a social environment in which:

◆ *all* people—whether they are theists, atheists or agnostics—are treated with *equal* respect;

◆ *all* people are free to follow their own convictions, as long as they do *not* interfere with the rights of others or cause them any harm.

Christian commentators writing on the impact of secularism claim that its widespread adoption by a society tends to lead to:

◆ a general decline in the prestige and influence of all religions, Christian and non-Christian, as social institutions;

◆ an increased focus on success in 'this world', which is measured in terms of material acquisition, and a decreasing interest in spiritual issues and any question of whether or not there is a reality beyond 'this world';

◆ an acceptance of the view that religion is a purely 'private affair', which tends to discourage active participation in community-based religious activity;

◆ a progressively greater willingness to consider only purely rational, scientific explanations of life and to exclude or trivialise others.

It is therefore claimed that the impact of secularism is *not* neutral. It is said to encourage a wholly naturalist, as opposed to supernaturalist, outlook on life. As it would appear to largely involve a discouragement or rejection of organised religions playing a direct role in the life of a state or its citizens, secularism is said to follow after *secularisation*. The sociologist Peter Berger has defined secularisation as:

> *The process through which sectors of society and culture have been freed from the decisive influence of religious ideas and institutions.*

We shall turn next to assess how far advanced this process is in contemporary Irish society.

Questions

1. Why is Ireland today said to be a more religiously diverse place than in the past? ➡️

2. How is the membership of a religion determined?

3. What is meant by '*secularism*'?

4. What do those who advocate secularism say they are seeking to achieve?

5. Why do critics of secularism claim that its impact is *not* neutral?

6. What is meant by '*secularisation*'?

The contemporary scene

An analysis of recent reports* reveals that:

◆ the number of Irish people who profess belief in a personal God stands at about three-quarters of the population;

◆ of the remaining quarter, between 4 per cent and 8 per cent identify themselves as atheists, while the remainder admit to belief in the existence of an impersonal 'life force';

◆ the overwhelming majority of people identify themselves as 'Christian', with the Catholic Church by far the largest Christian denomination;

◆ the number of active, committed Christians has declined, with rural attendances at religious services higher than those in urban areas;

◆ a significant minority of Catholics can be termed '*nominal*', i.e. using Catholicism largely as a badge of identity—showing up at churches for weddings, funerals, etc.—but are unwilling to make a firm commitment to its teachings and practices;

◆ a small but growing number of people describe themselves as '*spiritual*' rather than religious: they wish to explore the possibility that something greater than themselves exists, but they do *not* want to take on the challenging doctrinal and moral requirements of a religion;

◆ though regular attendance at religious services has declined, prayer remains a popular activity. Those least likely to pray are those most educated and most urbanised;

◆ an increasing number of Irish people are willing

to experiment with other belief systems, even if only vaguely 'spiritual' in character, such as yoga and transcendental meditation;

- many people's attitudes towards religion have changed in recent times, becoming more *individualistic* in keeping with the dominant liberal, free-market ideas, which strongly emphasise personal choice in all areas of life;
- there has been a noticeable diminution in the power of religious authorities and a sharp decline in vocations, especially to the Catholic priesthood;
- the waning influence of the Christian Churches has brought a change in laws on issues such as contraception, divorce and homosexual rights, and a change in attitudes on issues such as abortion and stem-cell research because people feel freer to make decisions within their own *personal* moral framework.

Though levels of fundamental religious belief remain very high when compared to those of our nearest neighbours, it is clear that Ireland has not remained immune to the same forces that have produced an increasingly *de-Christianised* Western Europe.

*Sources:
- *Census Report*, CSO;
- *Eurobarometer Polls*;
- *European Values Survey*;
- *International Social Survey Programme*;
- *MRBI Opinion Polls*.

Questions

1. Explain the term '*nominal*' when applied to membership of a religion.

2. Many European societies are now witnessing the emergence of a 'social church', where people seek and use religious rituals and symbols without the social commitment it should involve. Consider the following example cited by a Presbyterian minister, Dr Allen, who witnessed '*social baptisms*' among Spanish Anglicans:

> … *where families, suitably dressed, arrive at the church door, take photographs, and then proceed to the hotel for a meal, without ever going into church. This also happens at confirmation time. They keep the custom but refuse the commitment.*

(*The Irish Times*, 3 June 1999.)

Is there any evidence of such practices taking root in Ireland? Explain your answer.

3. (a) Why do a small but growing number of people describe themselves as '*spiritual*' rather than '*religious*'?
   (b) What evidence is there that this is a significant trend in contemporary Ireland? ➡

4. In what ways have people's attitudes towards religion become more *'individualistic'*?

5. Studies show that religious knowledge, specifically knowledge of the Christian religion, is highest among those aged over sixty-five and lowest in the group aged fifteen to twenty-four years.
Why, do you think, is this the case?

Causes of change

Sociologists have suggested a number of reasons for these recent changes in religious belief and practice:

◆ Ireland is merely experiencing an overdue convergence with other Western European societies, where increasing urbanisation has led to a loss of community, which is a corner-stone of religious faith;

◆ religious belief is viewed by a growing minority as superfluous in an era of great scientific and technological advances;

◆ the social pressures that may have caused some people to attend church in order to conform to communal expectations rather than to express sincerely held religious convictions have disappeared;

◆ the mass media has made many people aware of the variety of alternative belief systems of which they were previously unaware;

◆ the attractiveness of the consumer culture wherein people have many after-work options to pursue and gradually lose the habit of attending religious services and eventually abandon its belief system;

◆ the number and frequency of scandals involving the abuse of power and trust by authority figures within the religious establishments.

Romantic hero: at the top of the liberal agenda is the creation of a society in which the sovereign individual is free, like the romantic hero, to live life on his own terms.

The future

Despite the often gloomy predictions of certain social commentators, there is no reason why the decline of religious belief and practice in Western Europe should be viewed as irreversible or inevitable. Sociologists have recorded a remarkable upsurge of interest in religion across the rest of the globe. Furthermore, the world's religions, especially Judaism and Christianity, have shown an extraordinary capacity to endure, even in the most inhospitable of social climates.

Andrew Greely, Professor of Sociology at the University of Chicago, points out that while Christianity is on the wane in Western Europe, this is *not* the case elsewhere on the Continent. He warns us to be wary of sweeping generalisations about the decline of religion, and asks us to remember that of its very nature,

Religion is always declining and always reviving.

Over the centuries those who have sought spiritual nourishment and fulfilment have found it as members of one of the world's religions. This remains possible today, even in the fast-paced world of the twenty-first century, where we face an astonishing array of complex moral, social, political and economic challenges. Why? Because religion continues to provide people with a framework for responding to such challenges by offering them:

◆ a strong sense of communal identity and support

systems as they face questions about the meaning and direction of their lives;

◆ clear guidance when faced with making moral decisions;

◆ encouragement to act with generosity and be willing to make sacrifices so that, one day, people will be able to live in peace and harmony with one another;

◆ hope, by providing a window through which they can glimpse the possibility of life after death.

Contrary to the expectations of some commentators, secularism may in the long-term provide an unexpected opportunity for a renewal of interest in religious faith in Western European societies, including Ireland. This is because secularism does *not* in itself offer any answers to life's most profound questions. What it offers to individuals is an open space in which all are free to choose and follow their own convictions.

Another sociologist, Peter Berger, warns that to be religious in this new context will have to be the result of a *deliberate* choice. Even those who are born into a given religion will have to *consciously* choose it and commit themselves to it because the society will not be structured so as to support them in their faith.

Questions

1. Read the following extract:

   When I was a student in University College, Dublin, around 1960, an amazing scene took place every day in the library at noon: everyone there stood and in silence said the Angelus. Even a Buddhist girl from Thailand whom I knew quite well stood in silence. I would love to know when exactly the custom died, but I know that it now would be unthinkable for anyone to make such a public gesture; I wouldn't do it myself. Then only a brave individual would sit down; now only a brave individual would stand up. A different ethos is dominant, which entails the retreat of religion to a largely personal domain.
   (M.P. Gallagher, *Help My Unbelief.*) ➡

In the light of this writer's example, how would you explain the changes he witnessed in Irish people's attitudes towards a public expression of religious devotion?

2. Read the following extract:

As Irish society changes, a huge vacuum appears at the level of public policy and official ideology. At the moment, the only thing that appears to fill it is the consumer-driven ideology of Western capitalism, with its lack of concern for the vulnerable in society and its insensitivity to the social solidarity that holds society together. (C. Coulter, 'Women, Gender and the Divorce Debate' in A. Bradley and M. Valiulis (eds), *Gender and Secularity in Modern Ireland*.)

In the light of this commentator's concerns, what valuable role might the religions of Ireland play in the future? Explain your answer.

3. What, do you think, Professor Andrew Greely means when he says that

Religion is always declining and always reviving?

4. (a) What are the possible opportunities for a revival of religious faith offered by secularism?
   (b) What are the challenges secularism poses for the individual who is either born into or drawn towards a particular religious faith?

Humanism

The term '*humanism*' was originally used by Christian writers, such as Erasmus and St Thomas More, to denote their religiously grounded commitment to uphold human dignity. Since the Enlightenment (eighteenth century), the term 'humanism' has taken on a different meaning. It is now used to name an intellectual movement that offers itself as an *alternative* to the world's religions. Humanists are either atheists or agnostics, although *not* all atheists or agnostics subscribe to humanism.

The philosopher Baron d'Holbach (eighteenth century) was one of the first self-described atheists. He was the author of two influential books, *The System of Nature* and *Good Sense* (1772).

Tel Aviv, Israel, 1 November 2003: a young Israeli girl listens to peace songs during a rally marking the anniversary of the assassination of Israeli Prime Minister Yitzhak Rabin. He was killed in Tel Aviv, after a peace rally in the square, on 4 November 1995.

Atheism denies the existence of God. It claims that, as matter is the fundamental and final reality, *only* that which can be observed, managed or predicted is meaningful. There is therefore no need to postulate the existence of what Joseph Campbell refers to as 'the *invisible plane*' (i.e. God and the soul), which supports the visible context of everyday life.

Agnosticism claims that it is impossible for human beings to know whether God exists or not because there is insufficient evidence to warrant our reaching any definite conclusion one way or the other.

Some humanist writers have posed difficult, but legitimate, questions that have challenged religious thinkers to refine their arguments and, in some cases, re-think them entirely. For instance, humanists correctly highlighted the way in which the world's religions have for too long co-existed with *patriarchy*, i.e. those social structures that deny women equality of respect, opportunity and treatment. Fair-minded figures within religions, most notably in Judaism and Christianity, came to recognise the injustice of patriarchy and modified their social teachings in the light of this moral insight.

Generally, humanists tend to have little sympathy with the whole phenomenon of religious faith. This is largely due to their belief that religious doctrines are merely second-hand answers dealt out by powerful authority figures. In contrast, they claim that when searching for answers to the meaning of life, people should only accept those answers that they themselves have discovered from their own reflection on their life experiences.

Religious thinkers would respond to this assertion by pointing out that the two are *not* mutually exclusive. Some humanist writers, such as Richard Dawkins, have characterised the world's religions as essentially human—not divine—constructs. According to this view, religions exist primarily to tranquillise those among us who cannot face up to the hard facts of human existence. These facts are:

◆ we humans are the product of unguided evolutionary processes;

◆ we do not exist to fulfil any grand plan;

◆ when we die, that is the end of our existence.

Since we are without any form of supernatural guidance, each of us must accept the need to work out *for ourselves* what constitutes an authentic human existence. The philosopher John Dewey claimed that this could be achieved by utilising the scientific method to determine—by means of observation, experimentation and analysis—what our moral values should be. The outcome of such reflection is a choice. One can accept either:

a moral code based on the principle of enlightened self-interest

or

a moral code based on the idea that we should all act in a life-enhancing manner because it is, in itself, a good way to behave.

Both of these notions about the basis for morality are rooted in the fact that we are, by nature, *social* creatures, i.e. we find meaning in and through our relationships with others. Humanists argue that as we only have each other, we need to take care of each other. Only by co-operating with one another can we make our environment, and the lives we each live within it, a better place for all.

Humanists reject the tendency to despair and say we should face life with courage and dignity, believing that:

It is better to light a candle than to curse the darkness.

While in certain respects admirable, this outlook has been sharply criticised. One of its strongest critics, John Gray, is himself an atheist. In his controversial book *Straw Dogs*, Gray *rejects humanism* as merely

'a secular version of Christian faith'.

He claims that if we reject the Abrahamic faiths and accept humanism's key ideas, then we cannot escape the conclusion that

'human life has no more meaning than the life of slime mould'.

He asserts that humanism invites people to adopt a life-affirming and altruistic view of the world, but fails to provide us with good enough reasons for doing so.

Questions

1. Explain the origin of the term 'humanist'.

2. What is the contemporary meaning of the term 'humanism'?

3. Explain the following terms:
   (a) *atheism*;
   (b) *agnosticism*.

4. Identify a positive impact of humanism upon the world's religions.

5. (a) How do most humanists view the phenomenon of religious faith?
   (b) Why is this the case?

6. Outline the humanist view of human existence.

7. According to humanist thinkers, what should we accept as a basis for our moral code?

8. How might a humanist respond to the following questions:
   (a) *Why should I value human life?*
   (b) *Why should I consider other people when making moral decisions?*

9. (a) What are John Gray's criticisms of humanism?
   (b) Do you agree/disagree with his assessment? Give reasons for your answer.

New Religious Movements and Cults

The emergence of NRMs

The nineteenth and twentieth centuries witnessed the growth of many new religious movements, or *NRMs*. Most of these have their roots in one or other of the existing major world religions, though some do not and are more a product of recent secular culture. Consider:

1. The following have their roots in Christianity:
   - the 7th Day Adventists;
   - Mormonism;
   - Christian Science;
   - Jehovah's Witness.

Each of these religions asserts that Christianity, as currently practised, has been corrupted. Each one claims that it *alone* offers the only authentic, purified way to God.

2. The following draw on Islamic doctrine and practice:
   - the Baha'is;

Hare Krishna members.

- the Nation of Islam;
- the Sufi Order of the West.

3. These emerged out of Hinduism:
    - Élan Vital;
    - the Brahma Kumaris;
    - the Satya Sai Baba Society;
    - the Hari Krishna (or ISKCON).

4. These display the influences of contemporary secular western theories about how best to liberate human potential:
    - the Church of Scientology;
    - the Raelians.

The kinds of NRMs

Sociologists tend to divide NRMs into *two* groups:

1. World-affirming NRMs

These groups tend to be individualistic, life-positive and concerned with how each member can release his/her human potential. They usually encourage members to participate actively in secular society. These groups tend to appeal most to middle-class people who are disenchanted and disillusioned with materialism and searching for meaning, but who do not desire formal membership, participation in rituals or having to adhere to a strict moral code.

As such, these NRMs bear a greater resemblance to a therapeutic movement than to a formal religious community in the traditional sense. An example of this kind of NRM would be the Church of Scientology.

Example of a world-affirming NRM:

The Church of Scientology

As the new religions began to appear in the twentieth century, the religious fascination with the authority of 'science' broke free of its earlier linkage to Christianity in movements of the 'Christian Science' type. One result was the emergence of Scientology, founded by L. Ron Hubbard (1911–1986). Although born in Tilden, Nebraska, Ron Hubbard was exposed to Asian religion and culture as a child because his father was in the navy. As a young man with an adventurous spirit Hubbard was involved in three Central American ethnological expeditions. He received a commission in the navy during World War II, during which service he was pronounced dead twice. In one instance he apparently had something like a shamanistic out-of-body experience in which he acquired spiritual knowledge that gave him his life's mission.

In 1950 Hubbard published *Dianetics: The Modern Science of Mental Healing*, in which he claimed to have discovered a cure for all

L. Ron Hubbard.

human psychological and psychosomatic ills through the realisation of a state of mind he called 'Clear'. Hubbard went on to establish the Hubbard Dianetic Research Foundation in Elizabeth, New Jersey. Later he moved the organisation to Phoenix, Arizona, where the Hubbard Association of Scientologists was founded in 1952.

Scientology goes beyond the psychological orientation of Dianetics to develop an elaborate mythology according to which all humans were once advanced beings Hubbard called Thetans: all-powerful, eternal and omniscient. The first Thetans relieved their boredom by playing mind games in which they used imagination to create different physical worlds. However, they soon forgot their true identity as creators and found themselves trapped in these worlds, living as mortals who died, only to be reincarnated again and again. At each reincarnation, people accumulated more psychological baggage, which Hubbard called engrams. To be liberated from this pattern and realise one's true identity, it is necessary to gain insight into one's engrams. Upon finally achieving the 'Clear' state of mind, a person gains control over both mind and life. The auditing process that leads to this liberation came to involve the use of a machine that works somewhat like a lie detector. This device, the E-meter, it is believed, measures reactions of resistance to words and other symbols that reveal undissolved engrams. After achieving Clear, one can go on to higher states that involve out-of-body experiences.

In 1954 Hubbard established the first Church of Scientology in Washington, DC, and in 1959 he started the Hubbard College of Scientology in England. Whereas many new religious movements stress individualism and are quite loosely organised, Scientology has an elaborate global organisation. In some ways it is similar to the modern international business corporation, with its penchant for technical language, efficient organisation, and the dissemination of polished communications to interface with the world. And yet all this organisation and efficiency is focused on bringing about a powerful experience of enlightenment or rebirth that perfects the self and opens it to the spiritual world that shamans have traversed throughout the ages.

Scientologists have also shown a keen

interest in Buddhist teachings, and of course, the parallels of the auditing practices to depth psychology are obvious. The description of Clear by one Scientologist shows the movement's affinity with both Western experiences of being 'born again' and Eastern experiences of enlightenment:

'There is no name to describe the way I feel. At last I am at cause. I am Clear – I can do anything I want to do. I feel like a child with a new life – everything is so wonderful and beautiful. Clear is Clear! It's unlike anything I could have imagined. The colours, the clarity, the brightness of everything is beyond belief. Everything is so new, I feel new born. I am filled with the wonder of everything.'

Scientology is, in many ways, the perfect illustration of the global eclectic integration of the elements that make up new age religions: science (especially psychology), technology (corporate and technical structure), Asian religions (reincarnation and the quest for liberation), and shamanism (out-of-body spiritual explorations). A Thetan, according to Hubbard, goes 'through walls, barriers, vanishes space, appears anywhere at will and does other remarkable things.'

(Adapted from J. L. Esposito *et al.*, *World Religions Today.*)

Questions

1. What is meant by a '*world-affirming*' New Religious Movement?

2. To whom does a world-affirming NRM appeal?

3. Who founded the Church of Scientology?

4. What did he claim in his book, *Dianetics: the Modern Science of Mental Health*?

5. Who are the *Thetans*?

6. What does Scientology teach about the relationship between Thetans and humans?

7. (a) Explain the concept of the 'Clear' in Scientology.
   (b) How does Scientology teach that this can be achieved?

8. From what sources does Scientology draw inspiration for its teachings?

9. Why, in your opinion, might some people be attracted to the Church of Scientology? Give reasons for your answer.

2. World-rejecting NRMs

These groups resemble existing conventional religions in that they require their members to:

◆ pray regularly;

◆ study religious texts;

◆ abide by a strict moral code.

They are always highly critical of those who are not members of their movement and typically refer to the secular world as *evil*.

These groups encourage the communal pooling of wealth and the total subordination of the individual to the movement's mission. They are usually *millenarian*, i.e. teach that God will soon intervene decisively in human history to bring about an earthly paradise, which only the particular NRM's members will enjoy. These NRMs have a strong appeal for the young and those living on the margins of affluent societies. An example of this kind of NRM would be the Unification Church.

Example of a world-rejecting NRM:

The Unification Church

The Unification Church was founded in South Korea by Sun Myung Moon. He established a religion of divine principle called Tong Il. Eventually, Tong Il became known in the West as the Unification Church. In its earliest form this movement drew heavily on Korean shamanism, emphasising out-of-body travels, healing, communication with spirits, and so on. As the religion moved from East to West, these elements have been downplayed. The church's global outreach really began with the emigration of Sun Myung Moon to the United States in 1971. Like Scientology, the movement showed a penchant for organisation and public relations. Just as Scientology developed a reputation for attracting famous entertainers, the Unification Church courted political and academic figures with some success.

Unification's teachings are based on Moon's book, *Divine Principle*, which is really a kind

Mr Sun Myung Moon.

of Asian interpretation of the Bible in terms of polarities, or opposites (divine-human, male-female, etc.), beginning with the polarity of

---

male and female in God. As in the Confucian traditions, these polarities are arranged hierarchically. The proper fourfold foundation of social order puts God at the top, then male and female as equals, with children at the bottom. The lowest order shows deference to the next higher, and all defer to God.

According to Moon's teachings, the 'original sin' was Lucifer's spiritual seduction of Eve, leading her to rebel against God, after which she seduced Adam, who had intercourse with her before the time God intended, undermining the proper order of love and deference. To restore the sacred order, says Moon, God has repeatedly sent great prophets – Abraham, Moses, Jesus – but none were able to succeed. If Jesus, for instance, had not been destroyed by his enemies, he (as the second Adam) would have married a second Eve and reinstituted the right order of family and society.

Moon teaches that God has sent three 'Israel's' to attempt to redeem the world. First he chose the Jews, then the Gentiles. In the twentieth century he chose the Koreans as the people of salvation, and a Korean (Moon himself) is the third Adam. Just as the early Hebrews, the first Israel, suffered persecution at the hands of the Babylonians, and the second Israel, in the days of the second Temple, at the hands of the Romans, so Korea, the third Israel, suffered at the hands of the Japanese during World War II. Finally, in Korea, Satan is making his last stand. For in Korea, the forces of God and Satan (democracy and communism) are engaged in the final apocalyptic conflict. But God has chosen as the divine centre for the salvation of the world Korea, where East and West have met. Confucianism, Buddhism, and Christianity have come together, and now God has sent Rev. and Mrs Moon, a third Adam and Eve, to restore the human race and complete the unification mission.

Moon's followers generally believe that Moon is the new Messiah and that he and his wife are the new and true parents who are regenerating the human race. To effect this regeneration, Sun Myung Moon chooses marriage partners for his followers and then, with his wife, officiates at mass wedding ceremonies, which have attracted considerable media attention. For the movement, every new crop of married couples furthers the struggle against the Communists, Satan's representatives on earth, who Moon depicts as arrayed against himself as demonic agents in a lifelong cosmic battle. Though famous globally, the Unification Church claims only a modest number of adherents in Korea.

(Adapted from J. L. Esposito *et al.*, *World Religions Today*.)

Questions

1. What is meant by a *world-rejecting* New Religious Movement?

2. To whom does a world-rejecting NRM typically appeal?

3. Who is the founder of the Unification Church?

4. What are the key ideas contained in his book, *Divine Principle*?

5. What does the Unification Church teach about '*the original sin*'?

6. Explain the role of Korea in the Unification Church's doctrine.

7. What does it teach about its leader?

8. What is the Unification Church's view of newly married couples?

9. Why, in your opinion, might some people be attracted to the Unification Church? Give reasons for your answer.

Controversy

Some NRMs have been the subject of considerable interest and sometimes have been ridiculed for their stated beliefs. In fairness, it must be said that some have displayed a solid track record for being caring and supportive of their members. In the case of those who have rituals, their worship is highly participatory and vibrant. A number of NRMs appear to meet the needs of some people for a sense of belonging and seem to enhance their personal sense of self-worth.

In recent decades, however, there has been a growing sense of unease among commentators, both religious and non-religious, about the activities of some NRMs that have been labelled '*cults*'.

The Cult Phenomenon

Cults come in three forms:

Benign — Friendly groups that do no harm and provide a temporary shelter at some point in a person's search for answers about the meaning of life.

Commercial — Those groups that cynically exploit the idealism of their members to engage in activities aimed at enriching the leadership under the guise of fulfilling some 'divinely inspired' mission.

Destructive — Those groups that have a dark, apocalyptic mindset and prepare their members for the imminent 'end time'.

The *latter* two, namely commercial and destructive cults, tend to share the following characteristics:

◆ they are often small, localised communities centred around a charismatic, self-appointed leader who exercises virtually absolute control over every aspect of its members' lives;

◆ the leader often uses whatever methods he/she deems necessary to attain certain goals he/she desires. The leader can never be held accountable to anyone but God;

- the cults' recruiting agents target a particular clientele and use psychologically coercive methods to attract, indoctrinate and retain members;
- all members must adhere to a strict code, as set out by the leader. Failure to do so results in humiliating public punishment;
- a radical elitism and disdain for outsiders is fostered by the leadership. Only cult members are deemed enlightened. Every other person or group is condemned as wicked and avoided. Some declare the outside world to be doomed and abandon all contact with it.

Generally, any attempt to engage in dialogue with such groups tends to be a *frustrating* and *unproductive* experience because:

- cult members are encouraged to develop a *single-minded, obsessive loyalty* to the leadership and therefore close their minds to even the consideration of any alternate viewpoint;
- the cult to which they belong is viewed as being, of its very nature, the *only* source of truth and therefore *not* to be questioned under *any* circumstances.

Further, since some of these cults believe that our entire planetary civilisation is doomed to destruction, they see absolutely no point in engaging in debate with those who, because they are *not* members of the cult, are destined both for destruction in this life and damnation in the next.

Questions

1. Explain the differences between the following:
   (a) *benign* cults;
   (b) *commercial* cults;
   (c) *destructive* cults.

2. What characteristics are *shared* by both commercial and destructive cults?

3. Why do those who attempt to engage members of such cults often find it a frustrating and unproductive experience?

Destructive cults

Over recent decades a number of appalling incidents have heightened public awareness of those particular cults that are categorised as *destructive*. We shall examine three of them.

1. The People's Temple

On 18 November 1978 some 913 members of a cult known as *the People's Temple* died in what was initially believed to be a mass suicide pact at their 300-acre commune at Jonestown, in the rainforest of Guyana, South America. Their leader, Jim Jones (1931–78) had ordered all of them to ingest a fruit drink laced with a deadly poison—cyanide. Most believed him when he declared that the world was about to end and that, after their deaths, they would all be rewarded with better lives on another planet.

Some of the cult members seem to have come to their senses, although it was too late to escape.

Jim Jones.

According to one survivor, Jones ordered his body-guards to either force those who objected to his demands to drink the poison or to kill them with a lethal injection. Once this was done, Jones took his own life with a single gunshot.

Those who predicted at the time that such an event was unlikely to ever re-occur were sadly proven wrong by subsequent events.

2. The Branch Davidians

On 28 February 1993 US federal agents of the ATF (the Bureau of Alcohol, Tobacco and Firearms) raided the property known as Mount Carmel, near the town of Waco, Texas. It was the headquarters of a previously little-known group called *the Branch Davidians*.

The federal agents were searching for a cache of illegal weapons and were also concerned about allegations that systematic child abuse was taking place in the compound. Subsequent investigations revealed their concerns about the latter to have been *justified*. However, they also revealed that these agents did not fully appreciate the unique difficulties of dealing with a group such as the Branch Davidians.

The initial raid on the Mount Carmel complex was a failure. The Branch Davidians were heavily armed with automatic weapons and had advance notice of the raid. They resisted the search and in the fierce gun battle that ensued, four agents and six Davidians were killed and several others wounded.

What followed was a tense stand-off that lasted for fifty-one days. Despite the best efforts of FBI negotiators, the Davidians' leader, David Koresh (originally Vernon Howell), refused to surrender. When reasoning failed, the authorities used various psycho-logical ploys to force Koresh to end the siege. This, too, met with no success.

Growing increasingly worried about the safety of the children still inside Mount Carmel, the authorities decided to act. They stated afterwards that they never expected Koresh to sacrifice either his followers or himself. They were tragically *mistaken*.

David Karesh.

Koresh believed that he and his fellow Davidians were living in the last days of human history. He interpreted what was happening as a sign that the end of the world had come. When the final assault took place, he and his followers would all die so that they could later be resurrected to rule *alone* over a future world cleansed by war of all other humans.

On 19 April 1993 federal agents used a special assault vehicle to break into the Mount Carmel compound and began to spray the buildings with tear gas. At that moment, fires broke out throughout the compound; it is believed they were started deliberately by Koresh. After a few minutes there was a series of massive explosions as the flames reached the large quantities of ammunition and fuel the Davidians had stockpiled within their wooden buildings. In the chaos that followed, eighty Branch Davidians died, including seventeen children. Only nine Davidians escaped the inferno.

It was later discovered that Koresh had shot himself in the head; the bodies of several other Davidians also bore gunshot wounds. It is unclear if they committed suicide or were killed trying to escape.

The profile of David Koresh later built up by investigators proved to be a distinctly unflattering one. Survivors and ex-members stated that Koresh was a handsome, charismatic figure, but that he was also cruel, devious, hypocritical, manipulative, paranoid and utterly selfish. His influence over his followers was so strong that *none* dissented when he declared that he would have sexual relations with any women in the group, married or not. This extended to the sexual abuse of underage girls.

Despite all of this, almost all of his followers seem to have believed Koresh when he declared himself to be '*the Sinful Messiah*'. Most were apparently quite willing to sacrifice their lives for him. A small group of survivors remain devoted to David Koresh even still. They believe that one day soon a massive earthquake will strike the Waco area and it will be devastated by floods.

3. Aum Shinrikyo

On 20 March 1995 a dozen commuters on the Tokyo subway died and thousands more were hospitalised when they were poisoned by sarin nerve gas that was deliberately released into the city's underground rail system. Police investigations led them to a secretive organisation called *Aum Shinrikyo* (meaning *Supreme Truth*), which was led by a wealthy business tycoon named Shoko Asahara.

Beginning in the 1980s, Asahara (originally named Chizuo Matsumato) attracted followers by promising to teach them how to read minds, predict future events and teleport from one location to another. He had a highly charismatic personality and his movement, which had an extraordinary appeal to young, middle-class professionals, grew rapidly, gaining an estimated 10,000 members in Japan by 1995.

Shoko Asahara.

Asahara organised his followers into a number of secretive, monastic-style communities at various locations around Japan. Each follower had to sever all contact with his/her family, hand over all finances and property to the organisation and swear absolute obedience to the leader.

In the early days of Aum, Asahara taught that its followers had been entrusted with a sacred task: to save humanity. But after Asahara and his closest advisors failed to win seats in the Japanese parliamentary elections in 1990, he changed his mind. He decided to obtain the means to *destroy* what he believed to be the evil forces seeking to prevent him from fulfilling his mission.

From this point onwards, Asahara told his followers that he was Jesus Christ and that he had returned to judge the human race. He declared that the USA would soon trigger a nuclear war that would devastate the northern hemisphere. He purchased land in Australia, where he and his followers could wait until radiation levels dropped low enough for them to take control of a vast landscape devoid of any other human beings.

By 1993 Asahara had employed scores of scientists and engineers in high-security plants. They began producing chemical and biological weapons that he would later claim were developed solely to protect Japan from foreign attack. He also sent Aum members abroad to investigate the possibility of acquiring a nuclear weapon. Most of the organisation's members believed that all of this was done in the interests of national defence; very few seem to have had any inkling of his terrorist plans.

The Japanese government became concerned about Asahara's activities when, in 1994, it was revealed that Aum Shinrikyo's assets exceeded $1 billion. Once Asahara became aware that he was arousing suspicion, he tried to instil fear in any opponent by ordering the assassination of three judges. The attacks, which involved the use of poison gas, failed to kill their intended targets, but caused the deaths of several innocent bystanders. The following year, after the Tokyo subway attack, Asahara was arrested.

Asahara was tried and found guilty of murder. He is currently serving a life sentence for his crimes. The movement he founded has apparently regrouped under the title *Aleph* (meaning 'the beginning') and still reveres Asahara as its leader. It is thought to be closely monitored by the Japanese authorities.

Questions

1. From what you have read, draw up a profile of a typical leader of a destructive cult.

2. Asahara justified his murderous activities to his followers by saying that they were only killing those who had acquired 'bad karma' and that by killing these people, they were actually doing them a spiritual *favour* because it stopped them from creating any more negative karma.
   Why, do you think, were many of his followers willing to accept this line of thinking? Explain your answer. ➡

3. In her autobiographical work *Seductive Poison*, People's Temple survivor Deborah Layton recounts how, even after the leader Jim Jones had physically and sexually abused her, she

> '*stayed deaf to the warnings ringing in my ears, because I believed I could not be that wrong*'.

Why, do you think, was this her reaction at that time?

4. It has been said that

> *Religions have members, cults have victims.*

Do you agree/disagree? Explain your answer.

5. Read the following extract

> *Quite often, the unpaid debts of the Christian Churches end up on the doorsteps of the cults. No doubt the widespread success of cults is due in part to their frequently manipulative methods of recruitment. But the main reason for their success seems to be the fact that in our society people are more and more being treated like mere numbers; rarely are they treated as people. The result is a coldness and a loneliness that can become unbearable. This is where cults come on the scene, with an approach that is emotional rather than rational. They nourish the logic of the heart rather than the mind.*
>
> (Joseph Cardinal Daneels, *Christ or Aquarius?*)

(a) What does Cardinal Daneels identify as the main reason for the success of cults in the Western world?

(b) Do you think he is reading the situation correctly? Explain your answer.

(c) What steps do you think the Christian Churches should take to help people feel part of a community in which they are considered important and wanted?

Section

d

Introduction to Morality

Introduction

In the novel *The Day of the Triffids*, the hero, a scientist named Bill Masen, awakens one morning in a private room of a London hospital. He had been unconscious for some time after undergoing an operation to repair damage to his eyes. He eagerly awaits a visit from his specialist to confirm that the operation has been a success. After an hour he becomes impatient and calls for a nurse, but no one responds. Then he realises that his floor of the hospital is completely quiet; there are none of the usual sounds of daily activity.

Eventually, Masen becomes anxious and decides to remove his bandages himself. To his immense relief, he discovers that his eyesight has been fully restored. He quickly dresses and goes to investigate why he has been left to his own devices.

Masen discovers that the hospital has been abandoned, that he is the only patient left. The medical staff are nowhere to be found. He decides to venture out into the city and makes a shocking discovery: everyone he meets is *blind*, apparently due to the effects of a bizarre meteor shower that occurred while he was unconscious. Worse still, he soon discovers that this is *not* some local phenomenon—most of humanity is now blind.

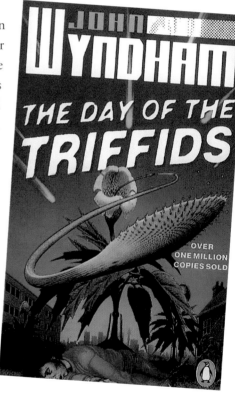

Masen looks on in increasing horror as he witnesses the civilisation he has taken for granted collapse all around him. He is shaken to the core and feels he is being over-whelmed by a sense of hopelessness.

It is only when Masen finally meets up with a few other sighted people that he begins to regain some sense of purpose and hope. He is brought to a rude, but profound, awareness of a central fact of human existence: we are *relational* beings. In other words, we readily take for granted how much we *need* and *depend on* others.

Consider:

◆ our very existence is the fruit of the relationship

between our parents;

- our survival depends from the outset on some form of sustaining relationship with others;
- we need a network of care, guidance and support from others to facilitate our development into mature adults.

We need *community*. We *cannot* live in a social vacuum. We need to interact with other human beings. We know that what we say and what we do affects others. So this leads us to ask:

- how should we behave towards others?
- how should we treat the world we share?

These are moral questions.

Meaning

If you ask someone what the term '*moral*' means, you will probably be told that it involves

'Doing what is right and avoiding what is wrong'
or
'Doing good and avoiding evil'.

Once you ask people to explain precisely what they mean, you quickly realise that some of them have

quite different ideas about what constitutes right/good and wrong/evil. However, you will discover that most people* recognise that:

- it is meaningful to talk in terms of right/good and wrong/evil;
- it is possible to distinguish one from the other;
- we experience an obligation to do the former and to avoid the latter.

*N.B.

Those people who:

- *cannot* appreciate the meaningfulness of talk about right/good and wrong/evil;
- are *unable* to make such a distinction;
- do not experience any sense of obligation to do the former and avoid the latter;

are considered to suffer from a form of *mental disorder*.

Notice that we are talking about '*doing*' and '*avoiding*'. These are terms denoting *action*. Morality is concerned with specific kinds of action, namely those that are *deliberate*, i.e.

those actions that are under the control of the person doing them.

We can distinguish between three different kinds of deliberate actions:

- Obligatory actions: those that must always be done, regardless of the consequences.
- Impermissible actions: those that must never be done, under any circumstances.
- Permissible actions: those that can either be done or not done, as they may be good either way.

Therefore, we can say that morality:

is concerned with the evaluation of deliberate human actions and the justification of this assessment.

By our actions we demonstrate that we value one way of living over another and reveal the *kind* of people we really are, i.e. whether we are generous or selfish, open-minded or prejudiced, altruistic or calculating.

Questions

1. Read the following extract from the poet John Donne:

   No man is an island, entire of itself. Every man is a piece of the continent, a part of the main. If a clod be washed away by the sea, Europe is the less, as well as if a promontory were, as well as if a manor of thy friends or of thine own were. Any man's death diminishes me, because I am involved in mankind. And therefore never send to know for whom the bell tolls: it tolls for thee.

   How does the novel *The Day of the Triffids* support this claim?

2. What is meant by a *deliberate action*? Give an example of your own.

3. Explain each of the following kinds of deliberate actions:
   ● *obligatory;*
   ● *impermissible;*
   ● *permissible.*

4. What is *morality*?

The foundations of morality

It is sometimes claimed that it is necessary to believe in God in order to be a person of high moral principles. This is *not* the case. Both religious and non-religious alike share a sense of obligation to do good and avoid doing evil. Indeed, there is considerable evidence to show that *all* people—even criminals—appeal to what they perceive to be some universal standard of right and wrong when trying to justify or excuse their behaviour. Even those who profess *relativism* (the

belief that right/good and wrong/evil are merely human conventions) will almost instinctively appeal to this standard when they are themselves wronged. Why so?

In his book *The Abolition of Man*, C.S. Lewis explored this question in detail. He claimed that making moral judgments is an inescapable part of being human. Every deliberate act we perform *presupposes* a goal we seek to attain, and this goal represents a value judgment on our part. The only question is which direction we choose to take—whether we follow the path of good, or the path of evil.

Lewis proposed that the foundation of all our moral judgments is one set of moral first principles that we all know *intuitively* (i.e. insights that are grasped immediately, that are known without reasoning). These first principles include such obligations as:

◆ to treat others fairly;
◆ to be honest in our dealings;
◆ to keep our promises.

Clearly, moral right and wrong are *not* based exclusively on some command of God, any more than on the approval or disapproval of a particular community. Certain acts, such as dishonesty or treachery, are judged as right or wrong *in themselves* because they are perceived as running contrary to the proper order of things. Thus, it is only by acting in certain ways that we can *flourish*, i.e. live a truly human existence.

What role does this leave for the world's religions in the area of morality?

All of the great religious figures have taught that the heart of true religious faith does not consist of rituals and texts, but in living a good life. For those who are open to finding answers to life's great questions, a religion can be an indispensable guide. Religious faith *strengthens* and *inspires* people on their journey through life because once we seek to understand morality, we soon find ourselves asking questions about the very meaning and purpose of human life on Earth.

Questions

1. What is *relativism*?

2. Read the following extract:

   Some people have said that morality is nothing more than the customs and conventions of those around us, and that the only foundation of our ideas of right and wrong is what we are told by our parents and others who influence us. These people say that there is no fixed standard of morality and that the feeling of guilt we have after doing an evil action comes from the fear we used to have of being punished when we were disobedient as children.

   (Nano Brennan, *The Moral Life*.)

   How would C.S. Lewis respond to this claim?

3. Read the following extract:

> *Sister Sarah is an Indian Catholic nun. Sisters from her religious order are scattered around the world; the headquarters are in London. For some years Sister Sarah worked in India, where she was born and brought up. She became expert in primary health care in rural areas. Her success in raising standards gave rise to invitations to speak at International Health Conferences. Now she lives and works in rural Peru. Her aim is to show the love of God in practical ways—through health care and feeding programmes. By means of a simple 'come and collect' system, she and her American colleague, Sister Antonia, provide a daily breakfast for 1,000 Peruvian farmers—in no more than 30 minutes! The intention is not to make these families dependent; rather to help provide the necessary energy required for long hours of survival-farming in arduous conditions.*
> *Two things remain in my memory from my conversation with Sarah: her tranquillity and her laughter.*
>
> (John Young, *Christianity.*)

What is the role of religion, specifically Catholicism, in Sr Sarah's moral vision? Explain your answer.

On being human

In his book *Heretics*, G.K. Chesterton claims that the most important and practical thing about a person is his/her view of the universe and the place of human beings within it. He states that the historical record demonstrates clearly that *our beliefs govern our actions.* Consider the following examples:

◆ it was because Adolf Hitler believed that the German people were a superior race with a destiny to rule the world that he waged a war of conquest;

◆ it was because Dr Martin Luther King Jnr believed in the equal dignity of all human beings and the sacredness of human life that he led the campaign to obtain civil rights for negroes and encouraged the use of non-violent methods to achieve this.

There is strong evidence to support the assertion that our understanding of what it means to be human has immense implications for the way in which we treat our fellow human beings. So, what does it mean to be human?

Let us begin our search for an answer by comparing ourselves with the other creatures on this planet. We shall do so under a number of headings:

1. Technology

◆ A chimpanzee can use a stick to probe an anthill for food, or to defend himself against attack. However, humans are the *only* creatures that can take natural materials, like iron, stone and wood, and turn them into machines, houses and furniture.

◆ This human capacity to *design* and *make* things is without parallel in the animal kingdom. It has allowed people to change the face of the Earth with massive construction projects.

2. Language

◆ Animals do *not* tell stories, write poems, read or keep historical records. They do *not* learn new languages, reconstruct lost ones or invent new ones.

◆ Only *humans* are capable of thinking about and communicating complex ideas between one another by means of speech, gesture or writing.

3. Art

◆ Animals cannot compose music, write lyrics, paint landscapes, appreciate the beauty of a sunset nor enjoy a joke. Only *humans* are capable of such things.

◆ Birds do not truly sing, nor do hyenas really laugh. It is *human beings* who hear music in the sounds of a songbird and laughter in a hyena's cackle.

4. Freedom

◆ Animals act on *instinct*, i.e. patterns of behaviour that they have inherited biologically from their ancestors. For example, a squirrel stores food for the winter, but he/she is guided by instinct rather than by any freely chosen plan. A squirrel cannot change his/her way of behaving any more than an ant can resign from its community and set up a home on its own.

◆ In contrast, human beings are *not* completely dominated by their instincts. People can *learn* from their own experiences and those of others. They can *evaluate* their actions and distinguish between good and evil. People can form their own *plans* for the future and make their own *choices* about how to live their lives. This is called *free will*.

◆ As far as science can tell, animals are *not* capable of making their own plans for the future *nor* can animals make decisions about the rightness or wrongness of certain actions. For example, a dog can be trained to bark and growl at a burglar, but the dog could not work out why stealing is wrong nor could he choose to change sides and become the burglar's assistant.

◆ These characteristics of human beings—*rational thought* and *free will*—are the foundation of morality. The former allows us to understand life and the latter allows us to decide how to live it.

5. Self-Awareness

◆ There is some evidence to suggest that some animals—such as apes and dolphins—exhibit a limited form of knowledge. However, only human beings can reflect on their knowledge, i.e. '*know*

that they know'.

◆ Humans can communicate this knowledge in an astonishing variety of ways, e.g. architecture, law, literature, mathematics, medicine, painting, philosophy and poetry.

◆ Only humans can distinguish between the various *degrees* of certitude as to whether a statement should be understood as proven beyond all reasonable doubt or not.

◆ Only humans can consider their origin and their ultimate destiny. Human beings are the only creatures who are aware that they will one day *die*. Humans are also the only creatures who speculate on their status *after* death.

◆ Related to this human characteristic is the fact that only humans have some form of *religion*, involving belief in, communication with and worship of a Supreme Being.

It is clear from all the above that human life is qualitatively very different from the rest of the natural world. We have evolved into creatures capable of thinking and acting at an altogether higher level than any other life-form on this planet.

Why has this happened?

A survey of the many books written in response to this question reveals that they all tend to offer answers that are essentially variations of two opposing points of view:

Viewpoint 1: Human beings are packages of genes formed by entirely random forces and set adrift in a world where they exist without any purpose, other than that which they construct for themselves.

Or

Viewpoint 2: Human beings are uniquely privileged creatures who have reached their current level of evolution as a result of the deliberate creative action of a loving God. Though creatures of this world, their ultimate destiny lies *beyond* it.

The latter view is that held by the Abrahamic faiths. They teach that, alone among the vast array of creatures on Earth, humans have been made in God's '*image and likeness*' (Genesis 1:27). To be a human being is both a great privilege and an enormous responsibility. It requires humans to treat each other with the utmost respect and to protect one another from injustice in all its many forms. This is what it means to say that human life is *sacred*.

Questions

1. Read the following statement:

   We are right to value sincerity, but false beliefs—even sincerely held false beliefs—can be disastrous.

   (John Young, *The Case Against Christ*.)

   Do you agree/disagree? Why?

2. What evidence is there to support the claim that *human life is qualitatively very different from the rest of the natural world*?

3. Explain the view of the human person held by the Abrahamic religions.

Moral development

People have been thinking, talking and writing about morality for many centuries, but it is only quite recently that there have been any scientific studies conducted into the *way* human beings form their notions of right/good and wrong/evil, and *how* they can be encouraged to develop into morally mature persons.

One of the most influential writers in the field of moral development is Lawrence Kohlberg (1927–87). He was a psychologist who undertook an extensive investigation of the moral growth of young people in

many different cultures around the world. He concluded that it follows the *same* pattern *everywhere*.

Kohlberg asserted that humans progress in their moral reasoning through a series of six stages, which can be generally categorised into three levels.

Kohlberg taught that we can only progress through these stages one at a time.

For example:
A person cannot move from an orientation towards self-interest (Stage 1) to a willingness to abide by the law (Stage 4), without progressing through the stages in between. This is because we are only capable of comprehending a moral rationale (i.e. set of reasons for doing right/good) one stage above our current understanding.

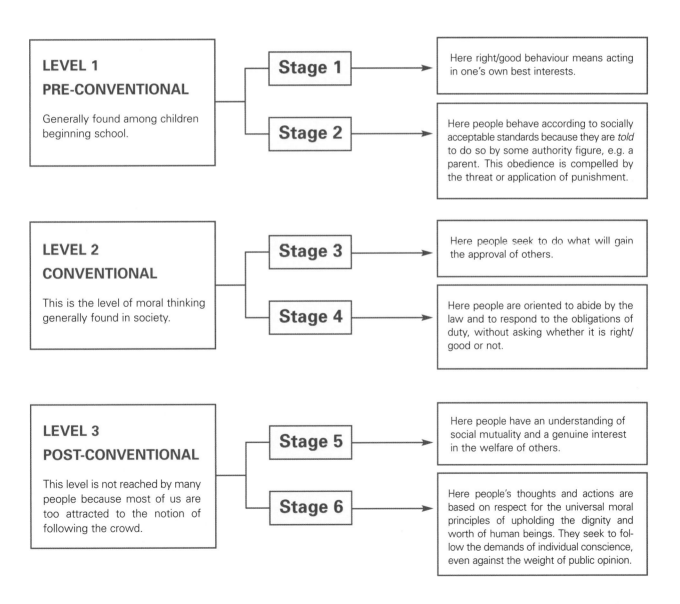

Moral Development

LEVEL 1
PRE-CONVENTIONAL

Generally found among children beginning school.

Stage 1 → Here right/good behaviour means acting in one's own best interests.

Stage 2 → Here people behave according to socially acceptable standards because they are *told* to do so by some authority figure, e.g. a parent. This obedience is compelled by the threat or application of punishment.

LEVEL 2
CONVENTIONAL

This is the level of moral thinking generally found in society.

Stage 3 → Here people seek to do what will gain the approval of others.

Stage 4 → Here people are oriented to abide by the law and to respond to the obligations of duty, without asking whether it is right/good or not.

LEVEL 3
POST-CONVENTIONAL

This level is not reached by many people because most of us are too attracted to the notion of following the crowd.

Stage 5 → Here people have an understanding of social mutuality and a genuine interest in the welfare of others.

Stage 6 → Here people's thoughts and actions are based on respect for the universal moral principles of upholding the dignity and worth of human beings. They seek to follow the demands of individual conscience, even against the weight of public opinion.

Questions

1. Lawrence Kohlberg identified three levels of moral development: *pre-conventional*, *conventional* and *post-conventional*.
   In each of the following examples, identify the level of moral development to which the person belongs:

   (a) 'X' has fully thought out and freely accepted the principles of moral life. She holds to these principles even when those around her do not.
   (b) 'Y' acts from self-interest and considers an action good if it brings her pleasure or praise, and bad if it brings her pain or punishment.
   (c) 'Z' follows the morality he learns from those around him. Thus, he is not yet able to make up his own mind on moral matters, but has to rely on the judgment of others.

Moral example

All the world's religions teach 'the Golden Rule', namely that:

You should treat others as you would have them treat you.

A person who has attained stage 6 in Kohlberg's scale of moral development is one who accepts the Golden Rule not because the world's religions teach it but because he/she acknowledges it as the only morally authentic way to live. Giving concrete expression to such a belief involves *doing* what one knows one *ought* to do. This can be enormously challenging, but there have been some shining examples of people who have lived up to the demands of the Golden Rule.

The Courage of Raoul Wallenberg

During the waning months of World War II, even as the prospects for an Axis military victory dimmed, the Nazis grew more determined to complete the 'final solution'. Death camps operated at maximum capacity in a feverish effort to rid Europe of Jews and other target groups. Until a complete military triumph could be secured, nothing could halt the genocide

Raoul Wallenberg.

raging inside Nazi-occupied Europe. Therefore, a volunteer was sought—someone who could disrupt the insidious Nazi death machine. No one could have been a less obvious choice for this mission than Raoul Wallenberg. Wallenberg was 32 years old in 1944, a wealthy upper-class Swede from a prominent, well-respected family. Sweden's neutrality in the war was only one in a long series of ready-made excuses life had handed young Wallenberg, had he wanted to use them to refuse the rescue mission. He was not Jewish; he was rich; he was well-connected politically; he was in line to take the helm of the vast Wallenberg financial empire; he had everything to lose and nothing to gain by accepting this challenge.

Wallenberg was recommended for this endeavour by Koloman Lauer, a business partner who was involved with the new War Refugee Board. Lauer felt that Raoul possessed the proper combination of dedication, skill, and courage, despite his youth and inexperience, and that his family name would afford him some protection. Wallenberg proved eager to serve, but he boldly demanded and was granted a great deal of latitude in the methods he would use.

When he learned that Adolf Eichmann was transporting roughly 10,000-12,000 Hungarian Jews to the gas chambers each day, Wallenberg hastily prepared to travel to Budapest. His 'cover' was that of a diplomat, with the official title of first secretary of the Swedish legation. He conceived a plan whereby false Swedish passports (*Schutzpasse*) would be created and used to give potential victims safe passage out of Nazi-controlled territory. In conjunction with this, a series of safe-houses would be established within Hungary, in the guise of official Swedish legation buildings under diplomatic protection. With this scheme still forming in his mind, 'Swedish diplomat' Wallenberg entered Hungary at the request of the United States War Refugee Board and his own government on 6 July 1944, with a mission of saving as many of Hungary's Jews as possible from Nazi liquidation.

He designed the fake passports himself. They were masterpieces of the type of formal, official-appearing pomp which was so impressive to the Nazis. Wallenberg, though young, had travelled and studied extensively abroad,

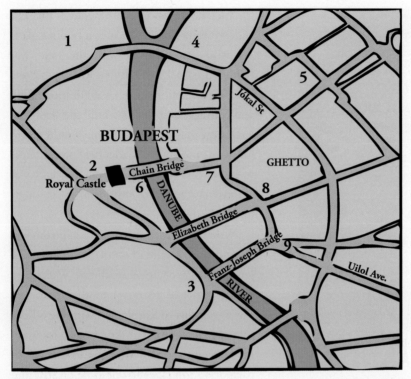

Map of Central Budapest, 1943–5.

1. Rose Hill, where Eichmann lived in a villa and from where he supervised the destruction of the Hungarian Jews.
2. Castle Hill, from where Raoul Wallenberg watched the Russian forces close in around Budapest.
3. Gellert Heights, location of the Swedish Embassy.
4. Area of Wallenberg's 'Swedish Protective Houses and Hospitals'.
5. Benczur Street, location of the American Red Cross.
6. Budapest Chainlink Bridge, which connects the cities of Buda and Pest.
7. Hamincad Street, where Wallenberg lived.
8. The Dohany Synagogue, where thousands of Jews were assembled before Wallenberg secured their release.
9. One of Wallenberg's headquarters, at which many of his staff members lived.

both in the United States (where he attended the University of Michigan as a student of architecture) and in Europe, and he knew how to deal with people and get things done. He worked hard at understanding enemies as well as allies, to know what motivated them, what they admired, what they feared, what they respected. He correctly concluded that the Nazis and Hungarian fascists with whom

he would be dealing responded best to absolute authority and official status. He used this principle in fashioning his passports as well as in his personal encounters with the enemy.

Wallenberg began with forty important contacts in Budapest, and quickly cultivated others who were willing to help. It is estimated that under Wallenberg's leadership he and his associates distributed Swedish passports to

Passport created by Wallenberg.

the last remaining urban enclaves was critical. And so Wallenberg himself plunged into the midst of the struggle.

Sandor Ardai was sent by the Jewish underground to drive for Wallenberg; Ardai later told of one occasion when Wallenberg intercepted a trainload of Jews about to leave for Auschwitz. Wallenberg swept past the SS officer who ordered him to depart. In Ardai's words,

'Then he climbed up on the roof of the train and began handing in protective passes through the doors which were not yet sealed. He ignored orders from the Germans for him to get down, then the Hungarian Fascists, known as the Arrow Cross, began shouting at him to go away. He ignored them and calmly continued handing out passports to the hands that were reaching out for them. I believe the Arrow Cross, men deliberately aimed over his head, as not one shot hit him, which would have been impossible otherwise. I think this is what they did because they were so impressed by his courage. After Wallenberg had handed over the last of the passports he ordered all those who had one to leave the train and walk to the caravan of cars parked nearby, all marked in Swedish colours. I don't remember exactly how many, but he saved dozens off that train, and the Germans and Arrow Cross were so dumbfounded they let him get away with it!'

20,000 of Budapest's Jews and protected 13,000 more in safe houses that he rented and which flew the Swedish flag. However, Eichmann continued to pursue his own mission with fanatical zealous devotion, and the death camps roared around the clock. Trains packed with people, crammed eighty to a cattle car, with nothing but a little water and a bucket for waste, constantly made the four-day journey from Budapest to Auschwitz and back again. The Hungarian countryside was already devoid of Jews, and the situation in

US congressman Tom Lantos and his wife. When Lantos was a child, Wallenberg saved him from the Nazis in Budapest.

As the war situation deteriorated for the Germans, Eichmann diverted trains from the death camp routes for more direct use in supplying troops. But all this meant for his victims was that they now had to walk to their destruction. In November 1944 Eichmann ordered the 125-mile death marches, and the raw elements soon combined with deprivation of food and sleep to turn the roadside from Budapest to the camps into one massive graveyard. Wallenberg made frequent visits to the stopping areas to do what he could. In one instance, Wallenberg announced his arrival with all the authority he could muster, and then,

'You there!' The Swede pointed to an astonished man, waiting for his turn to be handed over to the executioner. '*Give me your Swedish passport and get in that line*,' he barked, 'And you, get behind

him. I know I issued you a passport.' Wallenberg continued, moving fast, talking loud, hoping the authority in his voice would somewhat rub off on these defeated people ... The Jews finally caught on. They started groping in pockets for bits of identification. A driver's license or birth certificate seemed to do the trick. The Swede was grabbing them so fast; the Nazis, who couldn't read Hungarian anyway, didn't seem to be checking. Faster, Wallenberg's eyes urged them, faster, before the game is up. In minutes he had several hundred people in his convoy. International Red Cross trucks, there at Wallenberg's behest, arrived and the Jews clambered on ... Wallenberg jumped into his own car. He leaned out of the car window and whispered, 'I am sorry,' to the people he was leaving behind. 'I am trying to take the youngest ones first,' he explained. 'I want to save a nation.'

This type of action worked many times. Wallenberg and his aides would encounter a death march, and, while Raoul shouted orders for all those with Swedish protective passports to raise their hands, his assistants ran up and down the prisoners' ranks, telling them to raise their hands whether or not they had a document. Wallenberg 'then claimed custody of all who had raised their hands and such was his bearing that none of the Hungarian guards opposed him. The extraordinary thing was the absolutely convincing power of his behaviour,' according to Joni Moser.

Wallenberg indirectly helped many who never even saw his face, because as his deeds were talked about, they inspired hope, courage, and action in many people who otherwise felt powerless to escape destruction. He became a symbol of good in a part of the world dominated by evil, and a reminder of the hidden strengths within each human spirit.

Tommy Lapid was 13 years old in 1944 when he was one of 900 people crowded 15 or 20 to a room in one of the Swedish safe-houses. His account illustrates not only vintage Wallenberg tactics, but also how Wallenberg epitomised hope and righteousness, and how his influence extended throughout the land as a beacon to those engulfed in the darkness of despair.

'One morning, a group of these Hungarian Fascists came into the house and said all the able-bodied women must go with them. We knew what this meant. My mother kissed me and I cried and she cried. We knew we were parting forever and she left me there, an orphan to all intents and purposes. Then, two or three hours later, to my amazement, my mother returned with the other women. It seemed like a mirage, a miracle. My mother was there—she was alive and she was hugging me and kissing me, and she said one word: 'Wallenberg.' I knew who she meant because Wallenberg was a legend among the Jews. In the complete and total hell in which we lived, there was a saviour-angel somewhere, moving around. After she had composed herself, my mother told me that they were being taken to the river when a car arrived and out stepped Wallenberg—and they knew immediately who it was, because there was only one such person in the world. He went up to the Arrow Cross leader and protested that the women were under his protection. They argued with him, but he must have had incredible charisma, some great personal authority, because there was absolutely nothing behind him, nothing to back him up. He stood out there in the street, probably feeling the loneliest man in the world, trying to pretend there was something behind him. They could have shot him then and there in the street and nobody would have known about it. Instead, they relented and let the women go.'

Virtually alone in the middle of enemy territory, outnumbered and outgunned beyond belief, Wallenberg worked miracles on a daily basis. His weapons were courage, self-confidence, ingenuity, understanding of his adversaries, and ability to inspire others to achieve the goals he set. His leadership was always in evidence. The Nazis and Arrow Cross did not know how to deal with such a man. Here was someone thickly cloaked in apparent authority, but utterly devoid of actual political or military power. Here was a man who was everything they wished they could be in terms of personal strength of character, but for the fact that he was their polar opposite in purpose.

It is impossible to calculate precisely how many people Raoul Wallenberg directly or indirectly saved from certain death. Some estimate the number saved as close to 100,000, and countless more may have survived in part because of the hope and determination they derived from his leadership and example. Additionally, he inspired other neutral embassies and the International Red Cross office in Budapest to join in his efforts to protect the Jews. But the desperate days just prior to the Soviet occupation of Budapest presented Wallenberg with his greatest challenge and most astonishing triumph.

Eichmann planned to finish the extermination of the remaining 100,000 Budapest Jews in one enormous massacre; if there was no time to ship them to the death camps, then he would let their own neighbourhoods become their slaughterhouses. To cheat the Allies out of at least part of their victory, he would order some 500 SS men and a large number of Arrow Cross to ring the ghetto and murder the Jews right there. Wallenberg learned of this plot through his network of contacts and tried to intimidate some lower-ranking authorities into backing down, but with the Soviets on their doorsteps, many ceased to care what happened to them. His only hope, and the only hope for the 100,000 surviving Jews, was the overall commander of the SS troops, General August Schmidthuber.

Wallenberg sent a message to Schmidthuber that, if the massacre took place, he would ensure Schmidthuber was held personally responsible and would see him hanged as a war criminal. The bluff worked. The slaughter was called off, and the city fell out of Nazi hands soon thereafter when the Soviet troops rolled in. Thus, tens of thousands were saved in this one incident alone.

But while peace came to Europe, Wallenberg's fate took a very different path. He vanished, and the whole truth of what happened to him has not been revealed even to this day. From various sources, though, the following seems to have occurred.

The Soviets took Wallenberg into custody when they occupied Budapest, probably because they suspected him of being an anti-Soviet spy. For a decade, they denied any involvement in Wallenberg's disappearance. Then they admitted having incarcerated him, but claimed he died in prison of a heart attack in 1947, when he would have been 35 years old. Since then, however, many people who have served time in Soviet prison have reported seeing Wallenberg, conversing with him, or communicating with him through tap codes. Others have heard of him and his presence in the prisons, but had no direct contact. The Soviets denied the accuracy of all of these reports and never deviated from their official position. But in 1989, Soviet officials met with members of Wallenberg's family and turned over some of his personal effects. Reportedly, a genuine investigation was launched in an effort to determine the truth. Whether the years and the prisons will ever yield up their secrets remains to be seen.

In Israel there is today a grove of trees, planted by the Martyrs' and Heroes' Remembrance Authority, or Yad Vashem. Known as The Avenue of the Righteous, each tree memorialises a 'righteous Gentile', someone who risked his or her life to help Jews during the Holocaust. The trees stand in silent testament to those who, in the words of a former speaker of Israel's parliament, 'saved not only the Jews but the honour of humanity'. Along with Raoul Wallenberg's tree, there is a medal. His medal bears the language of the Talmud and summarises his mission in the words, 'Whoever saves a single soul, it is as if he had saved the whole world.'

The chairman of Yad Vashem, Gideon Hausner, who also prosecuted Adolf Eichmann, summarised his feelings for Raoul Wallenberg in this way:

'Here is a man who had the choice of remaining in secure, neutral Sweden when Nazism was ruling Europe. Instead, he left this haven and went to what was then one of the most perilous places in Europe, Hungary. And for what? To save Jews. He won his battle and I feel that in this age when there is so little to believe in—so very little on which our young people can pin their hopes and ideals—he is a person to show to the world, which knows so little about him. That is why I believe the story of Raoul Wallenberg should be told and his figure, in all its true proportions, projected into human minds.'

(Adapted from J.C. Kunich and R.I. Lester, 'Profile of a Leader' in *The Journal of Leadership Studies*, Vol. 4, No. 3.)

Questions

1. Who was Raoul Wallenberg?

2. What was the purpose of his mission to Budapest in 1944–5?

3. Read the following statement by Dr Martin Luther King:

Courage is an inner resolution to go forward despite obstacles; cowardice is submissive surrender to circumstances.
Courage breeds creative self-affirmation; cowardice produces destructive self-abnegation.
Courage faces fear and masters it; cowardice represses fear and is mastered by it ...
Cowardice asks the question, is it safe?
Expediency asks the question, is it politic?
Vanity asks the question, is it popular?
But courage asks the question, is it right?
And there comes a time when one must take a position that is neither safe, nor politic, nor popular, but one must take it because it is right. ➡

Define each of the following:
- *cowardice*;
- *expediency*;
- *vanity*;
- *courage*.

4. All historians readily agree that Raoul Wallenberg was a courageous man. Can you identify any courageous acts performed by him in this extract?

5. What, do you think, motivated Wallenberg to be courageous?

6. What did his actions achieve?

7. The United Nations declared Raoul Wallenberg to be

'the greatest humanitarian of the 20th century'.

Do you think he merits this title? Give reasons for your answer.

8. Why might Raoul Wallenberg's story be considered an example of a person who has reached stage 6 of Kohlberg's scale of moral development?

The human condition

The Denial of St Peter, by Pensionante de Sarceni.

Some writers have speculated that, in time, we humans may evolve beyond such dysfunctional behaviour as envy, greed and violence. Others describe such musings as, at best, examples of wishful thinking.

It requires only a cursory glance over our historical record to determine that human beings have always found it an enormous struggle to do the right/good thing when faced with a moral choice. There is very little reason to think that this is ever likely to change. When confronted with a difficult moral choice, we all experience an *inner tension* pulling us in *opposite* directions: do we stand our ground and do what is right/good? Do we turn away and do what is wrong/evil?

St Paul wrote about his own experience of this:

I cannot understand my own behaviour. I fail to carry out the things I want to do, and I find myself doing the very thing I hate.
(Romans 7:15–16)

The story of St Peter's denial of ever knowing Jesus of Nazareth provides a powerful illustration of this. Peter had been one of Jesus' closest friends for several years. He had witnessed Jesus working miracles and even restoring the dead to life. Yet none of this in any way lessened the inner struggle Peter experienced on Holy Thursday night. In the end, Peter gave in to his fears and abandoned his friend at the very time the latter needed him most.

Like Peter, we too find it very difficult to consistently choose and follow the path of goodness. It is often so much easier to take the path of least resistance and give in to some desire of the moment.

Original sin

The Abrahamic religions agree that all people find choosing and doing good instead of evil to be a serious challenge. However, they reject any suggestion that God created humans with some kind of built-in tendency to do bad things. They teach that God can only create what is *good*. Therefore, all people are created

The impact of sin upon the sinner.

good. But experience shows that people *do* find it difficult to follow the path of goodness. Why?

For Jews and Christians the key to answering this question can be found in the story of *the Fall*, as recounted in the Old Testament (see Genesis 3). This begins by describing the original goodness and first perfection of God's creation, including humanity. It then describes how Adam and Eve deliberately disobeyed God, thereby destroying the harmony that had existed between them and God, and between humankind and nature. As an immediate consequence of this, human beings were exiled from the Garden of Eden into a world of hardship, suffering and death.

While *not* intended to offer a literal historical narrative, this story contains a profound message:

◆ the first humans openly abused their capacity for making free choices. As a result of *their* actions—*not* God's—sin and the suffering it causes came into the world;

◆ by choosing to pursue their own petty, selfish goals and desires rather than do God's will, our ancestors threw away the gift of perfect happiness. They rejected the state of innocent goodness in which God had wanted them to live and became estranged from God. They refused to acknowledge that, in and of themselves, human beings are *not* whole. It is only by living in harmony with the will of God, as expressed in his commandments, that human beings can be complete;

◆ the first—or *original*—sin committed by our ancestors is the source of all evil in the world. It has affected all of subsequent human society because its effects have been passed down from one generation to the next. It has given rise to two related forms of sin:

(a) *personal* sin, i.e. where the individual puts the attainment of selfish goals before the love of God and others;

(b) *social* sin, i.e. where human institutions are hindered by selfish attitudes, structures and values.

Islam has no belief that equates to the Christian doctrine of original sin. Muslims believe that human beings are born pure and lean towards goodness, so that to incline towards evil is to go against one's human nature. Muslims divide sins into two categories:

◆ first order sins: these concern offending the honour of Allah by associating Allah's divine attributes with anything inferior;

◆ second order sins: these are acts against one's fellow human beings, such as murder, rape or theft.

Reasons for hope

Both Jews and Christians believe that God is utterly good, loving and wise in ways that surpass all human understanding. As such, it would be unthinkable for God to create human beings and then abandon them, even after our ancestors rejected God's love. While Jews and Christians agree on humanity's need to return to God and renew our bond of loving obedience to God, they *disagree* as to *how* God himself is effecting this restoration.

Christians believe that:

◆ God redeemed (rescued) humanity from the power of sin by becoming a human being in Jesus of Nazareth;

◆ Jesus has shown us the way in which God has always *intended* us to live. This is the only way in which we can achieve peace and harmony with God, one another and nature;

◆ Jesus extends an *invitation* to follow him, but does not coerce anyone to follow him. The choice is up to each individual to make;

◆ we are called to live lives of *virtue*, i.e. to develop and act upon our capacity for treating each other with compassion, honesty, love and respect;

However, Christianity teaches that humans are *incapable* of achieving this goal entirely by their own efforts. We need God's *grace* (i.e. strengthening love) to encourage and guide us in the pursuit of goodness;

In the sacrament of Baptism, Christians receive the grace to combat their inherited tendencies and to choose the right path. Despite being redeemed by Jesus, humans still suffer from the effects of original sin and therefore are still vulnerable to temptation. Thus, Christians are taught to:

◆ *pray to and co-operate with God, who gives them the strength to conquer their weakness;*

◆ *draw on the support and moral guidance provided by active membership of the Christian community.*

St Peter Baptising New Converts, a fresco painted *c.* 1427 by Tommaso Masaccio.

Questions

1. Explain the following statement by St Paul:

> *I cannot understand my own behaviour. I fail to carry out the things I want to do, and I find myself doing the very thing I hate.*

2. Many modern novelists have taken as their theme the dramatic tension between choosing good or evil within each and every human being. Reacting against those ideologies which claim that humans can be conditioned to live perfect lives here on Earth, these writers paint a distinctly unflattering portrait of human nature.

    (a) In his novel *The Lord of the Flies*, William Golding appears to offer little hope for the human race. He portrays humans as all too often vicious and murderous, driven by dark, destructive urges that can quickly rise to the surface whenever people drop their guard, either individually or as a community. The many wars in human history would seem to bear this out.

Do you agree/disagree with Golding's view? Is he too pessimistic? Explain your answer.

    (b) In his novel *Animal Farm*, George Orwell claims that even reform movements that seek to build a better world inevitably lose their original idealism as they are taken over and led off course by a clever, unscrupulous minority. All the while, the majority of people, apparently overcome either by apathy or wickedness, just sit back and allow it to happen.

Is Orwell correct in his assessment of *all* reform movements? Does the 'silent majority' *always* just sit back? Consider the work of people such as Mahatma Gandhi and Martin Luther King Jnr in your answer.

3. What is the message contained within the story of 'the Fall' about the relationship between God and human beings?

4. What is meant by *original sin*?

5. What are said to have been the effects of the original (i.e. first) sin?

6. Explain the following terms:
(a) *personal* sin;
(b) *social* sin.

7. How do Muslims differ from Christians regarding original sin?

8. What do Christians believe is the role of Jesus of Nazareth in restoring the relationship between humans and God?

9. Explain the term *grace* in reference to God.

10. What do Christians believe about the sacrament of baptism?

Making Moral Decisions

Introduction

Vincent Teresa was a Mafia gangster in the Boston branch of the Patriarca crime family. After his arrest, he turned informer and entered the FBI's witness protection programme. When interviewed by journalist T.C. Renner, Teresa admitted that he had chosen to pursue a life of crime partly because it was '*the family business*', but primarily because it was an easy way to get what he most desired: wealth and power. When asked about the violent acts he had committed during his criminal career, Teresa responded:

> *If you gotta go out and kill a guy, you gotta make yourself believe it was him or you. You justify it to yourself, but you never confess it to a priest.*
> (Vincent Teresa, *My Life in the Mafia.*)

Teresa's words reveal that he was well aware that certain acts he had committed were wrong/evil, no matter what excuse or justification he had conjured up, and that he might be answerable for what he had done. Some observers might say that Teresa's '*conscience*' was troubling him.

The meaning of conscience

The term '*conscience*' is employed frequently by people when discussing moral decisions, but what does it mean?

'My conscience tells me that ... '
'Always let your conscience be your guide'

Such statements give conscience the characteristics of some mysterious, independent entity existing inside each of us. This is *not* the case. Perhaps the best explanation of conscience is to be found in the writings of St Thomas Aquinas. He described conscience as:

the ability to make practical judgments about what is the right or wrong thing to do when faced with a particular moral issue.

Conscience is sometimes thought of as a strictly religious phenomenon, i.e. as *'the voice of God'* in each person that tries to keep us on the right path in life. While containing some merit, this idea is misleading. Conscience is not solely a religious idea, it is an integral part of what it means to be a human being. Much of the confusion about conscience stems from the way in which we often use the word, for example:

Normally, our conscience operates with such swiftness and efficiency that we are rarely aware of how it functions. Indeed, often our response to certain situations is *habitual*, which is why moral educators stress the importance of encouraging children to acquire good habits and dispense with bad ones.

Let us turn now to consider a slow-motion example, which illustrates the way in which we should apply a general moral principle to a particular moral problem.

Problem	I am tempted to make a statement that is malicious gossip about a person I dislike.
Principle	But it is always wrong to spread malicious gossip.
Conclusion	Therefore, if I make this statement, I am doing something wrong.
Decision	A morally good person would then say: I wish to help, not to injure others, even those I dislike, so I will not make this statement.

Questions

1. What is meant by 'conscience'?

2. Imagine that you are sent to the school office by your teacher to collect some photocopied material. When you get there, you find the office unattended. The door is open, so you walk in and spot the photocopies on top of the photocopying machine. As you are picking up the bundle, you notice a copy of the end-of-term maths exam paper you are due to sit next week. There is no-one around. You appear to be presented with a 'golden opportunity'. But are you?

(a) Explore the implications of each of the following:
  - stealing the paper and keeping it secret;
  - photocopying it and giving copies to your friends or selling it to members of your class;
  - refusing to steal it, but looking at it;
  - refusing to either steal it or to look at it.

  Which of these is the correct course of action to take?
  Explain your answer.

(b) Examine the reasons you gave. What do they tell you about your *own* set of *values*, i.e. those things you consider important and worthwhile?

3. Read the following:

Hugh Thompson, who has died aged 62, was the US Army helicopter pilot who tried to halt the My Lai massacre of more than 500 villagers by American troops during the Vietnam war. At one point, he rescued 15 defenceless civilians while training his machine guns on US infantry-men commanded by Lieutenant William Calley, threatening to shoot if they did not stop the slaughter.

Hugh Thompson Jr., helicopter pilot, 1943–2006.

By the time he arrived in Vietnam in late December 1967, Thompson was a 25-year-old chief warrant officer reconnaissance pilot with the 123rd Aviation Battalion. On 16 March 1968, he was flying his H-23 scout helicopter, with its three-man crew, over a part of Quang

Ngai province known as Pinkville, supporting a three company search-and-destroy assault on several villages, which faulty intelligence had indicated were heavily defended by Vietcong troops. The US 120th Infantry Battalion was led by Charlie Company, commanded by Captain Ernest Medina, who sent in the 1st platoon, led by Calley, to clear out My Lai and several neighbouring hamlets.

Charlie Company was bent on revenge; days earlier several of its members had been killed by Vietcong mines and booby traps. Without a shot being fired against them, Calley's men began slaughtering anyone they could find—old men, women and children. Groups of villagers, 20 and 30 at a time, were lined up and mown down. In the four-hour assault, the men of the 2nd and 3rd platoons joined in.

Early on, Thompson spotted a young woman injured in a field. He dropped a smoke canister to indicate she needed medical help; he claimed in a court martial later that Medina went over and shot her. During the massacre, Thompson discovered the bodies of 170 executed villagers in a drainage ditch. One of his crew rescued a child and they flew it to hospital.

In another incident, he challenged Calley to help a group of civilians hiding in a bunker rather than attack them. When Calley refused, Thompson ordered his helicopter gunners to open fire on the 1st platoon if they advanced any closer. He then called down gunships to rescue the civilians.

On returning to Chu Lai military base, Thompson reported everything to his commanding officer. But a local inquiry whitewashed his complaints, claiming the civilian deaths had been caused by artillery fire. An elaborate cover-up ensued and Thompson was awarded the Distinguished Flying Cross for saving the lives of Vietnamese civilians 'in the face of hostile enemy fire'—he threw the medal away, believing his commanders wanted to buy his silence.

A year later, the Pentagon learned the truth and a high-level inquiry was conducted by Lieutenant General William Peers. Thompson later appeared as a witness at the courts martial of several men involved in the massacre or the cover-up, though the only person convicted was Calley, who served a few months in jail before having his life sentence reduced and being given parole.

During his time in Vietnam, Thompson was shot down five times, finally breaking his backbone. He received a commission, but back in America some colleagues regarded him as a turncoat. When evidence of the atrocity was finally made public in late 1969, he was castigated by pro-Vietnam war politicians in Washington.

It was only 30 years later that Thompson was recognised as a genuine American hero by the Pentagon, after a nine-year letter-writing campaign. The US army had initially wanted his Soldier's Medal, the military's highest award for bravery in peacetime, to be presented quietly, preferring to keep what happened at My Lai in the background. But Thompson resisted. He wanted a ceremony at the Vietnam memorial in Washington DC, and the bravery of his fellow crew members recognised as well. In March 1998, he finally got his wish.

After his role in trying to stop the massacre was recognised in the US, Thompson and his surviving crew-member, Larry Colburn, were taken back to My Lai, where they were introduced to three women who had survived the massacre. On a second visit three years later, he met an electrician from Ho Chi Minh City who, aged nine, had been one of the children Thompson had rescued from the bunker.

(Adapted from: http://www.guardian.co.uk/)

(a) Describe the state of mind of the US troops entering the village of My Lai on 16 March 1968.
(b) What was the role of Hugh Thompson in this military operation?
(c) What actions did he take to save the lives of unarmed Vietnamese civilians?

(d) How did Hugh Thompson react to being awarded the distinguished Flying Cross soon afterwards?

(e) Why did he react in this way?

(f) How was Hugh Thompson treated by some people when he gave testimony at the trial of those responsible for the massacre at My Lai?

(g) Journalist Seymour Hersh, who won the 1970 Pulitzer Prize for his exposé of the My Lai massacre, described Thompson as

'one of the good guys'.

He went on to commend Thompson's courage both at the time of the massacre and afterwards, saying:

'You can't imagine what courage it took to do what he did.'

Do you agree/disagree with this assessment? Explain your answer.

(h) When asked about why he had done what he did at My Lai, Hugh Thompson simply responded:

These people were looking to me for help, and there was no way I could turn my back on them.
(Associated Press Interview, 1998.)

What set of values lay behind Hugh Thompson's response that day at My Lai?

(i) When researching for his book *The Forgotten Hero of My Lai* (2006), journalist Trent Angers discovered that the story of Hugh Thompson's heroic rescue of civilians is now being used in US and European military training manuals to teach soldiers how to conduct themselves on the battlefield.
What lesson do you draw from this about the example he set for members of the world's military?

The members of the Abrahamic religions accept the Ten Commandments as their basic moral guide. These are:

1. I, the Lord, am your God; you shall have no other gods besides me.

2. You shall not take the name of the Lord your God in vain.

3. Remember to keep holy the Sabbath day.

4. Honour your father and your mother.

5. You shall not commit murder.

6. You shall not commit adultery.

7. You shall not steal.

8. You shall not bear false witness against your neighbour.

9. You shall not covet your neighbour's husband/wife.

10. You shall not covet anything that belongs to your neighbour.

(Source: R. McBrien (ed.), *Encyclopedia of Catholicism*.)

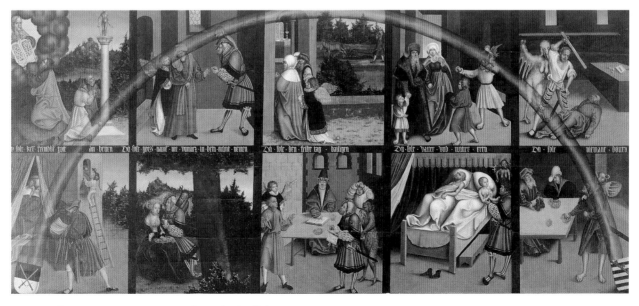

The Ten Commandments, by Lucas Cranach the Elder.

Christian morality

Christian morality is founded on:
◆ the Ten Commandments in the *Old Testament*; and
◆ the teachings of Jesus in the *New Testament*.

Jesus taught his disciples that, in essence, the Ten Commandments could be summarised as follows:
◆ Commandments 1–3
You should love the Lord, your God, with all your heart and mind.
◆ Commandments 4–10
You should love your neighbour as yourself.

Jesus did *not* leave his followers a detailed set of instructions covering every conceivable moral challenge that might arise. Indeed, people today are confronted by an array of issues undreamt of 2,000 years ago. Developments in medicine, technology and communications have both enriched and complicated our lives. However, Christians can make moral decisions based on the values Jesus taught and lived by, namely:
◆ love of God and neighbour;
◆ respect for all members of the human family at all stages of their lives;
◆ commitment to defend their dignity and welfare;
◆ gratitude for and stewardship of the world people have been given to share.

Over the centuries the Christian Churches have sought to:
◆ build on these moral principles;
◆ determine what is and what is not the morally right thing to do;
◆ provide guidance as to how Christians can best follow Jesus' command to 'love one another as I have loved you'.

Temptation of St Thomas Aquinas, by Diego Rodriguez de Silva y Velásquez.

Obstacles

We are said to have achieved moral maturity when we can think for ourselves, honestly evaluate situations and determine a course of action consistent with our values. But we must ever be on our guard against those things that can cloud our judgment and lead us into error, namely:
◆ where we are unaware of the true nature of the issue confronting us, either because we have not or could not obtain the advice or information we require;
◆ where we allow our emotions and prejudices to unduly influence our decision-making;
◆ where we do something for the sake of conformity with others;
◆ where we have made a mistake in our reasoning, e.g. War involves killing people: *Problem*;
It is always wrong to kill another person: *Principle*;
Therefore, war is wrong: *Conclusion*.

The problem here is that this principle is *not* true for *every* situation. In some circumstances it may, regrettably, be both necessary and correct to take a life, for example in defence of yourself or your loved ones in times of extreme danger, when there is no other course of action open to you.

Questions

1. (a) Which of the Commandments centre on our relationship with God?
    (b) Which Commandments centre on relationships between ourselves and other people and vice versa?

2. What do you think is the meaning and importance of the Ten Commandments for people living today? Explain your answer.

3. (a) Can you identify any situations where ignorance of the true nature of the problem we may face could have unfortunate consequences for ourselves and others?
    (b) In what circumstances can our emotions cloud our judgment?

4. (a) List the most common types of conformist behaviour or thought (i.e. going along with the crowd) among people in your age group.
    (b) Why do people think and behave in this way?
    (c) What are the consequences of this conformist behaviour for them and for others?

5. In most circumstances, it would be true to say, '*It is wrong to cut another person with a knife*'.
    (a) Can you identify any situation in which it would be morally correct to do so *other* than in defence of oneself or one's loved ones? Why?
    (b) What does this say to you about applying general moral principles to particular moral problems? Explain your answer.

Law and morality

We may define '*law*' as:

a rule enacted and promulgated by the governing authority that enjoins or prohibits certain actions, which is enforced by the imposition of penalties.

The legal definition of a crime is:

an act forbidden by law and done with wrongful intention.

All the major world religions teach that their members are not only legally bound to obey the law but are *morally* bound to do so. However, this applies *only* where the law is *just*; it does *not* hold where the law is deemed to be unjust.

For a long time Judaism and Christianity have emphasised that our legal system should always strive to enshrine in law and apply in practice the principles

Nicolas Poussin's painting *The Judgement of Solomon* illustrates that moral decisions can be difficult.

of sound reasoning and moral integrity. The law of the state should have as its focus the protection of the individual's rights and the upholding of the common good.

However, the law is sometimes revealed to be inadequate in helping people to attain *justice*, i.e. that to which they are entitled. In other situations, the law can be used to actively *deprive* people of justice. As a result, what is legal need not necessarily be moral.

History provides many examples of unjust practices that were quite legal in a particular country. For example:

- the anti-Jewish Nuremberg Laws imposed by the Nazis on Germany in the 1930s and 1940s;
- the racist laws imposed by the apartheid regime in South Africa for much of the twentieth century;
- the anti-Catholic Penal Laws imposed on Ireland in the eighteenth century.

When making a moral decision we need to bear in mind the distinction between what is legal and what is moral.

Questions

1. Define the following terms:
   (a) *law*;   (b) *crime*.

2. Are law and morality one and the same thing? Explain your answer.

3. Can you identify any forms of behaviour, past or present, which, though legal, are considered morally wrong according to the teachings of all the major world religions?

Making a moral decision

Many of our actions do *not* require a great deal of thought before we perform them. But there are some situations where we do need to pause and think carefully about what is the right course of action to pursue. What follows is a checklist of questions we should ask ourselves before making a moral decision on an important life issue:

◆ what exactly is the issue at stake?

◆ do I possess all the relevant facts?

◆ what does the law of the state say?

◆ what can my previous experiences or those of trustworthy advisors tell me?

◆ what are my motives—are they in harmony with the Golden Rule?

◆ what methods may I use? There are certain actions (e.g. murder) that are morally wrong and can never be justified;

◆ what are the likely effects of a particular course of action on both myself and others?

◆ is there any morally acceptable alternative course of action open to me?

A religious person will add two other questions to this list:

◆ what does my religion teach about this?

◆ have I prayed for guidance?

Only after going through this process should a person act according to his/her conscience because it is then an *informed* conscience.

N.B.

Some religions offer more specific guidance on moral matters than others, which their members are obliged to consider before making a moral decision. Catholics are expected to accept as their guide the Magisterium, i.e. the teaching authority of the Church, which consists of the Pope and the bishops. When making a moral decision a Catholic must carefully consider the teachings of the Church. These teachings aim to help Catholics fulfil Jesus' command to 'Love one another as I have loved you'.

Outlook

In order to make good moral decisions a person must strive to think clearly, consistently and without prejudice. There is *more* to morality than this, however. Good moral decisions require courage, determination, honesty and humility on the part of those making them.

It is important to keep in mind that no one can be 100 per cent certain in matters of morality. Further, moral development takes time: it is a life-long project. All one can do is try to think clearly, stay true to one's values, act responsibly and strive honestly to do what is right.

Many members of the world's religions draw great comfort and strength from their faith. For almost 2,000 years many Christians have been drawing enormous inspiration and encouragement from the example of Jesus of Nazareth, firm in the belief that what he taught is true: that God's love is infinitely more powerful than sin and death, and that all those who have lovingly served God in this life will share eternal life with God in the next.

Questions

1. Imagine that you are a trade union leader representing healthcare workers in a hospital. You have received a request for immediate strike action from members opposed to a management proposal to: (a) freeze pay at current levels for two years, and (b) make some people redundant to save money. Explain:
   (a) Explain:
       how you would go about arriving at a decision as to whether you would recommend a '*yes*' or '*no*' vote in a strike ballot; and
       the difficulties you might encounter in making your decision.
   (b) What, in your opinion, would be a fair and mutually acceptable compromise agreement? Give reasons for your answer.

2. Read the following statement:

   In most cases when we act wrongly our failure is a failure of will, not a failure of knowledge.

   (Nano Brennan, *The Moral Life*.)

   (a) What does this mean?
   (b) Do you agree/disagree? Give reasons for your answer.

3. Read the following extract:

   Franz Jagerstater owned a small farm and was married with four children when the Germans invaded Austria at the beginning of the Second World War. The invasion was widely popular in Austria and many people supported the Nazis. Jagerstater rejected them utterly. He was required to sell his crops through a local Nazi-owned co-operative but he refused to do so as this would have meant co-operating with evil-doers. Then a call went out that everyone of military age was required to join the army, Jagerstater refused to go. His friends told him that he had to go and the mayor of the local town came out to try and persuade him, saying that if he did not go he would be put to death. Still he refused.

The mayor said that if he would volunteer to work in the local hospital he would be exempted from service and would therefore be safe. Still he refused—he considered that to compromise would be to give into evil and he rejected this. He felt a duty to something absolute. But this was something that his friends and family were unable to understand.

Jagerstater was duly killed and almost forgotten. His action seemed to have no point and no significance, yet today, years later, his integrity and bravery are remembered long after all those who collaborated are forgotten.

Yet it is not whether he is remembered or whether he is forgotten that is significant—many more died making similar stands against the Nazis—what is important is that he lived an accountable life. His conscience was informed of what it would mean to go with the flow of Nazi imperialism and such compliance would have been a denial of his humanity. He would not have been able to live with the knowledge that he was siding with evil, so accountable did he feel for his decision. The accountability he felt to a higher authority superseded accountability to his wife, his family, his community and even to himself. If more individuals had had the informed developed conscience of this man, the events of the Holocaust might well have been avoided.

(Adapted from P. Vardy, *Being Human*.)

(a) In what ways did Franz Jagerstater refuse to co-operate with Nazi rule?
(b) Why did he do so?
(c) Do you agree/disagree with the assessment that if others had followed his example, the Holocaust might have been avoided? Give reasons for your answer.

The Crown v Sir Thomas More 1–6 July 1535

By 1534 England's King Henry VIII had been battling the Catholic pope for eight years, unsuccessfully petitioning to annul his marriage to his first wife, Catherine of Aragon. Finally, Henry decided to proclaim himself head of the Church of England. On 23 March 1534, Parliament passed the Act of Succession, declaring Henry's marriage to Catherine void and validating his second marriage to Anne Boleyn. The act carried with it a stiff penalty for any who challenged it: it called for a charge of treason and a sentence of death. To ensure total support, Henry ordered that all adult subjects take an oath of allegiance.

A summons was issued on 7 March 1534 requiring Sir Thomas More, a prominent statesman and author, to take the oath the following day at Lambeth Palace. More was privately opposed to Henry's split with Rome and had resigned as lord chancellor in 1532. When he arrived at Lambeth Palace, he found the archbishop of Canterbury, the lord chancellor, the king's chief adviser, Thomas Cromwell, and other friends of the king waiting to see what he would do. They strongly urged More to take the oath and showed him a list of influential people who had already signed it. More insisted that although Parliament had the right to name Henry's successor, it was wrong to declare Henry's first marriage invalid. He could not in good conscience take the oath. When More was offered a second opportunity to swear allegiance in April 1534 and once again refused, he was imprisoned in the Tower of London along with a leading churchman, Bishop John Fisher.

More had been in prison without trial for seven months when Parliament passed a series

Sir Thomas More, by Holbein.

of acts intended to force any still hesitant about the oath to a decision. The Act of Supremacy, which finalised the break with Rome, declared that the king was the '*Supreme Head*' of the Church of England, but omitted the former conditional clause '*so far as the law of Christ allows*.' The Second Act of Succession enshrined the controversial oath of allegiance in the statute books. The Act of Treasons extended the definition of treason to include words either spoken or written against the king, the queen, or their heirs. Finally, the Act of Attainder – which was specifically designed to put pressure on More, Fisher, and five other recalcitrant churchmen – proclaimed that those refusing to take the oath of allegiance forfeited all their possessions.

More was brought for interrogation before Thomas Cromwell and other members of the ruling council on 30 April 1535. They informed More that the king wanted to know his opinion on the new statutes, particularly the Act of Supremacy. When More was unable to give a satisfactory answer, Cromwell warned him that Henry would let the law take its course. Meanwhile, word came from Rome that the pope had made Bishop Fisher a cardinal. 'Let the pope send him a hat when he will,' King Henry stormed, ' … head he shall have none to set it on.' Now Henry was determined that More and Fisher be trapped into explicit treasonable denial of the Act of Supremacy. On 3 June a gathering of king's men—including Cromwell, Cranmer, and Thomas Boleyn, the new queen's father—interrogated More in the Tower. Cromwell

told More that the king commanded him to answer plainly: he must either acknowledge Henry as supreme head of the Church or 'utter plainly his malignity.' More replied that he was a loyal servant of the king, but added: '*for if it were so that my conscience gave me against the statutes* (wherein how my mind giveth me I make no declaration) … *it were a very hard thing to compel me to say either precisely with it against my conscience to the loss of my soul, or precisely against it to the destruction of my body*.' In other words, if he spoke out, it would cost him dearly whether he told the truth or a lie. Unable to trap More, they asked him why, if he was prepared to die for his beliefs, he would not condemn the statute. More replied: '*I have not been a man of such holy living as I might be bold to offer myself to death, lest God for my presumption might suffer me to fall*.'

Infuriated by More's refusal to co-operate, Cromwell sent for Sir Richard Riche, an agent provocateur who had already trapped Fisher into an explicit denial of the Act of Supremacy. Riche tried to corner More:

Riche: '*Admit there were, Sir, an act of Parliament that all the realm should take me for king. Would not you, Master More, take me for king?*'
More: '*Yes, sir, that would I.*'
Riche: '*I put the case, further, that there were an act of Parliament that all the realm should take me for pope. Would you then, Master More, take me for pope?*'
More: '*Suppose Parliament should make a law

that God should not be God. Would you then, Master Riche, say that God were not God?'
Riche: *'No Parliament may make any such law.'*

More fell silent, leaving Riche to draw the obvious conclusion. Still lacking an outright statement from More, Cromwell and the king decided that this exchange with Riche would form the basis of an indictment against him. On 17 June 1535, More received the news that Fisher had been tried and convicted. Fisher was beheaded five days later.

More's trial took place in Westminster Hall on 1 July. The formal indictment stated that More had *'traitorously and maliciously, by craft imagined, invented, practiced, and attempted wholly to deprive our sovereign lord the king of his dignity, title and name of Supreme Head on Earth of the Church of England.'* Four pieces of evidence were offered to the court: More's silence when interrogated by Cromwell, Cranmer and Boleyn; his correspondence with Fisher, which had been burned; an allegation that he wrote to Fisher that the Act of Supremacy was a two-edged sword; and his conversation with Richard Riche on 12 June.

More, speaking in his own defence, made short work of the first point: *'Your statute cannot condemn me to death for such silence, for neither your statute nor any laws in the world punish people except for words or deeds.'* Any discussion of his correspondence with Fisher could only be speculation, but More denied that he had written that the statute was *'like a sword with two edges, for if a man*

answer one way it will confound his soul, and if he answer the other way it will confound his body.' He had, he said, only written conditionally: *'If the statute cut both ways like a two-edged sword, how could a man behave so as not to incur either danger?'*

Riche was called in to give evidence on the final count. He described the exchange, but added a fictional, damning sentence: *'No more than Parliament could make a law that God were not God could Parliament make the king Supreme Head of the Church.'* More addressed the jury: *'If this oath of yours, Master Riche, be true, then pray I that I never see God in the face, which I would not say were it otherwise to win the whole world.'*

More then gave his own version of the conversation. He accused Riche bluntly of perjury and, turning to the bench, asked his accusers: *'Can it therefore seem likely unto your honourable lordships, that I would in so weighty a cause so unadvisedly overshoot myself as to trust Master Riche, that I would unto him utter the secrets of my conscience touching the king's Supremacy?'*

The jury took just fifteen minutes to find More guilty. They were unanimous in their verdict. The lord chancellor rose to pass sentence, but More interrupted him with the reminder that every prisoner should be asked why judgment should not be given against him. Granted permission, More spoke freely at last. He argued that sentence should not be passed because he had been found guilty by a statute that was not valid. *'This indictment is grounded upon an Act of Parliament directly* repugnant to the laws of God and his Holy Church... it is therefore, in law among Christian men, insufficient to charge any Christian man.'

More was condemned to death. Although the penalty for high treason was to be hanged, drawn, and quartered, More's sentence was commuted by the king to beheading by the axe, widely considered to be a more noble end. Early in the morning on 6 July 1535, he walked to his death on Tower Hill, dressed in a coarse grey gown and carrying a red wooden cross. After giving a short address to the onlookers, in which he asked the people to pray for him and bear witness that he suffered death for the Catholic faith, he knelt at the block and told the executioner to be of good cheer: 'Pluck up thy spirits man and be not afraid to do thine office; my neck is very short; take heed therefore thou strike not awry, for saving of thine honesty.' His head was severed with a single stroke.

After he had been condemned to death he spoke the following words to the members of the court:

'I verily trust and right heartily pray that though your lordships have now here in Earth been judges to my condemnation, we may yet hereafter in heaven all merrily meet together; to our everlasting salvation.'

Four hundred years later, Thomas More was canonised a saint by the Catholic Church.

(Adapted from Frank McLynn, *Famous Trials*.)

Questions

1. (a) What was the Act of Succession 1534?
   (b) Who was required to take an oath of allegiance to express support for it?
   (c) What were the penalties for denying this act?

2. Who was Sir Thomas More?

3. How did Sir Thomas More respond to the demand that he take an oath of allegiance?

4. Why did he respond in this way?

5. What was the Act of Supremacy 1534?

6. How did King Henry VIII punish those who refused to take the oath of allegiance?

7. What was Sir Thomas More's attitude towards the king?

8. Why did Sir Thomas More choose to remain silent when asked to accept or deny the Act of Supremacy?

9. Who was Sir Richard Riche and what did he try to do when questioning Sir Thomas More?

10. Why was Sir Thomas More put on trial in July 1535?

11. What were the charges brought against him?

12. How did Sir Thomas More defend himself against these charges?

13. Describe the role played by Sir Richard Riche in the trial.

14. Was the verdict of this court a foregone conclusion even before the trial began? Explain your answer.

15. How did Sir Thomas More die?

16. What message, do you think, is contained in his final comments to the members of the court that had condemned him?

17. Why, do you think, was Sir Thomas More prepared to refuse King Henry VIII's wishes even though he knew that to do so was to put his life at risk?

18. In 2000 Pope John Paul II declared Thomas More to be the patron saint of politicians. What relevance does his example have for contemporary politics? Give reasons for your answer.

Life Issues: Abortion and Cloning

A. ABORTION

Introduction

Abortion is a disturbing subject, one that many people are inclined to avoid. Studies reveal that attitudes towards abortion are deeply divided in almost every nation. Many people claim to find the whole matter perplexing. However, it would be wrong to attempt to ignore such a crucially important moral issue because it has such serious consequences for the lives of so many human beings.

Meaning

Broadly speaking, the term abortion refers to:

any death of a child in the mother's womb and/or its expulsion from the mother's womb before it is viable, i.e. able to live outside the womb without artificial support.

There are *two* types of abortion:

◆ spontaneous;

◆ procured.

We shall examine each in turn.

Confrontation at an anti-abortion protest rally.

1. Spontaneous Abortion

Spontaneous abortion is usually referred to as a *miscarriage*. It is a *natural* event that happens on its own *without* any medical intervention. It can cause great sorrow when a woman wants to have a child. Some miscarriages may happen so early in a pregnancy that the woman is unaware it has happened. Some studies claim that up to 30 per cent of all pregnancies end in miscarriage, with the vast majority occurring in the first ten weeks. (Source: British Medical Association, *Complete Family Health Encyclopaedia*.)

2. Procured Abortion

Procured abortion is also referred to as *direct* abortion, *therapeutic* abortion or *termination*. It is an artificially *induced* event caused by the use of either drugs or surgery, or a combination of both, depending on the stage the mother's pregnancy has reached.

A *procured* abortion may be defined as: *any medical procedure the direct and deliberate purpose of which is either to prevent the implantation of an embryo or to remove it from the mother's womb before it is viable.*

In this chapter, we shall focus on the issues raised by procured abortion, which from this point on will be simply termed *abortion*.

Why Choose Abortion?

Usually, a pregnancy is a cause for celebration. Sometimes, however, it may *not* be welcomed and the woman may choose to have an abortion. This decision may be made for one or more of the following reasons:

- ◆ it might seem to offer the best and most immediate solution to a distressing personal situation. For example, where a long-term relationship has broken down and ended in acrimony or, more tragically, where a woman has become pregnant due to rape or incest;

- ◆ sometimes poverty and/or pregnancy late in life, especially where there is a higher-than-usual risk of the child being born with a disability such as Down's Syndrome, may lead a woman to believe that abortion provides the only solution to her problem;

- some people have currently incurable genetic disorders, e.g. Cystic Fibrosis, Haemophilia, which can be passed on to their children. Where a woman and her husband/partner know that there is a considerable risk of their child being born with a disability or a severe illness, it can cause great confusion, uncertainty, fear and worry. The couple may decide that the best course of action is for the woman to have an abortion and spare all concerned from the suffering they believe will result from the child being born;

- in some cases powerful psychological pressure may be applied to the pregnant woman by another interested party. This could be the father of the unborn child, who does not wish to support a child, or wishes to conceal what he later considers an embarrassing error. Or, in the case of a young woman, it may be some or all of her relatives who fear that her pregnancy could have a damaging impact on her future educational, employment and social opportunities;

- pre-marital sexual intimacy is now more widely practised than ever before. This has led to more many pregnancies that are the result of contraceptive failures. A woman who has become pregnant after a casual sexual encounter may be frightened and alone. Indeed, the majority of abortions are performed on young, single women. The father of the unborn child may be indifferent and unsympathetic to her situation, leaving her emotionally very vulnerable. Her decision to abort the baby might well be taken in desperation and against her own beliefs that abortion is wrong. Often such a decision is bitterly regretted later.

Statistics

In most countries abortion is legal and is on the increase. It is estimated that between 40 and 50 million abortions are performed each year across the globe. According to the UK Office for National Statistics, an average of 6,000 women giving Irish addresses obtain an abortion in British hospitals or clinics each year. The largest number of these abortions occurs among women in the 20–30 age group.

Determining the *true* number of Irish women who have had an abortion is difficult because:
- a number of Irish resident women do not give their real addresses when having an abortion in Britain;
- some women may take advantage of internet booking services and lower airfares to avail of abortion services in other European countries.

As a result, the actual number of Irish women who have an abortion is most likely higher than the official figures indicate; how much higher is a matter of conjecture.

Questions

1. What is meant by the following terms:
(a) *spontaneous abortion;* (b) *procured abortion*?

2. Identify five reasons why some women choose to have an abortion.

3. Why is it difficult to determine the exact number of abortions carried out on Irish women each year?

Different Views

Opinion is sharply divided as to the morality of abortion.

◆ Humanists advocate what is termed the *'pro-choice'* approach, namely that the decision whether or not to seek an abortion is one best left to the pregnant woman and should not be subject to any involvement by others.

◆ Muslims are divided on the issue of abortion. Many believe it is wrong, should never be allowed under any circumstances and should be actively discouraged.

◆ Some Muslims disagree, however, believing instead that an abortion is permissible if it is performed before the point in foetal development when the soul is infused into the body (*c.* day 120) and in circumstances where the mother's life is believed to be at risk.

◆ A number of Buddhist and Hindu sects have publicly stated their opposition to abortion at any stage of foetal development and under any circumstances. They believe that as all life is sacred, the destruction of an unborn child's life will create bad karma for the next life.

◆ The Catholic Church, Evangelical Protestantism, Conservative Judaism and Jehovah's Witness have all declared abortion to be wrong under any circumstances because they believe that it involves the direct and intentional destruction of unborn human life. This is often referred to as the *'pro-life'* stance.

Catholic teaching on abortion

From the very outset, Christianity has opposed abortion:

◆ The first-century document called the Didache (i.e. the Teaching of the Twelve Apostles) taught that:

You shall not kill the embryo by abortion nor cause the newborn to perish.

◆ In AD 175 the Christian philosopher Athenagoras wrote of how:

We regard the foetus in the womb as a created being and therefore an object of God's care.

The Catholic Church has consistently taught that *unborn* human life is *innocent* life. As such, it has always condemned abortion as *immoral* because it violates the Fifth Commandment, which grants the innocent human being an absolute right to life.

The medical evidence

Although opinions differ among medical experts, a strong case, consistent with science, can be made for the idea that human life begins at conception.* Consider how an adult human being is the result of a long process of *continuous* growth, then reflect on the various stages of this process in reverse order:

◆ before one is an *adult*, one is a *teenager*;
◆ before one is a *teenager*, one is a *child*;
◆ before one is a *child*, one is an *infant* (i.e. newborn baby);
◆ before one is an *infant*, one is a *foetus* in the womb;
◆ before one is a *foetus*, one is an *embryo*;
◆ before one is an *embryo*, one is a *zygote* (i.e. a fertilised ovum), which is smaller than the full stop at the end of this sentence.

From conception to adulthood, there is no break in the process of human development. Each stage of

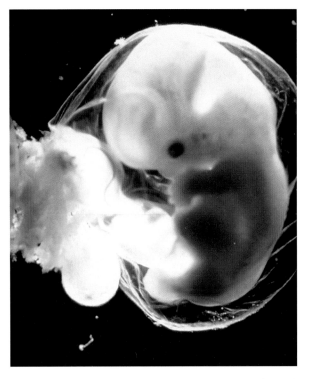

6–8 weeks: the embryo is now developing a sense of smell. Clearly visible are hands, with fingers. Hindbrain, midbrain, brain blood flow, forebrain, pigmented eye, hand, heart and liver, umbilical cord, foot plate.

development lies on a continuum and each is the full expression of humanity appropriate to its own stage.

It is reasonable to choose conception as the start of human life because conception marks a clear and momentous *qualitative change*. The entire genetic plan that directs our development into mature adults is present in the zygote: no new genetic information is added at any later stage. Therefore to select any other point on the subsequent continuum would be an arbitrary choice.

Accordingly, the child in the womb should *not* be referred to as 'a potential person'. Pregnancy is the period in which a new human being can *mature*. He/she does not become human, rather he/she is *already* human, possessing all the capacities necessary to grow into a full adult. Thus, it is reasonable and equitable to argue that there is a moral obligation on each of us to maintain the utmost respect for human life from conception onwards and to do all that is possible to protect the right to life of the unborn child.

Actual size: the embryo grows rapidly throughout the first trimester.
By week 12, most of the body systems are already present, albeit in miniature form.

28 days	32 days	36 days	40 days	42 days	44 days	51 days	52 days	56 days
4 mm	4.5 mm	6 mm	8 mm	11 mm	13–17 mm	18–22 mm	22–24 mm	27–31 mm

Questions

1. Explain the following terms:
   (a) 'pro-choice';
   (b) 'pro-life'.

2. Read the following statement:

   Abortion is one of the most emotive and politically charged issues.
   (Andrew Goddard, *A Pocket Guide to Ethical Issues*.)

   Do you agree/disagree with this assessment? Give reasons for your answer.

3. 'Christianity has opposed abortion from the very outset.'

   What is the evidence to support this claim?

4. The Catholic Church teaches that:

   There is a moral obligation on each person to maintain the utmost respect for human life from the moment of conception onwards.

   Why does it hold this view?

5. Read the following statement:

   The difference between the day-old or hour-old embryo and the human adult is one of degree of maturity only; not of essential nature; the adult is a mature member of the species, whereas the embryo is a human person whose characteristic human powers and potentialities have only just begun to be developed and actualised.

   (Agneta Sutton, Linacre Centre.)

   (a) What point does Agneta Sutton make about the *humanity* of the unborn child?
   (b) What evidence is there to support this view?

Abortion:
Arguments For and Against

FOR	AGAINST
1. It is sometimes claimed that: *A woman has an absolute right to do with her body whatsoever she chooses.* Many people who personally oppose abortion and many women who would never consider having an abortion themselves nevertheless support a woman's right to choose on this issue. They do so on the basis that it is her body and she is therefore entitled to decide whether or not she will have the baby and all that this would mean for her life afterwards.	**1.** There are a number of difficulties with this argument: **A.** If one accepts that women, or indeed men, have absolute rights over their own bodies, this can lead to supporting unacceptable situations, such as: <ul><li>a person is free to mutilate him/herself;</li><li>a man could insist that it is his absolute right to do what he wants with his body, even if this involved committing rape.</li></ul> Therefore, this argument cannot be sustained. A person's right over his/her own body is not absolute. **B.** The foetus is *not* a part of the woman's body. Consider the following: <ul><li>the unborn child has his/her own separate gender identity from the moment of conception. It would be very difficult to account for a differently gendered (i.e. male) part of a woman's body if the foetus were a part of her;</li><li>the unborn child has his/her own unique genetic code and from early on in the pregnancy has his/her own heart and circulatory system;</li><li>the foetus is *not* part of the woman. He/she is attached to the mother and carried within her body.</li></ul> **C.** It is wrong to concentrate solely on the issue of rights here. One must also take *responsibilities* into account. If a man and a woman mutually consent to sexual intercourse, they should not selfishly choose to ignore the consequences of their action. They are responsible for a new human life.

FOR	AGAINST
2. It is sometimes asserted that: *A woman should not be forced to continue with her pregnancy when it may cause her overwhelming hardship.* This assertion holds that, without the option of abortion, a woman (especially if she is young, poor and single) would be condemned to a life of poverty and lost opportunities. An abortion, it is argued, might save her from any damaging long-term consequences, in terms of career, education and relationships, caused by giving birth to a child.	**2.** There are two difficulties with this argument: **A.** This argument assumes that the unborn child is *not* a person. The argument can only work by making this assumption. Otherwise, this argument could be used as the basis for killing all those people who place any kind of burden, financial or otherwise, on our society. Obviously society refrains from doing so because it is accepted that those people who are a financial burden are persons with rights, especially the right to life. The fact that they are a cost on the state is irrelevant to their right to continue living. Only if one can demonstrate that the foetus in the womb is not a person can this argument stand up. **B.** This argument confuses finding a solution with the elimination of the problem. True, a woman may become so desperate that she believes that abortion is the only course open to her. However, there is an alternative to abortion in the case of an unwanted pregnancy. The woman can have the baby and offer him/her for adoption. There are many couples only too willing to offer her child a loving home.
3. It is sometimes said that: *It is wrong to force a woman to bring an unwanted child into the world.* This view is held by those who claim that unwanted children are more likely to be born into and reared in deeply troubled and unhappy circumstances. As a result, these unwanted children are claimed to be more likely than others to be victims of abuse and neglect. It is therefore proposed that abortion is the best option in the case of an unwanted pregnancy as a child born in such circumstances would have little chance of having a happy, healthy and fulfilling life.	**3.** There are a number of difficulties with this line of argument. **A.** It assumes that the unborn child is *not* a person. He/she *is* a human being with a right to life. **B.** It also assumes that the value of any child's life is determined by the degree to which he/she is wanted. However, the question of whether or not the unborn child is wanted has no bearing on his/her right to life. Otherwise, this line of argument could be used to justify the killing of other unwanted groups in society.

FOR	AGAINST
	C. There is no evidence to support the claim that there is a necessary link between a child being unwanted and being abused or neglected later.
	D. Again, this argument confuses eliminating a problem with solving it. The unborn child is a person with a right to life. If the mother is unable, for whatever reason, to care for or cope with her child, she has the alternative of putting the child up for adoption.

4. It is sometimes claimed that:

A woman who has become pregnant due to rape or incest should not be forced to continue with the pregnancy.

This is undoubtedly one of the most powerful arguments in support of a woman's right to choose to have an abortion.

A woman who is a victim of rape or incest did not consent to becoming pregnant. She is the victim of a brutal and vicious crime where a sexual act was forced upon her against her will. She is *not* responsible for what has happened. Consequently, she should not be forced to continue with a pregnancy due to rape or incest.

For society to force a woman to carry a child conceived as a result of rape or incest to term would, it is claimed, be an act of unjustifiable cruelty. It would only inflict further pain and victimise the woman a second time by asking her to continue the pregnancy against her will.

For this reason, many people maintain that the law of the state should allow an exception to permit abortion in cases of rape and incest.

4. Rape is a horrendous crime. It is a violent, brutal and dehumanising act. Besides the physical harm and violation of rape, it often leaves long-term emotional scars that can damage a victim's capacity to build intimate relationships.

However, the argument that a woman who is a victim of rape or incest should be permitted to have an abortion if she becomes pregnant as a result of such crimes is based on two incorrect assumptions:

A. It assumes that the unborn child is *not* a human being.

B. It assumes that one can justify the killing of another human being when it is done to relieve the mental anguish endured by the woman who is a victim of rape.

The number of pregnancies that result from rape and incest are very few, but, though rare, they do sometimes occur. This places the victim in a cruel dilemma. She needs support and understanding. However, she is now carrying a new human life. This child has a right to life that deserves to be protected.

One action that is wrong (i.e. the rape) should *not* be considered as justification for another act that is also wrong (i.e. an abortion).

FOR	AGAINST
	Rape is a despicable act and the victim deserves the utmost sympathy and support. However, the child in her womb is *not* at fault. His/her life should not be ended because of the circumstances surrounding his/her beginnings. The unborn child has done nothing wrong and deserves to be nurtured and protected, rather than punished for the crime of his/her father. Further, there is a real danger that having an abortion could only serve to compound the trauma of the rape victim. Some women who have given birth to babies after rape have stated that at least something good has come out of such a terrible experience.
5. It is sometimes claimed that *abortion is needed where there is a risk of maternal suicide.*	**5.** Suicide, either during pregnancy or in the early post-natal period, is a very *rare* event. • Pregnancy seems to be *protective* against suicide. Indeed, UK government statistics indicate that the risk of suicide associated with pregnancy is one-eighteenth that of a non-pregnant woman of the same age. This may be due to hormonal changes caused by a pregnancy or by some other, as yet undiscovered factor(s). • If a woman is feeling suicidal during her pregnancy, she is *more* likely to respond to appropriate psychiatric treatment if she continues the pregnancy to term than if she has an abortion. Proceeding with an abortion would most likely serve only to deepen her depression. Indeed, a woman is more likely to commit suicide after an abortion than during a pregnancy. (Sources: 1. *Psychiatric Journal of the University of Ottawa*, Vol. 14, 1989. 2. *Irish Medical Journal*, Vol. 75, 1982. 3. *British Medical Journal*, Vol. 30, 1991.)

FOR	AGAINST

FOR

6. It is sometimes claimed that:

A woman should be permitted to have an abortion where the unborn child is diagnosed as disabled.

Pre-natal tests are now medically routine. The two most widely used tests are:

- *Ultrasound scanning*

Here very high-frequency soundwaves are passed into the uterus and the returning echoes are converted into moving pictures of the foetus, which are displayed on a monitor. This is usually an exciting and reassuring experience for an expectant mother.

- *Amniocentesis*

In this procedure, a small sample of the amniotic fluid surrounding the developing baby is removed and the foetal cells within it are examined to detect any abnormalities. (There is a one in 100 chance of amniocentesis causing a miscarriage.)

Usually these tests give reassuring results. Sometimes, however, they can give heartbreaking news that the unborn child has a severe disability.

Since currently there are very few disabilities treatable once detected, abortion is often considered as an appropriate course of action in such a tragic situation. For example, a survey has revealed that 96 per cent of French women who were informed that their unborn children had a disability subsequently had an abortion. Usually such abortions are conducted late in pregnancy (see *The Tablet*, 2 March 2002).

Sometimes the woman and/or her husband/partner may simply not want to raise a child with a particular disability. Again, powerful pressure may be applied to the woman to get her to agree to an abortion.

Often, it is argued that choosing abortion is the best choice for all concerned. The woman may recognise that the foetus is a human being. However, she may genuinely believe that being born with a particular disability will make the child's life 'not worth ▶

AGAINST

6. It is an enormous shock to discover that one's child is disabled, particularly when one has little or no experience of disability. There can be no down-playing the seriousness of the situation or any underestimating the enormous, life-changing consequences of such news. However, there are a number of serious difficulties with the argument to permit abortions in the case of detected foetal disability.

Consider the following:

A. It assumes that the unborn child is *not* a human person. The disabled child in the womb is no less a human being than one who is not disabled. Who has the right to end his/her life?

B. This argument assumes that a disabled person's life, both unborn and born, is *not* worth living. As a result, it could be used to justify killing disabled children not only before but also after birth (i.e. infanticide).

C. This argument is *inconsistent*. How can society support the rights of born disabled people (e.g. access to education, employment, housing, transport), while at the same time denying them the most basic human right—the right to life—while they are still in their mothers' wombs?

D. There is a danger that by accepting abortion in such admittedly tragic circumstances, it may, albeit unintentionally, foster the idea that children are possessions that should be subject to quality control and, if necessary, rejection. This would mean a complete abandonment of the whole notion of the child as a gift from God who is to be welcomed unconditionally and cherished, whether disabled or not.

Families who have to care for a disabled child ▶

FOR	AGAINST
living'. She might therefore think that it would be irresponsible for her to give birth to a child who, in her opinion, would enjoy so little quality of life. She might also be concerned about other factors, such as her own ability to cope with and care for the child, and her responsibilities towards her husband/partner and any other children she might have. As a result, the woman faced with such a crisis pregnancy could believe, or be convinced, that she has a moral obligation to have an abortion.	need a great deal of long-term support. This does require investment of State resources, but as citizens of the State the disabled are entitled to it and should receive it. Appropriate educational, medical and residential facilities and support for their carers should be provided. All too often, however, the families of the disabled have to struggle to secure their basic entitlements. This is clearly wrong. In addition to doing an injustice to the disabled person, this sends a message to the wider society that some lives are *not* of equal value. A society that genuinely wishes to live up to its claim of being fair and pluralist will *welcome* the disabled and do its utmost to help them to fulfil their potential and *support* those who care for them.

Questions

1. Examine the arguments for and against abortion in the light of the evidence presented. Which do you find the most convincing: the argument for abortion or that against it? Give reasons for your choice.

2. *Adoption* may be defined as: *the permanent legal transfer of parental rights and duties in respect of a child from one person or institution to another.*
   In recent years the number of Irish-born babies given up for adoption has fallen dramatically. In most cases, where a single woman is faced with a crisis pregnancy, she now tends either to accept *lone parenthood* or chooses *abortion* rather than adoption.
   What are the long-term benefits of adoption for each of the following:
   (a) the unborn child;
   (b) the woman with a crisis pregnancy;
   (c) the adoptive parents?

Reflection

Read the following poem by the Australian poet Bruce Dawe.

The Sticking Point

I am a man, I know
—but I still say
that life is life
and death is surely death
—to kill the growing child
in any way
is to rob the future
of its breath.

The means are many,
the result's the same:
life that already is
must cease to be
—I am not reassured
that when they came
such deaths were in the name
of liberty …

I only know
that every year the world
solves the insoluble
at infinite cost,
that every morning petals
part—unfurled
are brought to nothing by
a killing frost …

Questions

1. Explain the poet's attitude to abortion. Use quotations from the poem to support your statements.

2. What do you think he means by the line, 'the world solves the insoluble at infinite cost'?

3. How might this line be applied to issues such as the care of the elderly, the severely disabled or the mentally ill? Explain your answer.

B. CLONING

Introduction

Cloning may be defined as:

> *the process whereby an identical copy of a biological entity is produced.*

To date, a wide variety of animals have been cloned, ranging from frogs to sheep. Scientists are hoping to use cloning technology to preserve certain endangered species from extinction. Some even hope to use this technology in the future to re-introduce extinct species, such as the mammoth.

Although the experimental research necessary to produce a cloned human being is *banned* in most countries, this has *not* proven an effective barrier to the ambitions of some. Several scientists with considerable expertise in *genetics* (i.e. the study of heredity) have publicly declared their desire to be the first to achieve the cloning of a human being.

At this point it is necessary to distinguish between two forms of cloning:

◆ reproductive;
◆ therapeutic.

We shall examine each in turn.

Reproductive Cloning

The aim of *reproductive cloning* is to bring a cloned human child to full term. Why might people be tempted to do this?

Consider the following story:

The fog on the M4 was exceptionally dense as the Robinson family drove toward London on 20 November 2018. Their only child Susan, aged 4, was playing happily with her dolls on the back seat. After years of unsuccessfully trying for a baby the Robinsons had eventually decided to use in vitro fertilisation to have Susan, so she was especially cherished. Her long eyelashes and dimples were the spitting image of her mum, whereas even at that young age her long limbs held great promise of future athletic prowess, or so her proud father liked to think.

Suddenly a pile-up loomed out of the fog in front of them. Mr Robinson slammed on the brakes. His quick responses prevented their car diving into the mangled heap of wrecked cars ahead, but unfortunately the lorry driver behind was not so alert, sliding into their rear with a sickening thud. Seconds later the shocked parents found themselves clutching Susan's lifeless form as they huddled on the embankment, waiting for help to arrive.

Minutes later, after a short but fevered discussion, Mrs Robinson called CLON777 on her mobile and as the fog began to clear a helicopter landed in a nearby field, CLONE-AID emblazoned across its fuselage. A white-coated medical technician leapt from the helicopter and was soon taking tiny skin samples from Susan's limp body. Minutes later the samples were being stimulated in a nearby CLONE-AID laboratory to establish cell cultures.

Several months went by whilst the Robinsons grieved for little Susan, but finally they could contain themselves no longer. They wanted a replacement Susan and they wanted her now. Fortunately Mrs Robinson already had viable eggs frozen as a result of her cycle of in vitro fertilisation. The great day came. In the CLONE-AID laboratory, with its picture of Dolly the sheep proudly displayed on the wall, the process of 'nucleus transfer' began (see figure for a description of how cloning can be carried out). A nucleus was removed from one of Susan's cultured skin cells. This single nucleus contained the cell's DNA with its genetic instructions to build a new Susan. Carefully the nucleus was placed in a small dish with one of Mrs Robinson's eggs from which the nucleus had been removed. A small electric current was zapped through the cell suspension and the nucleus fused with the egg cell to produce a tiny embryo. This procedure was repeated several times, to generate several embryos that were carefully screened over the next few days to check for any abnormalities before one of them was implanted in

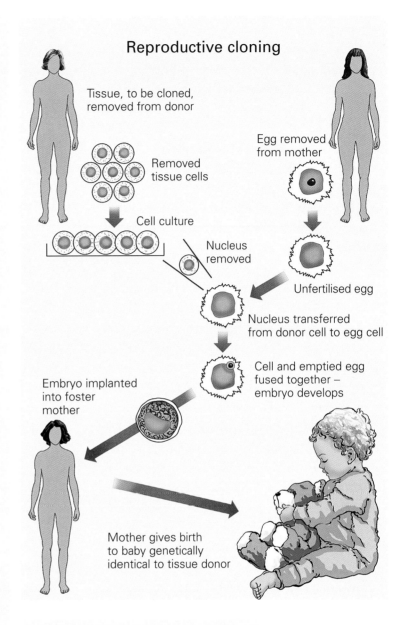

Reproductive cloning

Tissue, to be cloned, removed from donor

Removed tissue cells

Cell culture

Egg removed from mother

Nucleus removed

Unfertilised egg

Nucleus transferred from donor cell to egg cell

Cell and emptied egg fused together – embryo develops

Embryo implanted into foster mother

Mother gives birth to baby genetically identical to tissue donor

Mrs Robinson. Nine months later the Robinsons held in their arms a pink and gorgeous looking 'replacement Susan,' complete with dimples, prominent eyelashes and long limbs.

(From D. Alexander and R.S. White, *Science, Faith and Ethics.*)

Only science-fiction? At the moment, yes, as well as illegal. But technology advances and legal prohibitions can be lifted, given sufficient public demand.

The traumatic loss of a child in such tragic circumstances might cause some grieving parents to at least consider, if not actually proceed with, reproductive cloning. But if it were possible for them to pursue the cloning of their deceased child, would the cloned child produced be the *same* person?

The answer is *No*. Although the clone would have the same DNA as the original, deceased donor, he/she would be a different person.
Consider:

◆ the character of every human being is shaped by a *complex interplay* between each individual and his/her environment. Identical twins, for instance, are notable for their *differences* as well as their similarities;

◆ the donor and his/her clone would each undergo a different childhood. There would be no way to exactly replicate all the significant events that took place during the donor child's life. Thus, the clone would inevitably have a different set of life experiences, which would mould his/her personality in *different* ways from that of the donor;

◆ although physically identical, a clone of Leonardo da Vinci might become an accountant rather than emulate his donor by becoming a great artist.

All of this gives rise to certain questions.

For the parents

◆ Would they be disappointed to find out that the clone had different talents and interests from the donor child?

◆ Would they accept the clone once they discovered that he/she was a different person from the donor?

◆ How would they react to the discovery that each child, each human being, is unique and unrepeatable?

For the clone

◆ How would he/she react to the knowledge that he/she is a copy of someone else?

◆ Would he/she be able to cope with the parents' expectations for his/her future?

◆ How would all of this affect his/her mental health?

Clearly, the introduction of reproductive cloning could have serious and harmful consequences for people's lives. These do not stop here, however. As Dr Ian Wilmut of the Roslin Institute, which cloned Dolly the Sheep in 1996, has pointed out, there are enormous medical and moral problems inherent in the entire cloning process. It took 277 attempts before one cloned lamb was delivered: all the others either aborted spontaneously or resulted in malformed animals. Further, cloned animals suffer from premature ageing.

The creation of a new human life is too awesome a mystery to be meddled with in such a destructive fashion. Cloning is, and is likely to remain, experimental, with high risks of:

◆ miscarriage;

◆ deformities in newborn children;

◆ premature ageing.

As we saw earlier, there are strong grounds for arguing that human life is entitled to protection from the moment of conception onwards. The loss of human life inflicted to achieve one viable cloned offspring would be staggering.

Certainly, there is a need to treat the plight of those who lose a child in tragic circumstances with compassion and understanding. But experimenting with children—physically and psychologically—is *not* a morally justifiable way forward. If, however, a cloned human being is ever born, as may well happen in the future, then he/she should be accepted as a person in his/her *own* right and treated as being as much a member of the human community as anyone else.

Questions

1. What is *cloning*?

2. What is the aim of *reproductive cloning*?

3. Why is it claimed that, although a clone would have identical DNA to its donor, the clone would be a *different* person?

4. Examine the possible consequences of reproductive cloning for both:
   (a) the parents of a cloned child;
   (b) the clone him/herself.

5. Consider the following statement:

   Cloning is, and is likely to remain, highly experimental.

   What are the risks involved in reproductive cloning?

Therapeutic Cloning

Every human body contains stem cells. These cells develop into some 200 or more different kinds of cells that make up the different organs of the human body. The aim of therapeutic cloning is to produce cloned human embryos that are intentionally killed and their stem cells harvested, cultivated and programmed for specific medical purposes, e.g. the treatment of a number of debilitating diseases, such as AIDS, cancer, diabetes and Parkinson's. It is claimed that stem-cell therapy has already been used to enable Michael May, an American who has been blind since the age of three, to have his eyesight partially restored.

Advocates of therapeutic cloning point out that they are *not* seeking to create babies and bring them to term. Their opponents point out that once a woman's ovum has been implanted with a new nucleus and stimulated to begin its development, a new human life is present.

Some supporters of therapeutic cloning claim that if it helps to find cures for fatal diseases, this would justify the destruction of some human embryos. However, this line of thinking reduces people to their *usefulness*. The human embryo is treated as nothing more than a *pawn* in medical research, with no value of his/her own. Science has revealed that a human embryo is *not* some blob of tissue without purpose or plan. At the moment of conception a *new* human being is formed, with a *unique* genetic make-up that is *distinct* from both the father and the mother. The embryo only requires time in order to grow and develop into a recognisable human being.

There are strong grounds for arguing that unborn

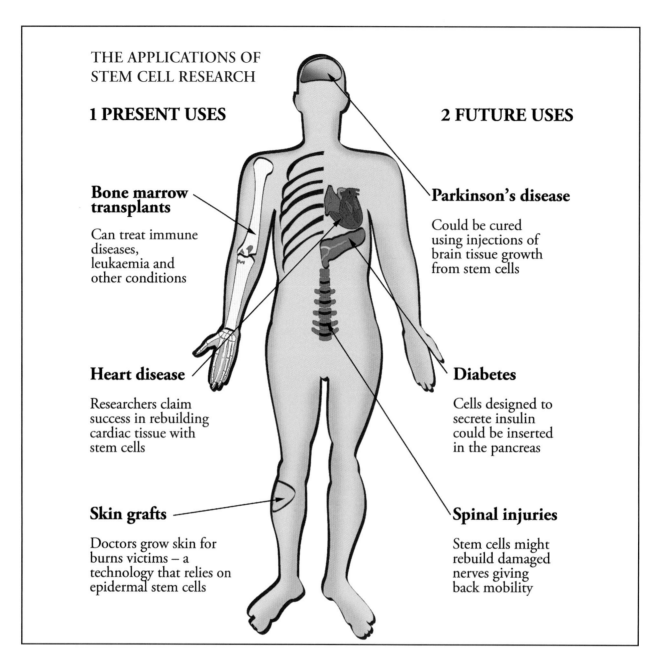

THE APPLICATIONS OF STEM CELL RESEARCH

1 PRESENT USES

Bone marrow transplants

Can treat immune diseases, leukaemia and other conditions

Heart disease

Researchers claim success in rebuilding cardiac tissue with stem cells

Skin grafts

Doctors grow skin for burns victims – a technology that relies on epidermal stem cells

2 FUTURE USES

Parkinson's disease

Could be cured using injections of brain tissue growth from stem cells

Diabetes

Cells designed to secrete insulin could be inserted in the pancreas

Spinal injuries

Stem cells might rebuild damaged nerves giving back mobility

life is innocent human life and that, as such, has an absolute right to life. To kill an innocent human being, at whatever point in his/her life, even with the intention of helping another person, can *never* be morally justified.

Therefore, cloning human embryos to kill them and harvest certain stem cells from them is *morally unacceptable*. This does *not* mean that there is a need to oppose all stem-cell research—only that which

involves the destruction of human embryos. There are *other*, morally acceptable routes for obtaining stem cells: they can be taken from *adult* individuals.

Although embryonic stem cells are said to be easier to reproduce and manipulate in the laboratory, it would appear that adult stem cells have a broader range of options for being re-programmed into other cell types than was previously thought. Adult stem cells are now being used to treat leukaemia, juvenile diabetes, spinal chord injury, immune deficiency and corneal damage. This is a very promising field of research, which one day might yield great medical benefits.

The Moral Dimension to Scientific Research

Scientific developments that offer genuine service to the human community are always to be welcomed because they can materially improve the lives of everyone in society. However, as Philippe Busquin, the former EU Research Commissioner, has commented:

Not everything scientifically possible and technologically feasible is necessarily desirable or admissible. (*The Tablet*, 1.12.2001.)

The Abrahamic religions teach that God commands human beings to transform the natural world, but *not* to toy with it. Each new human life is a gift from God to be cherished. The practice of cloning—whether reproductive or therapeutic—fails to respect the dignity of the human person.

Questions

1. What is the aim of therapeutic cloning?

2. What reasons do its supporters put forward to justify it?

3. What are the arguments raised against therapeutic cloning?

4. What is the alternative to using stem cells harvested from cloned embryos?

5. Since the time of Hippocrates, doctors have accepted that they should

   First, do no harm.

   Does cloning—both reproductive and therapeutic—violate this rule? Give reasons for your answer.

Life Issues: Euthanasia

On death and dying

Most, if not all, people are anxious about death, whether they are theists or atheists.

Death is defined as

the permanent ending of all the functions that keep an organism alive.

A person is pronounced *dead* when it has been established that:
- his/her brain has ceased to control the vital functions of his/her body;
- there is no evidence of muscular activity or blood pressure;
- he/she is unable to breathe without the aid of a life-support machine.

The word **dying** refers to:

the way in which a person's life comes to an end.

Human beings are the only creatures on Earth that

Dance of Death (sixteenth century).

can appreciate that all things have a limited lifespan and that death is *inevitable*. Nevertheless, talk of death often makes many of us feel *uncomfortable*. Perhaps it is because we realise that:
- death may come without warning, even for those in good health, through accident or act of violence inflicted by another;
- death may not occur until a person is quite elderly, but then after a prolonged battle with illness;

even though we may be surrounded by our loved ones when we die, each of us has to face death *alone*.

Meaning

Euthanasia is a very controversial issue about which many people have strong feelings and hold sharply opposing views.

The term *euthanasia* is derived from two Greek words:

- *eu*, meaning *good*;
- *thanatos*, meaning *death*.

A literal translation would be *a good death*. However, the term *euthanasia* is often used in contemporary debate with quite different meanings. Consider the following diagram:

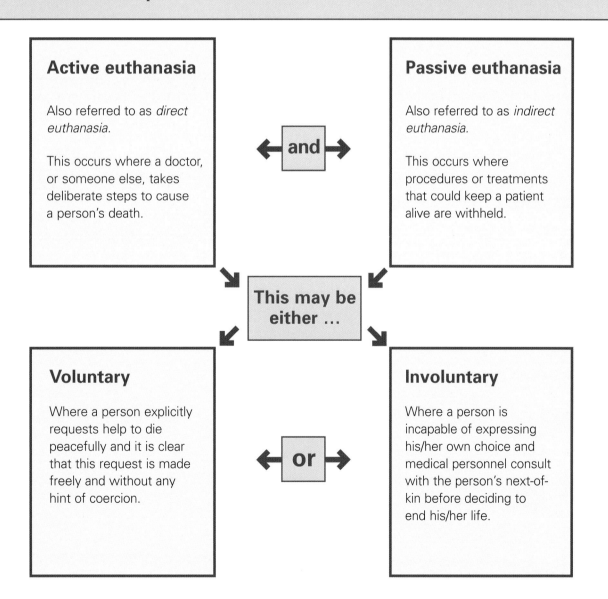

There is an important distinction that must be made between …

Active euthanasia

Also referred to as *direct euthanasia*.

This occurs where a doctor, or someone else, takes deliberate steps to cause a person's death.

and

Passive euthanasia

Also referred to as *indirect euthanasia*.

This occurs where procedures or treatments that could keep a patient alive are withheld.

This may be either …

Voluntary

Where a person explicitly requests help to die peacefully and it is clear that this request is made freely and without any hint of coercion.

or

Involuntary

Where a person is incapable of expressing his/her own choice and medical personnel consult with the person's next-of-kin before deciding to end his/her life.

Examples of how these terms are applied to concrete situations are:

◆ where a terminally ill person freely requests that he/she be given an overdose of pain-killing drugs to cause his/her immediate death:

➡ **Active voluntary euthanasia;**

◆ where someone gives a comatose person a lethal injection, causing his/her death:

➡ **Active non-voluntary euthanasia;**

◆ where a doctor accedes to the previously stated wishes of a person *not* to be resuscitated in the event of another heart attack:

➡ Passive **voluntary euthanasia.**

◆ where a doctor withdraws an intravenous feeding drip from a comatose person causing him/her to die from dehydration and starvation:

➡ **Passive non-voluntary euthanasia.**

Contemporary Interest

Euthanasia is usually advocated for reasons of compassion for anyone afflicted with a terminal illness.

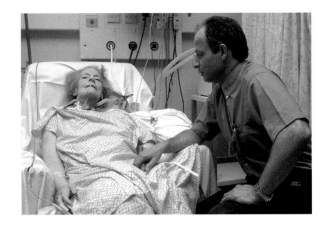

Pro-euthanasia activists argue that it should be an option for anyone in such a tragic situation. Indeed, many people in the developed world have grown frightened by the prospect of having to endure an agonising, lingering death while hooked up to machines and mostly cut-off from human contact in the unfamiliar surroundings of a hospital ward. The idea that euthanasia offers a person the means to liberate him/herself from undergoing such an experience makes it seem an attractive one to a growing number of people.

Euthanasia is currently *illegal* in Ireland, but there has been a significant change in public attitudes towards it in other EU States in recent years. In 2001 The Netherlands legalised euthanasia as an option in terminally ill cases; Belgium followed suit in 2002.

Questions

1. What is a literal translation of *'euthanasia'*?

2. Explain the meaning of each of the following:
active euthanasia;
passive euthanasia;
voluntary euthanasia;
involuntary euthanasia. ➡

3. Give examples of each of the following:
active voluntary euthanasia;
active non-voluntary euthanasia;
passive voluntary euthanasia;
passive non-voluntary euthanasia.

4. Why might euthanasia appear to be an attractive course of action to some people today?

Different views

Opinions are divided within the major religions as to the morality of euthanasia.

◆ Most Hindus are opposed to euthanasia in any form and in any circumstances because they view it as a harmful act that creates bad karma.

◆ Other Hindus disagree with this. They follow the teaching of Lord Krishna in the *Bhagavad Gita* that the soul cannot be harmed and claim that where the patient has no quality of life, euthanasia is an acceptable course of action.

◆ The overwhelming majority of Muslims reject euthanasia in any form and in any circumstances because:
(a) they believe it is forbidden in the Qur'an;
(b) they view life as a testing-ground where we must learn to cope bravely with whatever life brings until it reaches its natural end.
A small minority of Muslims accept euthanasia, though only in very limited circumstances.

◆ Most Jews are opposed to euthanasia in any form and under any circumstances. They believe that it is forbidden by the Fifth Commandment. Some Jews disagree with this. They believe that striving to keep a patient alive in a situation where doctors no longer believe treatments offer any

Dr Jack Kevorkian is a controversial, US-based advocate of the right of patients to opt for euthanasia or assisted suicide.

improvement is mistaken. To maintain a person's life any further in such circumstances would be to act against God's will, as it would unnecessarily delay the person's soul from being received into the afterlife by God. Accordingly, in certain tragic circumstances, euthanasia would be permissible.

Most Catholics, Orthodox and Evangelical Protestants are firmly opposed to euthanasia in any form and in any circumstances. We shall turn now to consider why this is the case.

Catholic teaching on euthanasia

The Catholic Church teaches that:
- God alone is the creator of life;
- human beings have a special dignity and worth because they are made in the image and likeness of God (Genesis 1:26–27);
- the deliberate killing of an innocent human being can *never* be morally justified, whether he/she is an embryo in the womb, an infant, an elderly person or someone who is enduring a terminal illness;
- human beings are called by God to *cherish* and *protect* life. They should *avoid* any action that unjustly seeks to destroy it.

It is because of this that the Catholic Church has declared euthanasia to be *morally unacceptable* (Catechism of the Catholic Church, No. 2277). This view is shared by the overwhelming majority of other Christian denominations. Contrary to opinions expressed by some of their critics, these Christian Churches readily admit to the complexity of the issues involved in euthanasia. Further, they acknowledge the awful plight of the tormented and incurably ill person. However, they ask us to remember that:
- any response to another person's needs should seek to respect and uphold his/her human dignity;
- true compassion leads us to share another person's pain; it does not accept deliberately ending the life of a person whose sufferings *other* people either cannot or will not bear;

- the person who requests euthanasia is really crying out for loving care and support in a time of terrible emotional upheaval and physical suffering.

At this point an important distinction needs to be made between *proportionate* treatment and *disproportionate* treatment.

Proportionate treatment
This refers to all medicines, treatments and operations that offer a reasonable hope of benefit for a person and *can* be obtained *without* inflicting excessive pain or burden on him/her.

Disproportionate treatment
This refers to all medicines, treatments and operations that do *not* offer a reasonable hope of benefit for a person and *cannot* be obtained *without* inflicting excessive pain or burden on him/her.

There is said to be *no* moral obligation on medical personnel to use disproportionate means to prolong a person's life in cases where:

- there is *no* likelihood of the person recovering from this illness; and
- any attempt to prolong his/her life by means of painful procedures would *only* inflict further, unnecessary suffering on the person without any foreseeable benefit.

In such tragic circumstances there *is* a morally acceptable *alternative* to euthanasia that fully respects the dignity of the terminally ill person. This is referred to as *palliative care.*

Questions

1. Read the following statement:

   'Life belongs to God and should only be taken by God.'

   How would the members of the world's non-Christian religions react to this statement?

2. Why do the overwhelming majority of Christian denominations reject euthanasia as *morally unacceptable*?

3. Explain the difference between *proportionate* treatment and *disproportionate* treatment.

4. In what circumstances do the majority of Christian Churches teach that there is no obligation to use disproportionate means to prolong a person's life?

Palliative Care

There still persists a widely held, but *mistaken,* belief that a terminally ill person must either die slowly in unrelieved agony *or* accept euthanasia. Nothing could be further from the truth.

Palliative care as offered by *the Hospice Movement* shows that the skilful use of current techniques of pain management *can* provide relief from the suffering associated with most terminal illnesses, or at least make it tolerable. This has the great benefit of enabling a terminally ill person to properly *prepare* for his/her death.

In palliative care, medical personnel use drug therapy *solely* with the intention of relieving pain. They never deliberately set out to cause a person's death. In some *exceptional* cases palliative care may have the effect of hastening the person's death. However, this *differs* from euthanasia in that the person's death is *not* the intended result of any treatment given. Palliative care seeks only to relieve the pain being endured by a terminally ill person, so that he/she may prepare for death and die with dignity.

The Hospice

A hospice is a nursing home in which the medical staff and facilities are dedicated to the provision of

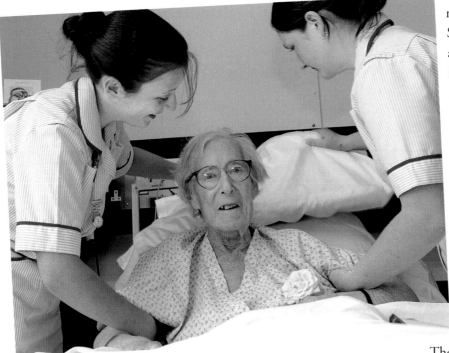

medicines. In contrast, Cicely Saunders introduced a new approach to pain control. This involves the needs of the terminally ill being anticipated to prevent the onset of pain. This usually enables a dying person to remain conscious and able to interact with loved ones for some time. Careful monitoring of his/her condition means the person's pain can be managed until his/her life comes to its *natural* end.

Though crucial, the medicinal care provided is only *part* of what the hospice has to offer. The hospice seeks to care for the *whole* person—emotionally, socially and spiritually, as well as physically. For this reason counselling and support are provided to help the terminally ill person and his/her loved ones *to prepare* for death.

Thanks to the inspiration of Cicely Saunders, there are now hospices dotted around the globe. But there are not yet enough of them. There is an urgent need for greater investment in the kind of palliative care provided by hospices, in particular the provision of more beds and trained medical personnel.

compassionate care for the terminally ill, who can either go there to live permanently or for short breaks to give their home-carers a rest.

The modern hospice movement began in 1967 when a Christian doctor named Cicely Saunders opened St Christopher's Hospice in London. Until then, doctors had generally responded to the pain endured by the terminally ill by giving them intermittent sedation, often rationed for fear that their dying patients would become addicted to such

Questions

1. (a) What does *palliative care* involve?
    (b) How is it *morally different* from euthanasia?

2. (a) What is *a hospice*?
    (b) Who founded the modern hospice movement?
    (c) How is a terminally ill person's pain managed in a hospice?
    (d) What does it mean to say that the hospice *seeks to care for the whole person*?

Founder of the hospice movement who transformed the care and treatment of the terminally ill

Cicely Saunders is regarded as the mother of the modern hospice movement. At St Christopher's Hospice, Sydenham, south London, founded in 1967, she charted new approaches in techniques for treatment of the terminally ill, based on her Christian belief that no human life, no matter how wretched, should be denied dignity and love.

Though the philosophy underlying St Christopher's was, from the outset, Christian, it welcomes patients of any persuasion or none.

Before St Christopher's opened its doors, there had been hospices, mostly run by nuns, which provided comfort for the dying; but they were backward in their understanding of medical techniques. Even on busy hospital wards where many people spent their final hours, very little was known about the management of pain. With a few exceptions, medical and surgical textbooks disregarded the problems of pain control; and chronic pain in the dying was usually either ignored or treated too late, by injection.

Cicely Saunders first had the idea of creating a modern hospice in 1948, when she was working as a lady almoner (medical social worker) at St Thomas's Hospital in London. There she met David Tasma, a young Polish waiter who, having escaped from the Warsaw ghetto, was dying of cancer, in great pain, on a ward she was visiting.

Though he had little English, they spent their time together talking about death and the care of the dying: 'He needed to make his peace with the God of his fathers, and the time to sort out who he was,' she recalled. 'We discussed the idea of somewhere that could have helped him to do this better than a busy hospital ward.'

Cicely Saunders fell deeply in love and, when he died, he left her all he had – £500 –

Dr Cicely Saunders.

and told her: 'I'll be a window in your home.' 'It was as though God was tapping me on the shoulder and telling me "You've got to get on with it",' she recalled.

Carrying Tasma's memory with her, Cicely Saunders became a physician and went on to found St Christopher's Hospice, where she hoped to 'help the dying to live until they die and their families to live on'. She had no new drugs, but showed how, by using them earlier in anticipation of, rather than in response to, the onset of pain, terminally ill patients could be kept comfortable until the end.

As a Christian, she saw dying not as something to be feared, but as a spiritual event which can bring meaning to life and provide an opportunity for reconciliation. In *Living with Dying* (1983), she explained that hospice care involves not only the alleviation of physical pain, but addresses patients' 'mental, social and spiritual pain'.

St Christopher's boasts, among other things, a hairdressing salon, and lays on activities such as creative writing, discussion groups and indoor gardening, reflecting its founder's belief that the last months of life can be lived happily and creatively.

Cicely Saunders believed in the importance of allowing patients to control their own treatment, and recognised the need to work closely with families of the terminally ill. The wards of St Christopher's were light and airy and often teeming with children and pets.

In her campaign to establish a hospice, Cicely Saunders encountered apathy, even outright hostility, from the medical profession.

Though she was widely revered as a sort of secular saint, it was only through being tough and authoritative, and often downright difficult, that she succeeded in forcing the medical profession to acknowledge what medicine can do for the dying.

The movement she began changed the face of death for millions of people, not only the dying, but also those around them.

Cicely Saunders viewed the relief of pain as a vital component in confronting the issue of euthanasia, which became a theme of public debate in the 1970s. She was the guiding influence behind a 1976 Church of England report on dying which argued that everyone should have the right to 'die well', without pain and with dignity.

In rejecting the argument that chronic pain justifies euthanasia, the report drew attention to the fact that correct medical and nursing treatment can usually remove pain or reduce it to a minimum and can help the survivors as much as the dying.

In 1985 Cicely Saunders handed over the reins as medical director of St Christopher's, but soon settled into the role of chairman, continuing to work there until she was well into her eighties. By this time, the hospice had established itself as a teaching and research centre. She also lectured all over the world.

By 1980 the principles of pain relief which she had set out in such works as *Care of the Dying* (1960), *The Management of Terminal Disease* (1978) and *Living With Dying* (1983), had become standard practice in the health service. In 1987 palliative medicine was recognised as a speciality in its own right. In 2000 she stepped down as chairman and became president.

Among numerous awards and honours, she became, in 1997, the first person for more than 100 years to receive an honorary doctorate of medicine from the Archbishop of Canterbury. In 1981 she was awarded the Templeton prize for Progress in Religion.

In 2002 she established the Cicely Saunders Foundation, an international research and education body dedicated to 'improving care at the end of life'.

Cicely Saunders died at St Christopher's Hospice, in July 2005.

(Adapted from *The Daily Telegraph*, 15.7.2005.)

Questions

1. What were the sources of Cicely Saunders' commitment to palliative care for the terminally ill?

2. How would you assess her impact on the issue of care for the dying?

3. Imagine that you are a hospice administrator seeking funding from the Department of Health and Children. Write a letter seeking to convince the relevant minister and his/her officials of the merits of providing this funding.

Euthanasia: Arguments For and Against

FOR	AGAINST
1. Patients with a terminal illness should be able to choose both the time and the way in which they die.	1. Patients with a terminal illness can be very vulnerable: • they are usually anxious about what the future holds for them; • they are often worried about the impact of their illness on their loved ones;

FOR	AGAINST
	• sometimes they may suffer from depression or a false sense of worthlessness. As a result, it can be difficult for a person with a terminal illness to be entirely objective about his/her situation. Those who regularly care for the terminally ill point out that, while people in great pain may request euthanasia, once effective symptom relief has been administered, they are usually very grateful that their request was not granted. Terminally ill patients can come to greatly value both the time they have left with loved ones and whatever quality of life is left to them.
2. Euthanasia ends the suffering of a terminally ill patient and makes death gentle, peaceful and easy.	**2.** The legalisation of euthanasia is often championed by people who have witnessed a loved one die in agony without the benefits of appropriate medical care. However, hospices offer precisely this care for the terminally ill. These special places allow people to die peacefully and without pain. Hospices also help relatives to cope with the death of their loved ones.
3. People should not have to live and endure pain if they have no chance of getting better. It makes more economic sense to allow patients who are terminally ill to die quickly than to keep them alive by using expensive treatments and drugs.	**3.** The legalisation of euthanasia on these grounds could have the following detrimental effects: • Some very ill people and some elderly people may feel that they are a burden both to their families and to a society that is cost-conscious and perhaps short of resources. They could feel under great pressure to request euthanasia. • People who are terminally ill need to know that they are valued and loved, not to feel that they are getting in the way and are considered a waste of time and money. It is important to remember that the way we treat the weakest and most

FOR	AGAINST
	vulnerable people speaks volumes about the true nature of our society.
	• One of the major driving forces behind the exceptional recent medical advances has been the desire to develop treatments for previously fatal illnesses, and to alleviate hitherto unmanageable symptoms. Medical research is essential if medicine is to advance further.
	• If the focus were to change from curing the condition to killing the individual who has the condition, then this whole process would be threatened. The increasing acceptance of prenatal diagnosis and abortion for conditions like spina bifida and cystic fibrosis in many Western countries is threatening the very dramatic progress made in the management of these conditions, especially over the last two decades. Rather than being employed to care and console, funds could be diverted to destroy human life.
4. The legalisation of voluntary euthanasia (i.e. where a patient with a terminal illness asks to die) would allow doctors to take the action they believe is in the best interest of their patients without fear of being prosecuted for breaking the law.	**4.** The Hippocratic Oath states: *I will give no deadly medicine to anyone if asked, nor suggest such counsel.*
	The International Code of Medical Ethics, adopted by the World Medical Association in 1949, declares that a doctor must always bear in mind the obligation to preserve human life from the time of conception onwards. Traditionally, medical ethics codes have rejected euthanasia. They have interpreted a patient's *right to die* to actually confer on a doctor the legal right to kill a patient.
	The reasons for refusing doctors the right to administer euthanasia are:
	• absolute certainty in medical diagnosis is

FOR	AGAINST
	impossible. Doctors are human beings who sometimes make mistakes;
	• some doctors may not be up-to-date in pain-relief techniques;
	• some doctors may be unaware of new treatments, or ones that are impending;
	• voluntary euthanasia could give doctors too much power, which could easily be abused and to which they are not morally entitled;
	• granting such a right to doctors could undermine the whole doctor-patient relationship. Some very ill patients might begin to suspect that they could not trust their doctors to give them appropriate care. They might worry that their doctor would opt for the quickest and most economical solution, even if that was to end their lives against their will;
	• the law is a very powerful educator of the public conscience. When a practice becomes legal, accepted and widely used in society, people cease to have strong feelings about it. This was demonstrated most dramatically in Nazi Germany. Many of those medical personnel involved in the Nazi euthanasia programmes were motivated initially by compassion for their victims. Their consciences, and that of the society which allowed them to do what they did, gradually became numbed and eventually involuntary euthanasia was permitted.
	• The answer is *not* to change the law, but rather to improve our standards of treatment for those who are terminally ill by providing appropriate palliative care.

Questions

1. Having considered the arguments for and against euthanasia, consider the following statements.
   In each case, state whether you agree/disagree. Give reasons for your answers.

   (a) Opponents of euthanasia point to what they consider to be two possible and important consequences of its legalisation:
   - a diminishing of attention to pain treatment;
   - a shifting of the burden of proof of every person's dignity and value, leading to a situation where a person must explain his choice not to request euthanasia to his relatives and to the medical staff.

   (b) The admission, in principle, of euthanasia can easily lead to the *crevasse effect* in as much as this step would create a precedent to extend the practice to the disabled (physically and mentally) who do not suffer so much themselves, but who could, in time, come to be seen as an unnecessary burden on society.

   (c) Euthanasia should be firmly resisted on the grounds that it side-steps true compassionate care and ultimately undermines, rather than respects, patients' dignity. Only the Hospice Movement offers a morally acceptable way forward.

War and Peace

Introduction

Jesus of Nazareth once remarked that there would always be 'wars and rumours of wars' (Matthew 24:6). Indeed, it has been estimated that since the first recorded battle at Armageddon, in 1469 BC, to the present day, there have only been 268 years without a war. Little wonder that Erik Durschmied has written that:

> To understand history, one must understand war, and its consequences.
> (Erik Durschmied, *The Hinges of Battle*.)

War may be defined as:

> *armed hostilities between two or more opposing groups, in which each side puts people forward to fight and to kill one another.*

There is *rarely* a single, clear-cut cause for the outbreak of war. People have fought, and continue to fight, for a complex mixture of reasons. Sadly, the *effects* of such conflicts are, in each case, the same: loss of life and a humanitarian crisis.

The precise *extent* of these effects depends upon:
- the duration of the conflict;
- the types of people and place targeted;
- the kinds of weapons used.

For example, consider one historian's summation of the impact of the First World War:

> *The consequences, both personal and international, of the 'Great War' spanned the world. The empires of Germany, Russia and Austria-Hungary fell, and the British Empire began its inexorable decline. It was a war which was industrial in*

scale and method, a war in which great advances were made in the technology of taking and saving life, a war waged on land, across the oceans, beneath the ground and, for the first time, in the air; it was the source of revolutions: social, scientific, political, medical, industrial and civil— and it laid the political, social and technical foundation for a second – and even more devastating – global conflict twenty years later.
(Peter Barton, *The Somme.*)

The First World War raged across three continents for four years and caused the deaths of more than 10 million people. The Second World War may have cost the lives of more than 60 million people. Recently, however, the consequences of war have become potentially *more* horrific than at any other time in history. Some nations now possess weapons of such destructive power that they are capable of extinguishing whole populations and may even threaten the continued existence of human life on this planet.

Non-proliferation Treaty factfile

Under the Nuclear Non-proliferation Treaty (NPT), 183 nations without nuclear arms pledged not to pursue them, in exchange for a commitment by five nuclear powers—the USA, Russia, Britain, France and China—to eventually eliminate their nuclear stockpiles.

 United States: maintains arsenal of some 7,000-plus operational nuclear warheads, about 1,600 of which are deployed on land-based systems, 1,660 on bombers and 2,880 on submarines. A further 1,120 are tactical 'battleground' weapons.

 Russia: thought to have 8,000 operational nuclear warheads. It is developing new-generation **Topol-M** intercontinental nuclear weapon capable of evading the US **National Missile Defence**.

 France: arsenal of about 348 nuclear warheads on sixty bombers and four nuclear-powered ballistic missile submarines. **Nuclear doctrine has changed since 9/11 to take into account threats from 'rogue states' with weapons of mass destruction**.

 Britain: arsenal of about 185 **Trident D-5** nuclear warheads on four Vanguard-class, nuclear-powered ballistic missile submarines. **The British Government plans to replace Trident with a new generation of nuclear weapons**.

 Israel: a non-NTP state, Israel's arsenal is put at around 200 weapons.

 China: estimated to have about 402 nuclear warheads, including copies of America's most sophisticated current warhead—the miniature **W-88**—deployed on Trident D-5 missiles.

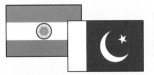 **India, Pakistan**: non-NTP members are said to have some forty warheads each.

 Iran: USA says uranium enrichment programme is cover for nuclear weapons plans. Article IV of NPT guarantees non-weapons states the right to peaceful nuclear technology.

 North Korea: signed NPT, but withdrew in 2003. **Recently announced it has nuclear weapons.**

(Sources: Physicians for Social Responsibility, Federation of American Scientists © Graphic News, *The Irish Times*, 7 May 2005)

Nuclear War

The *most* destructive form of conflict imaginable in human, economic and environmental terms is *nuclear war*.

Nuclear weapons are *uniquely destructive*. In addition to inflicting massive loss of life through the initial blast wave and by the searing heat of the fireball that accompanies it, nuclear weapons also produce lethal doses of radioactive fallout, the effects of which extend beyond the immediate theatre of war and long after the conflict has ended.

The capacity of nuclear weapons to destroy the human habitat and cause an ecological catastrophe is well summarised by the Indian writer Arundhati Roy:

If there is a nuclear war … Our cities and forests, our fields and villages will burn for days. Rivers will turn to poison. The air will become fire. The wind will spread flames. When every thing is burned and the fires die, smoke will rise and shut out the sun. The earth will be enveloped in darkness. There will be no day only interminable night. What shall we do then, those of us who are still alive? Burned and blind and bald and ill, carrying cancerous carcasses of our children in our arms, where shall we go? What shall we eat? What shall we drink? What shall we breathe?

(Arundhati Roy, *The End of Imagination.*)

To date, nuclear weapons have been used on only *two* occasions: at Hiroshima and Nagasaki in Japan in August 1945. There is now a growing concern that a set of circumstances, produced either deliberately or accidentally, might one day lead certain nations to use nuclear weapons against their opponents. Some commentators fear that as more and more states acquire nuclear weapons, the probability of a nuclear exchange becomes more likely.

Questions

1. What is *war*?

2. Read the following article and answer the questions that follow it:

   The Effect of a 15 kt Nuclear Bomb on Mumbai, India

   The effects of a 15 kt nuclear air burst at a height of 600 metres above Mumbai would include:

   The blast – would completely destroy a circle radius of 1.1 kilometres. If the attack were centred on the Fort area, the financial district and the secretariat would be destroyed. Many of the buildings in Mumbai are poorly constructed which suggests that the destruction to buildings outside of the immediate blast area would also be severe.

   Firestorm – in a high density city like Mumbai, with 23,000 people per square metre and where many homes are built of highly flammable substances, the firestorm is likely to claim many lives.

 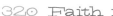

Prompt radiation would extend for approximately 4,000 feet which roughly corresponds to the area of the firestorm and blast zone, adding to the unlikelihood of anyone surviving in the immediate radius of the blast.

Fallout – if the bomb was an air burst then the amount of fallout would be quite small. But because Mumbai is close to the sea, there are high levels of water vapour in the atmosphere which could lead to water droplets condensing around radioactive particles and descending as rain, as occurred in Hiroshima and Nagasaki where black rain descended for several hours after the attack.

The total number of immediate deaths from these combined effects has been calculated at between 200,000 – 800,000 depending on where the air burst occurs over the city and what the population density is in the area.

Long-term effects – there would certainly be many more deaths from the long-term effects, due to radiation-related causes. These would include leukaemia, thyroid cancer, breast cancer and lung cancer.

(Source: M.V. Ramana, *Bombing Bombay? Effects of Nuclear Weapons and a Case Study of a Hypothetical Explosion,* Security Studies Programme, Centre for International Studies, Cambridge. Massachusetts Institute of Technology.)

(a) Identify the three ways in which a nuclear detonation inflicts loss of life.
(b) What would be the long-term consequences of such an event for the health of those who had survived the initial devastation?
(c) Do you think there is a likelihood of nuclear weapons being used in a war, or by a terrorist organisation, during your lifetime?
(d) What, do you think, would be the likely consequences of such an incident if it occurred?

3. Read the following statement:

Only total nuclear disarmament will rid humankind of this ultimate threat to its security.

(a) Do you agree/disagree? Give reasons for your answer.
(b) Is the abolition of nuclear weapons an achievable goal? Explain your answer.

Conventional War

Less destructive than the horror of nuclear conflict, but more likely to occur, are *conventional* wars, i.e. those fought without the use of nuclear, chemical or biological weapons.
Consider the following:

In the 21 major conventional wars that have taken place since 1900, more than 100 million people were killed. Wars in all their various forms result in the loss of human life, in the destruction of property, in social disruption, environmental damage and ecological disturbance.

The economic and social consequences of conventional wars are multiple and complex. They can be divided into immediate human costs and the longer-term development costs. This division is somewhat artificial because human costs such as the deterioration in nutrition and education, the loss of life and depletion of skills constitute development costs, while developmental costs such as destroyed infrastructure and negative growth are major factors contributing to human suffering and deprivation.

The direct economic costs of war include the loss of infrastructure, loss of economic output, destruction of both fixed and human capital, loss of livelihoods and medical costs. Human costs include the loss of life, followed by the loss of limbs and psychological trauma. There are also vital secondary effects — such as the forced displacement of civilians which has a destructive impact on social capital. At least two thirds of the world's refugees and internally displaced persons have fled their homes and countries because of conflict. Many refugees and displaced persons end up 'deskilled' as a result of extended leave from their communities. Those whose schooling is interrupted are excluded from formal labour markets and often resort to the gun as a source of livelihood. Even when armed conflict has terminated, the suffering and threat to civilians may continue.

The widespread availability of arms, especially small arms and light weapons and the 'cultures of violence' which emerge during protracted conflicts often prove durable and continue to undermine the rule of law and human security for years to come in post-war communities. Generations of children growing up in conditions of violence and conflict end up as victims of injury, or highly traumatised and unable to adjust to normal life. Women find themselves as heads of households often in societies based on a traditional division of labour that provides no basis for economic independence. Women who have been violated, a common occurrence during war, are often rejected by their communities altogether.

Landmines pose a particularly ghastly threat to the physical security of many communities around the world long after the violence of war has ceased. Currently there are some 87 countries in the world, suffering from varying degrees of land mine infestation. The worst affected countries include Afghanistan, Angola, Bosnia and Herzegovina, Cambodia, Croatia, Eritrea, Iraq (Kurdistan), Mozambique, Namibia, Nicaragua, Somalia and Sudan. Landmines are indiscriminate in the destruction they cause. They cannot distinguish between a soldier and a child. They can lie dormant for years and even decades after a conflict has been resolved, only to be triggered by a passing and unsuspecting human or animal. It has been estimated that each year landmines kill or maim over 26,000 men, women and children. Most mine victims die. In Cambodia alone there have been over 35,000 amputees injured by landmines — these are the survivors. Those who survive the initial blast inevitably require amputation, long periods of hospitalisation, the fitting of prosthetics and extensive rehabilitation. Many of the survivors, who lose legs, arms and eyes are condemned to a life with little dignity.

Mine deaths and injuries, over the last few decades, have totalled in the hundreds of thousands. Even if no more mines were to be produced or laid, landmines will continue to claim victims for years and even decades to come.

In general the economic legacies of war continue long after termination of conflict. The debt incurred through war and the process of reconstruction imposes a burden on generations to come. Children not yet born will have to pay the price of debt for wars they did not fight, for ideas they do not hold, for a regional and global system that no longer exists and for decisions made by regional and world leaders that are no longer in power.

(Adapted from Susan Willets, *Costs of disarmament – Rethinking the Price Tag*, Report by the United Nations Institute for Disarmament Research, UN Publications.)

Questions

1. What are the major factors that contribute to human suffering and deprivation following the end of a conventional war?

2. Assess the impact of such a conflict on those forced to become refugees.

3. What is the impact of the widespread availability of arms and *a culture of violence* in the aftermath of such a war?

4. How, in particular, are many women often affected by such conflicts?

5. (a) *'Landmines pose a particularly ghastly threat.'*
   Do you agree/disagree? Explain your answer.
   (b) How do landmines impede post-conflict reconstruction?

6. What is usually the impact of present, hugely wasteful conventional wars on *future* generations?

Approaches to War

Over the centuries people have tended to embrace one or other of the following:

◆ **Pacifism**: the belief that war can never be morally justified, no matter what the circumstances may be.
◆ **Crusade:** the belief that war can be authorised by God and required to fulfil some divine plan for humanity. (Also referred to as *a holy war*.)
◆ **Real politik:** the belief that war can be considered an acceptable method for furthering the economic, territorial or security interests of a state, or merely its ruling elite.
◆ **Just War:** the belief that, despite its often horrific and destructive character, war can be morally justified in certain circumstances and under certain conditions.

We shall now turn to examine the first and last of these approaches to war.

Pacifism

Pacifism is the belief that:
◆ participation in any form of violent military action is never justifiable, even if it is in self-defence;
◆ all funds currently expended on the military should be diverted to fund programmes to help the poor and vulnerable in society;
◆ evil should be resisted, but only by means that do not involve violence of any kind, i.e. passive resistance.

Those committed pacifists who refuse to fight in their country's armed forces in time of war are called

conscientious objectors. However, pacifists are divided on the question of what exactly is meant by *participation* in a war. Consider the following:
◆ some pacifists hold that this means that, while they cannot be involved in a war as *combatants*, i.e. front-line fighters, they can serve as *non-combatants*, i.e. as medical personnel, fire-fighters and even bomb-disposal experts;
◆ other pacifists claim that it is *always* wrong to take *any* part in a war, *either* as a combatant or as a non-combatant. They argue that there is little moral difference between direct involvement in a war and other indirect supporting roles, as *each* contributes in its own way to a nation's overall war effort.

This extends, for instance, to a person who works for a company that does business with the military, even if the majority of its business is not war-related, e.g. a company that sells rubber tyres to commercial airlines as well as to a country's airforce.

Questions

1. Explain each of the following approaches to war:
   (a) *pacifism*;
   (b) *crusade*;
   (c) *real politik*;
   (d) *just war*.

2. What is a *conscientious objector*?

3. Read the following extract:

   Jesus' lasting role in human history would be assured by his virtual invention of the strategy of non-violent resistance. The creative potential of this strategy has been widely recognised in our century outside the Christian Church. It was Mahatma Gandhi who first put it into practice, with stunning effect, in the struggle for Indian independence from the British. The moral challenge of non-violent resistance has been proved again and again. It really is very difficult to dominate people who refuse to accept that they are being dominated, who, by jokiness and lack of fear, force the aggressor to recognise them as human equals. Non-violent resistance is a nightmare to control because it inspires imitation, and the more people do it, the harder it is to repress. It was the way Nelson Mandela learnt to cope with his long imprisonment on Robben Island. Having a quick temper, his instinct was to rage against his captors, but he soon realised that this only gave them an excuse for seeing him as even less of an equal than they already did. His impotent rage actually boosted their sense of power. But behaving as an equal, insisting on simple dignities being respected and protocol observed to the letter, he gradually won the respect of his captors. It also reinforced among his fellow prisoners a sense of their own dignity and inner resources.
   (Angela Tilby, *Son of God*.)

   Answer the following questions:
   (a) How did Mahatma Gandhi put the strategy of non-violent resistance into effect against British rule in India?
   (b) How did the adoption of such a non-violent form of resistance assist Nelson Mandela during his long years of imprisonment by the apartheid regime in South Africa?

Interpreting the Fifth Commandment

The Abrahamic faiths share a common foundation for their moral teachings: the Ten Commandments. These are located in the *Tenakh*, the ancient sacred text of Judaism that Christians call the *Old Testament*. There it is stated that God instructed Moses to teach the people that:

> *'You shall not kill.'*
> (Exodus 20:13)

On first consideration, such a statement might appear inconsistent with other statements recorded in the Tenakh, as in its pages one can find approval for many different kinds of killing.

For example:

- capital punishment was permitted;
- war was allowed in certain circumstances;
- animals could be killed for food or to offer sacrifices to God.

The ancient Hebrews clearly understood that the Fifth Commandment was one with many qualifications. Many scholars believe that a more accurate rendering of the original Hebrew text would be

> *You shall not commit murder.*
> **or**
> *You shall not take an innocent life.*

Allegory on the Blessings of Peace, by Peter-Paul Rubens.

The Fifth Commandment, it is argued, was *not* intended to be understood as an absolute prohibition against taking human life in any circumstances. It is for this reason that the Catholic Church teaches that:

God alone is the master of life from its commencement to its end; no one in any circumstance can arrogate to him/herself the right to destroy an innocent human being.
(Catechism of the Catholic Church, No. 2258.)

This is a very carefully worded statement. Note its use of the word *innocent*, i.e. when someone is not guilty of wrongdoing. It implies that while it is always wrong to take the life of an innocent human being, there may be circumstances in which it could be morally permissible, though regrettable, for one person to take the life of another.

Consider the following situation:

Imagine that you are a parent of a young child. Late one night, someone breaks into your home. This person is extremely violent. Your child is woken by a sound and goes to investigate. She disturbs the intruder, who then attacks her. You arrive on the scene just as this person attacks your child. There is not enough time to call the police. Unless you intervene personally, your child will be injured and perhaps killed.

What should you do?

◆ you could attempt to overpower and detain the intruder until the police arrive. If that could be done, it would be the best option;

◆ for the pacifist, however, this would pose a difficulty because it would mean using a form of *violence*;

◆ what if it were *not* physically possible for you to overpower and subdue the intruder *without* harming him? The only means open to you may be to inflict injury on him in order to stop him from harming or even killing your child or yourself;

◆ in such circumstances a parent would be both morally and legally justified in using whatever degree of force was *necessary* to protect his/her child from injury or death, even if that resulted in the death of the intruder. However, it should be clearly understood that the physical force used to defend oneself or another should *never* be *excessive*, i.e. beyond what is required.

The situation outlined above illustrates the *difference* between killing in self-defence and murder, even though both result in the loss of human life. *Murder* involves the destruction of *innocent* human life, whereas killing in *self-defence* is justified when it is necessary to protect innocent human life from a lethal aggressor.

Just as the individual person has the right to defend his/her own life and that of others, so too does *the State* have the right, while respecting individual freedom, to employ force to protect its citizens:

◆ by keeping public order and promoting public justice through the enforcement of its laws *within* its borders;

◆ by defending its citizens from *external* military threats.

This is the basis for the just war doctrine and the legitimate use of force in international affairs.

Questions

1. What kinds of killing are permitted in the Tenakh?

2. What do many scholars believe would be a more accurate rendering of the original Hebrew text of the Fifth Commandment?

3. How does the Catholic Church interpret the Fifth Commandment?

4. Read the following statement:

Unconditional rejection of force in protection of right is nothing but the licence for might to prevail with impunity over right. And this means that humanity is to be abandoned to the disorder— which is far worse—of moral ravishment by brutal violence.

(Code de Morale International.)

Do you agree/disagree with its criticism of pacifism? Explain your answer.

5. (a) Explain the difference between murder and killing in self-defence.
   (b) Why is it argued that the State has the right to use force in certain circumstances?

6. Assessing the arguments for and against torture:

Torture may be defined as

the infliction of severe bodily pain, especially as a punishment or means of persuasion.

Very few people openly support the use of torture, yet many governments allow it to be used. Torture is prohibited by all international human rights treaties, but reports show that it is still used by the security forces of many countries. Read each of the statements on torture set out here:

- *Torture degrades the torturer as well as the victim.*
- *It's not really torture — just intensive interrogation.*
- *We need to find out about enemy agents and their friends.*
- *You can make anyone confess if you hurt them enough. As a result you could force innocent people to admit to things they have not done.*
- *A terrorist is not an ordinary soldier or criminal. If he gives information quickly, OK — if not, his secret must be forced from him. He must face suffering as part of his job.*
- *Torture is inhumane and is always wrong. It can never be justified.*

- *Torture may be useful in the short term. But some short-term methods must be forbidden in order to save the more important values of civilisation. Torture is never limited to 'just once'. Once we start to use it, it spreads to more and more cases.*
- *Torture is a regrettable act, but it is necessary for the good of everyone. If we are threatened by evil people, we have to use ruthless methods too.*
- *We must use torture to keep people afraid. If they don't fear us, they won't leave us in peace.*

(Source: J. Jenkins, *Religious Studies*.)

Now divide your page into two columns: one column for those points with which you agree, the second for those points with which you disagree.
(a) Choose those statements with which you agree and those with which you disagree and write them into the appropriate column.
(b) Give reasons for your choices.

7. Governments and security forces sometimes argue that the use of torture should not be ruled out completely. Do you agree/disagree with the view that torture could, *in certain circumstances and for certain purposes*, be justified?
Explain your answer.

A Moral Dilemma

Many people might have no doubts about being prepared to kill Hitler. But what if you were a prominent theologian? A noted pacifist? What then? That was exactly the dilemma that faced Dietrich Bonhoeffer, and one that led to his own death.

In the grey early morning of 9 April 1945, only weeks before the end of the war in Europe, a 39-year-old German Lutheran pastor was led to the gallows at Flossenborg concentration camp in Bavaria.

As he walked to his death, he could hear

Dietrich Bonhoeffer.

Adolf Hitler addressing a Nazi rally.

the American artillery, the liberators who would arrive just 11 days later.

An SS prison doctor, who witnessed the scene, described the condemned man 'kneeling on the floor praying fervently to his God'.

'At the place of execution, he again said a short prayer ... In almost 50 years that I worked as a doctor, I have hardly ever seen a man die so entirely submissive to the will of God.'

The man hanged that day was the theologian, writer and poet, Dietrich Bonhoeffer: his crime, belonging to an organisation which helped a group of Jews to escape from Nazi Germany to Switzerland.

But beyond that, the real reason for Bonhoeffer's death was for planning, as he freely admitted, to kill Adolf Hitler, and his implication in the July 1944 plot to assassinate the Nazi leader.

And it was Hitler, by this time sheltering in his bunker in Berlin, who personally ordered Bonhoeffer's execution.

Dietrich Bonhoeffer had been born in 1906 into a well-heeled family in Breslau, now Wroclaw in Poland. His father, a professor of psychiatry and neurology at Berlin University, was shocked when, aged just 13, Dietrich announced his intention to enter the Church.

And, after studying at Tubingen and Berlin and in New York, this is just what he did.

'Aryanised' church

Ordained a pastor in 1931, he served as a vicar in a German church in Barcelona. Having been deeply affected by a visit to Rome, Bonhoeffer became a champion of ecumenism, seeking to unify all the Christian churches. However, the coming to power of the Nazis in 1933 split the German Protestant community.

A large number welcomed Hitler as a stabilising force, bringing both social order and true German values to a country riven by political and social divisions.

They effectively '*Aryanised*' the church, preventing anyone without '*racially pure*' blood from holding any position within it and, most perversely of all, removing any Jewish influences from its liturgies and hymns.

Others, including Bonhoeffer and Martin Niemöller, broke away. Creating the Confessing Church, a rival to the officially-sanctioned Reich Church, they regarded Nazism as a blasphemy.

So affected was Bonhoeffer by these events that his response was immediate. Two days after Hitler became Chancellor, the pastor gave a radio talk which focused on the difference between a leader ('*Führer*') and a mis-leader ('*Verführer*'). He was cut off in mid-sentence.

Can Christians kill?

By 1935, Bonhoeffer had become the leader of the Confessing Church, which was outlawed in 1937, and set to work training a new generation of theologians while continuing to speak out against the Nazis.

With the coming of war, Bonhoeffer decided to remain in Germany and, surprisingly, became an officer in military intelligence, the Abwehr.

But, secretly, he also joined the ranks of those who wished to kill the Fuhrer, many of whom were also Abwehr officers.

Bonhoeffer's role in the conspiracy was one of courier and diplomat to the British government on behalf of the resistance, since Allied support was essential to stopping the war.

Between trips abroad for the resistance, Bonhoeffer stayed at Ettal, a Benedictine monastery outside Munich, where he worked on his book, *Ethics*, from 1940 until his arrest in 1943.

In *Ethics*, he wrestles with the essential problem: how can a Christian, essentially a pacifist, justify the taking of a human life?

His argument can be summarised thus:

Responsible action is how Christians act in accordance with the will of God.

The demand for responsible action — that is, acting in accordance with God's will — is one that no Christian can ignore.

Christians are, therefore, faced with a dilemma: when assaulted by evil, they must oppose it through direct action. They have no other option. Any failure to act is simply to condone evil.

Martyrdom

In a note to his fellow conspirators on New Year's Eve 1943, Bonhoeffer wrote: '*The ultimate question for a responsible person to ask is not how he is to extricate himself heroically from the affair, but how the coming generation is to live.*'

But how does Bonhoeffer's intention to kill differ from that of militants today who kill in the name of their faith?

Well, in a sermon at Westminster Abbey in 2002, the then Anglican Dean of Westminster, Dr Wesley Carr, said: '*The word martyr literally means a witness, and for Christians a martyr is a witness to Jesus Christ. Martyrs are not seeking to attract attention to themselves or their own cause, but like John the Baptist they point to Jesus as the one who gives himself fully and freely for the redemption of the world.*'

Dietrich Bonhoeffer was not the only member of his family to be killed by the Nazis. His brother Klaus and his brothers-in-law were also executed.

Today Bonhoeffer is honoured at Westminster Abbey in London as one of ten 20th-century martyrs, including Martin Luther King Jr and the murdered Archbishop of San Salvador, Oscar Romero.

His final prison letter attests to the strength of Dietrich Bonhoeffer's faith: 'This is the end, and, for me, the beginning of life.'

(Adapted from an article by the BBC News Profiles Unit in *BBC News/UK/Magazine*, 14.4.2006.)

Questions

1. Who was Dietrich Bonhoeffer?

2. When and how did he die?

3. Who ordered his execution?

4. Why was he condemned to death?

5. Describe the impact of the coming to power of the Nazis on the German Protestant community?

6. What was the *Confessing Church*?

7. What do you think Bonhoeffer meant by describing Hitler as a *verführer*, i.e. *mis-leader*, in an interrupted radio broadcast?

8. What was Bonhoeffer's role in the conspiracy to assassinate Hitler?

9. How did Bonhoeffer justify his involvement in this plot in his book, *Ethics*?

10. What, do you think, he hoped to achieve by assassinating Hitler? How would this benefit Germany, in particular, and humankind, in general?

11. What does it mean to describe Bonhoeffer as a *Christian martyr*?

The Just War Doctrine

The just war doctrine has attained a considerable influence on political deliberations on the use of military force in international affairs. Proponents of the just war doctrine have sought neither to glorify war nor to minimise its horrors. They remind people of how, in the aftermath of his victory at the Battle of Waterloo (1815), the Duke of Wellington was widely congratulated. Yet Wellington cautioned his well-wishers against glamorising the horrors of war. He told them:

> *I have lost all my dearest friends. I hope to God*
> *I have fought my last battle. It is a bad thing*
> *always to be fighting. Next to a battle lost, the*
> *saddest thing is a battle won.*
> *I never wish for any more fighting.*

Both pacifists and advocates of the just war doctrine *agree* that human beings can only flourish and achieve their potential where there is *peace*. However, the latter reject pacifism because they claim that by not resisting aggression when it comes and by not deterring it *before* it comes, pacifism merely *encourages* the predatory instincts of other people, who may not hesitate to use the very forces of destruction that pacifism condemns.

As first formulated by St Augustine (*d.* 430) and later expanded upon by St Thomas Aquinas (*d.* 1274), the just war doctrine lays down the conditions that must be met if a particular conflict is to be morally

The Triumph of St Augustine, by Claudio Coello.

justified. These conditions fall into two main categories:

- *Ius ad bellum:*
Latin, meaning: *the right to go to war*;
- *Ius in bello:*
Latin, meaning: *what is right in a war.*

According to advocates of the just war doctrine, moral justification for a conflict is:

- *needed*—because of the enormous harm and risks inflicted on others; and
- *possible*—because of the serious public values of justice, peace and order that are at stake.

Ius ad Bellum

In preparing to wage a just war, a state must meet the following criteria:

1. Just cause: the war must be a defensive action that seeks to confront an undoubted danger. The criterion of just cause has now been complicated by the availability of weapons of mass destruction (WMD). Some

A US Navy aircraft carrier.

philosophers argue that if a country has such weapons and has made known its intent to use them not for defence but in an act of aggression or terrorism, and this intent is serious, then a *pre-emptive strike* by the nation so threatened may be justified. With weapons of mass destruction the attacked country would not be able to defend itself and correct the wrong after the fact; a pre-emptive strike might be the only way to stop the unjust aggressor or terrorist. This criteria remains highly controversial.

2. Proper authority: there must be a formal declaration of war by the legitimate authorities of the State. Only a duly elected government has the authority to wage war on behalf of the people. Paramilitary groups or lone vigilantes operating outside the legitimate government do *not* have the authority to do so.

3. Right intention: the reasons for declaring the war must be to achieve a just and lasting peace and *not* to mask ulterior motives, such as to seize another nation's natural resources.

4. Last resort: all reasonable peaceful alternatives must have been exhausted or have been deemed impractical or ineffective. The contentious parties must strive to resolve their differences peacefully before engaging in war, e.g. through negotiation, mediation, or even embargoes.

5. Proportionality: the good that is achieved by waging war must not be outweighed by the harm. What good is it to wage war if it leaves both sides in total devastation, *with no one really emerging the winner*? Modern means of warfare (i.e. nuclear, chemical and biological weapons) give great weight to this condition.

6. Probability of success: there must be a reasonable hope of accomplishing the good purposes for which the war is being fought.

If a state can meet these criteria, then it may justly enter a war. Moreover, a country could come to the assistance of another country that is not able to defend itself, as long as these criteria are met.

Ius in Bello

Once war has broken out, the idea that all means of waging war are acceptable, i.e. 'all is fair in love and war', is incorrect. During war, a country must also meet criteria to ensure that justice is preserved:

1. Discrimination: armed forces ought to fight armed forces, and should do everything possible to avoid harming non-combatants. Sadly, innocent people will always suffer and die in war because of mistakes or accidents. However, armed forces should not deliberately target civilians or seek to destroy the enemy's countryside, cities, or economy simply for the sake of punishment, retaliation or revenge.

2. Due proportion: combatants must use only those means necessary to achieve their objectives. For example, no one should use nuclear missiles to settle a dispute over fishing quotas! Due proportion also involves *mercy*—towards civilians, in general, and towards combatants—when the resistance stops (as in the case of surrender and prisoners of war), and towards all parties when the war is finished. Moreover, the victors must help the vanquished to rebuild a stable government and economy, so as to ensure a *lasting* peace.

Comment

The just war doctrine begins with a strong presumption *against* the use of force. While a state has the right to defend the lives of its citizens, it should strive to avoid war and to settle disputes peacefully and justly. It can establish the conditions when this presumption may be overridden, for the sake of preserving the kind of peace that protects human dignity and human rights. In a disordered world, where peaceful resolution of conflicts sometimes fails, the just war tradition provides an important moral framework for restraining and regulating the *limited* use of force by governments and international organisations.

In this view, war involves resorting to a lesser evil, but only with the aim of *preventing* a far greater evil and with the intention of *restoring* justice and peace.

Some writers also caution that it is one thing to offer the just war doctrine as a set of ideas, but another thing to *put it into practice* as an effective set of constraints on the actual use of force. Once combat begins and the longer combat continues, respect for human life and any restraint on violent actions tends to *diminish*. Some commentators wonder if modern war, with all its savagery, can live up to the high standards set by the just war doctrine.

Regarding the morality of war, there are, as in so many areas of human life, no easy answers. Indeed, as Patrick Comerford cautions:

It is only long after a war is over that we have the time and the luxury to determine whether all the conditions have been met. In the meantime, we can only accept that all moral decisions are contingent and, at best, penultimate. We are left to *confess that war is evil, and accept that many people of good will resort to a lesser evil in the hope of preventing the perpetration of a further greater evil.*

Questions

1. Why do advocates of the just war theory reject pacifism?

2. Explain the meaning of each of the following:
   Ius ad bellum;
   Ius in bello.

3. Who would you list as *innocent people* in a war situation? Explain your choices.

4. Consider the following situation:
   - the people of country X are starving to death due to massive crop failures;
   - their neighbours in country Y enjoy a huge surplus of food;
   - all attempts by country X to negotiate famine relief from country Y have failed.

   Answer the following questions:
   (a) Would country X be justified in going to war with country Y to secure food for its people?
   (b) Which do you think would involve *greater* misery and suffering: fighting such a war, or refusing to do so?

5. Consider the American nuclear attacks on the Japanese cities of Hiroshima and Nagasaki in August 1945. People have tended to adopt one or other response to these events:

- *they condemn them*—because they claim that the use of such weapons of mass destruction violated the just war doctrine by inflicting appalling and unnecessary civilian casualties and immense suffering from radiation sickness afterwards;
- *they reluctantly support them*—because they claim that if a conventional (i.e. non-nuclear) war had continued and an invasion of Japan had taken place, far more lives would have been lost than were lost as a result of these nuclear attacks.

Which of these responses would you support? Give reasons for your answer.

6. Identify two difficulties in relation to the just war theory.

Stewardship

A. CHERISHING THE EARTH

Is there intelligent life elsewhere in the universe?

Since ancient times people have speculated about the possibility of life, particularly *intelligent life*, existing elsewhere in the universe. Indeed, the very possibility that intelligent life-forms may exist on other worlds continues to exert a powerful influence on the popular imagination, as shown by the success of films such as *Independence Day* and *Star Wars*. Different scientists offer different answers to the question: *Does intelligent life exist elsewhere in the cosmos?*

For example:

◆ the late and highly influential astronomer Carl Sagan claimed that there may be as many as 1 million technologically advanced civilisations in the Milky Way Galaxy alone;

◆ in sharp contrast, the UCLA astronomer Ben Zuckerman thinks that the Earth may be the

The Milky Way galaxy is estimated to be about 100,000 light-years wide. It contains hundreds of billions of stars, many (though not all) of which have planetary systems. It is only one of countless galaxies swirling through the vastness of space.

only inhabited world in this galaxy, if not in the entire universe.

All such estimates are, of course, highly speculative. To date, no publicly known, verifiable contact has been made with any extraterrestrial intelligent life-forms, nor do scientists have any proof that such beings exist.

Nonetheless, a substantial number of scientists claim that there are good reasons to believe that

Frank Drake.

intelligent life-forms may have originated and evolved elsewhere in the universe. They say that the chemical and biological processes involved in the formation of life on Earth could also have occurred on other planets and similarly given rise to an extraordinarily rich variety of creatures, as happened on this planet.

The quest for detecting and/or contacting extra-terrestrial intelligence began with the invention of radio telescopes after the Second World War. It was thought that alien civilisations would transmit messages across the vast distances of interstellar space by microwave radio transmissions, which travel at the speed of light (i.e. 186,000 mps), which is the fastest velocity permitted by the laws of physics.

The first radio telescopic search was conducted by Professor Frank Drake of the University of California in 1960. The following year he devised a simple mathematical formula to guide astronomers exploring this field. This formula has since become known as '*the Drake Equation*'.

The Drake Equation is intended to help scientists to:

◆ determine the likelihood of intelligent life-forms existing elsewhere in the Milky Way Galaxy;

◆ estimate how many they may be;

◆ assess the likelihood of contact with them.

The Earth, as viewed by an astronaut on the moon.

The Drake Equation

This states that

$$N = R^* \times f_p \times n_e \times f_l \times f_i \times f_c \times L$$

Here the letter N signifies the number of civilisations in our galaxy that are trying to make contact with the human race. The symbols on the other side of the equation represent the separate factors that must be considered when addressing the question of whether or not there is intelligent life elsewhere in the universe.

Key to the Drake Equation

$R^* \quad=\quad$ the rate of star formation in the galaxy;

$f_p \quad=\quad$ the fraction of those stars thought to be able to support planetary systems;

$n_e \quad=\quad$ the number of planets capable of supporting life per star system with planets;

$f_l \quad=\quad$ the fraction of such planets that actually go on to develop life-forms;

$f_i \quad=\quad$ the fraction of the above that proceed to develop intelligent life-forms;

$f_e \quad=\quad$ the fraction of those intelligent life-forms that are willing and able to communicate;

$L \quad=\quad$ the expected average lifetime of such a civilisation, i.e. those that have *avoided* being destroyed either by nuclear war or by a natural disaster, such as an asteroid impact.

After much discussion with colleagues, Professor Drake has speculated that, given the vast size of the Milky Way Galaxy alone, there could be up to 10,000 technologically advanced civilisations in existence, with the closest one about 300 light-years away from Earth.

Other scientists have poured cold water on Drake's optimistic estimate, however. They claim that:

◆ even if such technologically advanced civilisations do exist and are aware of humanity's existence, they might consider human beings to be too primitive to be worth contacting;

◆ even if intelligent life-forms have originated on other worlds, some may not yet be sufficiently technologically advanced to either send or receive radio signals;

◆ further, given the age of the Milky Way Galaxy and this solar system's comparatively recent formation, other advanced civilisations may have already come and gone, dying out before human beings were ever able to detect their signals and respond to them.

The number of advanced technological civilisations capable of communication may be far fewer than Drake has estimated. Some scientists, notably Peter Ward and Donald Browne, disagree profoundly with Drake. In their book, *Rare Earth: Why Complex Life is Uncommon in the Universe* (2000), they claim that while it is true that the universe is vast, this does *not* necessarily imply that intelligent extra-terrestrial life must exist elsewhere in space. Indeed, radio telescopes have been scanning the stars for intelligent radio messages for decades and so *far none* has been detected. Ward and Browne ask people to consider the entire, complex chain of conditions that must be present to allow life, especially human life, to thrive on Earth.

Consider the following examples:

- the Earth is sufficiently far from the Sun to keep its water in liquid form;
- the Moon orbits the Earth at just the right distance to ensure climatic stability;
- there is just enough carbon present on Earth to allow life to emerge and thrive, any more and the planet would overheat;
- the giant planet Jupiter is so positioned in this solar system that it absorbs most of the large asteroids and meteors that would otherwise strike the Earth and render the development of civilisation impossible.

Ward and Browne agree that conditions allowing *primitive* microbes to thrive might well exist in other worlds, but they think that the complex combination of factors necessary for the development of an advanced technological civilisation produced by intelligent life-forms are most likely quite *rare*, if not wholly *unique* to this planet. Indeed, as the leading biologist Ernst Mayr has noted, the kind of intelligence possessed by humans had occurred *only once* on Earth—and that out of something approaching a billion species in this planet's ecological history.

Nonetheless, Drake and many other astronomers are *not* disheartened by such counter-claims. They believe that their critics are *too pessimistic*. They point out that the universe, which contains countless galaxies, is unimaginably vast. Further, on the one planet where life is known to exist—the Earth—intelligent life-forms did eventually emerge.

Perhaps one day human beings will know the answer to the question of whether there is intelligent life elsewhere in the universe; perhaps not. However, anyone who investigates this complex but fascinating question can only be struck by what it reveals about this planet. One is left with a renewed appreciation for the Earth and life upon it. As Joel Achenbach writes:

In a universe of empty space and stellar furnaces and ice worlds, it is good to be alive.

The Earth is a beautiful oasis of life in the cold vastness of space. It deserves to be cherished, not ravaged. It is humanity's *home*. Unfortunately, for millennia now human beings have been treating the Earth—its oceans, its landscape and its air—as essentially indestructible. This view is now known to be *utterly wrong*. The Earth has a rich, complex, but profoundly *fragile environment*.

Questions

1. What is the purpose of *the Drake Equation*?

2. (a) In what ways do Peter Ward and Donald Browne differ from Frank Drake on the question of whether or not there exists extraterrestrial life?
   (b) Why do they differ?

3. Read the following statement by the German astronaut Sigmund Jahn, who travelled on a NASA space-shuttle mission:

   Before I flew I was already aware of how small and vulnerable our planet is; but only when I saw it from space, in all its ineffable beauty and fragility, did I realise that humankind's most urgent task is to cherish and preserve it for future generations.

   Why do you think he reacted in this way? Explain your answer.

Environmental Vandalism

Following the scientific revolution of the eighteenth century, the dominant worldview portrayed the universe as a vast machine that operated *blindly*, i.e. without any purpose. From this many concluded that the only meaning the Earth has is whatever meaning is given to it by its human inhabitants. This planet came to be seen as existing solely to be exploited by human beings, usually with little, if any, consideration of the long-term consequences of their actions.

By the latter half of the twentieth century many people were becoming increasingly uneasy about the impact of rapid industrialisation on the environment. While science and technology had done much to raise living standards and reduce disease and famine, there was a growing awareness that great damage was being inflicted upon the Earth, particularly to the *biosphere*, i.e.

> *the narrow zone that harbours life on our planet, limited to the waters of the earth, a fraction of its crust, and the lower regions of its atmosphere.*

Within the biosphere there exists a number of interconnected ecosystems. By an *'ecosystem'* we mean:

> *an integrated unit consisting of the community of living organisms and the physical environment in a particular area.*

The relationships among species in an ecosystem are usually complex and finely balanced, and tampering with them may have disastrous consequences.

For example:
It is no longer possible to assume that the Earth's oceans

If Not, Not, by Ron Kitaj.

are so large that they can continue to soak up human waste without producing catastrophic effects on marine life. It is clear that human beings cannot continue with a 'business-as-usual' approach to the environment.

Although a few dissenting voices remain, there is now a broad consensus among scientists that:
- climate change is actually happening;
- human activity is causing this;
- climate change is the most serious issue facing the human community.

Few scientists now dispute that climate change will have adverse effects—only the extent of the effects is still at issue and whether they will be irreversible. Despite this, a large section of the Earth's political establishment has yet to seriously address the issue.

Extinct Species

The dodo was the first species in recorded history to be effectively wiped out by human intervention. Sadly, it was *not* to be the last. Many other creatures have since shared its fate:

The passenger pigeon: wiped out by 1914;

The Tasmanian wolf: exterminated by 1936;

Stellar's sea cow: extinct since 1769;

The dusky seaside sparrow: not seen since 1984.

The gift of the Earth

Scientific analysis has made it clear that *all* species, including humans, are part of a complex chain of life, wherein each thing relies upon and is linked to another. For example, the loss of a species of plant can result in the loss of the insects and animals that depended upon it. If enough links in the great chain of life were to be broken, then the survival of humanity itself might be at stake. This has led an increasing number of people to *reject* the mechanistic worldview that reduced nature to something that existed only to be exploited for human

consumption. They have become aware that:

The physical world is not simply the stage for human history, but an essential part of our human

story. Our life is continuous with the soil, the plants, the animals, the birds and the atmosphere.
(Sean Fagan, *Does Morality Change?*)

Thus, rather than accepting the idea that human beings confer meaning on the world, many people now realise that there is a *pre-existing* order to things, i.e. there is a meaning to all reality that was *already there*, but which people need to discover and acknowledge gratefully. Furthermore, we need to keep in mind the *aesthetic value* of the natural world. Whenever a species of plant or animal disappears into extinction, the world *loses* a little more of its beauty and richness. Industry and mining cannot be allowed to grind up the last natural beauty and wilderness before people realise, too late, what has been lost. Only *then* would some people grasp what the poet Gerard Manley Hopkins meant when he wrote:

'After-comers cannot guess the beauty been.'
(Binsey Poplars)

As intelligent beings, humans can *still* act to prevent environmental catastrophe while there is *still* natural beauty and wilderness around them, serving purposes they may one day be wise enough to appreciate and understand.

There is simply no point trying to turn back the clock to some earlier agrarian age, but *nor* is there any reason to despair. We face an enormous challenge, but *there are solutions*.

To begin with, there is a need for all nations to adopt and pursue policies of *sustainable* development, i.e.

development that meets the needs of the present without compromising the ability of future generations to meet their own needs.

This will *not* be easy to achieve. Any significant changes to current government policies will face considerable opposition from powerful vested interests, both individual and corporate. But experience shows that governments *will* respond to demands for change if those demands enjoy sufficient public support. Therefore, the responsibility for bringing about change rests with each individual citizen, who must consistently and actively seek it. The necessary popular support for this new direction in environmental policy will only occur if enough people undergo what Pope John Paul II once referred to as '*an ecological conversion*', i.e.

the adoption of a new and radically different way of thinking about and relating to the rest of the natural world.

The basis for this can be found in the teachings of the world's religions, particularly those of the Abrahamic faiths.

Questions

1. (a) What was the dominant view of the universe, particularly the Earth, following the scientific revolution of the eighteenth century?
   (b) Why have many people been *forced* to *reconsider* this view?

2. Explain the following terms: (a) the *biosphere* and (b) an *ecosystem*.

3. What do you understand by the phrase '*the delicate balance of nature*'?

4. Read the extract below and answer the questions that follow it.

Scientists are now afraid that the melting Greenland icecap and North Pole ice will dilute the waters of the Gulf Stream, making it less salty and less likely to sink when it reaches our latitudes. If the Gulf Stream stops bringing warmer waters to our shores, average year round temperatures will fall by an estimated five degrees. We will freeze over in winter.

Two years ago scientists were shocked at the speed with which a huge Antarctic ice sheet called Larsen B started to melt. Within weeks it had broken up into hundreds of icebergs. In a month, 500 million tonnes of ice had collapsed into the sea. So far there have not been catastrophes on that scale in the Arctic, where it might affect the Gulf Stream, but there are signs that Greenland's glaciers are starting to shrink, and sea ice no longer extends as far south in wintertime as it used to. More worryingly, some scientists say the Gulf Stream is already starting to slow down.

We need to worry about more than just how hot, or cold, it will be. We could also get our feet wet. One estimate of the billions of tonnes of ice in Antarctica suggests that, were it all to melt tomorrow, worldwide sea levels would rise by between 15 and 20 feet. That doesn't sound a lot until you realise that would deluge all of the centre of Cork City and devastate Dublin's docklands and quays plus most of its northern and southern coastal suburbs. The older part of Limerick City would also become uninhabitable. The disastrous floods which affected central Europe two years ago could become commonplace, instead of once a century events.

(Source: *Irish Independent* (Weekend section) 26.10.2004.)

(a) What do some scientists fear would be the consequences for the Gulf Stream of the icecaps melting?
(b) How would this affect Ireland?
(c) What steps, do you think, should be taken to prepare for such an eventuality?

5. What did Pope John Paul II mean by the need for many people to undergo *'an ecological conversion'*?

6. Read the following poem written by the medieval thinker Hildegarde of Bingen.

> *Glance at the sun. See the moon and the stars.*
> *Gaze at the beauty of Earth's greenings.*
> *Now, think.*
> *What delight God gives to humankind with all these things …*
> *All nature is at the disposal of humankind.*
> *But we are to work with it.*
> *For without it we cannot survive.*

(a) What is her message?
(b) How should we apply it to the present environmental crisis?

Stewards of the Earth

Joseph Interpreting Pharaoh's Dream, by Reginald Arthur.

The key to understanding the teachings of all the Abrahamic faiths can be found in the Jewish Tenakh (*Old Testament*). Its first book, Genesis, opens on a positive, uplifting note, informing the reader that:

> *God saw all that he had made and it was very good.*
> (Genesis 1:31)

It is also written that humanity enjoys a pre-eminent place and unique dignity among the Earth's many species because we alone are

> *made in the image and likeness of God.*
> (Genesis 1:28)

We are told that God commanded humanity

> *to increase and multiply and have dominion over the earth.*
> (Genesis 1:28)

The meaning of this statement has, on occasion, been either misunderstood or misrepresented. It was not intended to grant people a licence to exploit and abuse the Earth's resources. On the contrary, human beings were instructed

> *to work the earth and to take care of it.*
> (Genesis 2:15)

A Convent Garden, by William Leech.

People were at no time ever to consider themselves to be the owners of this planet. A later text clarified this point by having God inform Moses that

> *the land belongs to me and you are only strangers and guests.*
> (Leviticus 25:23)

For Jews, Christians and Muslims these texts are of enormous significance. They make it clear that we are not the Earth's proprietors. God has entrusted the planet to our care for a time. We are called to be what Jews and Christians refer to as *God's stewards*, or what Islam refers to as *Allah's vice-regents* (Arabic: *Khalifah*, see Surah 2:30).

A steward is someone who is entrusted with handling the affairs of another. In ancient kingdoms, stewards ran the country in the absence of the king. Upon the king's return, the steward gave a full accounting for his actions. Often the steward handled the day-to-day affairs of the kingdom even when the king was present. However, a steward did *not* own the kingdom. Further, the king decided when and for how long a steward would serve him.

The Tenakh records several examples of stewards being placed over the affairs of their masters. For example, in Genesis, chapter 41, we find the story of how the Egyptian pharaoh, struck by the wisdom and discretion of Joseph, a Hebrew, decided to appoint the latter as steward over his great kingdom.

If one carefully reads the biblical text where God grants humanity '*dominion*' over the Earth, one discovers that it implies that stewardship has three essential characteristics:

- ◆ it is collective, i.e. it involves all of us;
- ◆ it respects the purpose for which things exist;
- ◆ it respects the dignity of each person.

A steward, therefore, is someone who:

- ◆ has been entrusted to care for and to cultivate the Earth on behalf of its owner—God;
- ◆ is concerned for the quality of life of his/her neighbours and so seeks to ensure that its resources are distributed fairly;
- ◆ adheres to the Seventh Commandment, which enjoins respect for the integrity of creation by acting to fulfil the common good of all living things—human, animal and plant—upon the Earth;
- ◆ does not give in to selfish, short-term interests, but instead strikes a balance between the needs of the present generation and those yet to be born by passing on this planet in a living and fertile state;
- ◆ rejects the idea of dominating the natural world and instead lives in harmony and companionship with it.

In his book *Cry of the Environment*, Bernard Anderson describes God's call to be stewards as:

> *a privilege bestowed on humankind.*

However, he reminds people that:

as with all privileges, human beings will be held accountable for their stewardship.

For as St Paul has written:

Now it is required that those who have been given a trust must prove faithful. It is the Lord who judges ... He will bring to light what is hidden in the darkness and expose the motives of men's hearts.
(1 Corinthians 4:2–5)

Jews, Christians and Muslims alike are called to take their role as stewards seriously because they will be judged by God on how well they have performed this task. Being a faithful steward is seen as an integral part of the call to live a good life. As Bernard Anderson writes:

If people are caring and cultivate harmony in all their dealings with each other and the Earth, then they will grow in the image and likeness of God.

The monotheistic faiths do *not* claim a monopoly on concern for the health of the natural world. Buddhists' belief in the oneness of all things has led some of its followers to actively intervene to preserve the environment.

Consider the following example:

Phra Boonsong (1941–), who has been the head monk of Phranon Wat, in central Thailand, since 1972, is a dedicated environmentalist who is also an effective lobbyist. When he arrived in the area, the ecosystem was sick. Runoff from the Chin River, which flows by the monastery, was polluting paddy fields, and declining agriculture and fishing yields were causing men and women to seek employment in the cities. Phra Boonsong has worked tirelessly to improve the region's ecological balance. Appealing to the traditional Thai prohibition against killing inside a monastery, he began by declaring the river adjacent to it a 'pardon zone' for all water creatures. Next, from profits made by selling fish food to local Buddhists (who in turn gave it to the fish, earning merit), he was able to add fish stock. The fish multiplied in that nearby stretch of the river, slowly adding to the breeding population available for harvest by many fishermen living along the river. This success enabled Phra Boonsong to convince the National Assembly to enact laws allowing monasteries nationwide to establish similar breeding zones, and over one hundred have done so. More recently the monk has begun planting fruit trees on long-deforested hills and having the orchards reduce the use of expensive, water-polluting chemicals. The expertise of the Phranon Wat monks in species use, grafting, fertilisers and marketing is now being shared across the region, allowing other monks to spearhead similar efforts and promote environmental awareness across Thailand's rural hinterlands.

(J.L. Esposito *et al.*, *World Religions Today.*)

Questions

1. Explain the notion of 'steward' in the ancient world.

2. What does it mean to be *a steward of the Earth* today?

3. Read the following statement:

   Wilful and selfish abuse of the environment is indicative of a deeper lack of respect for all life, and a genuine contempt for one's fellow human beings.

   Do you agree/disagree? Give reasons for your answer.

B. THE TREATMENT OF ANIMALS

Introduction

In recent years there has been considerable debate as to *how* human beings should treat animals. This debate centres on six controversial areas:

- the breeding and killing of animals for food;
- the use of animals in medical research;
- the testing of cosmetics, detergents and non-medical household goods on animals;
- the breeding and killing of animals for fur;
- the hunting and killing of animals for sport;
- the breeding and training of animals for entertainment.

Changing Views

Until quite recently, most societies have viewed animals as existing primarily, if not solely, for the purpose of serving human beings. As the ancient Greek philosopher Aristotle wrote:

Plants exist for the sake of animals, and animals for the sake of man—domestic animals for his use and food, wild ones for food and other accessories of life such as clothing and various tools. Since nature makes nothing purposeless or in vain, it is undeniably true that she has made all animals for the sake of man.
(Aristotle, *The Politics.*)

Following the scientific revolution of the seventeenth century, some influential thinkers went *much further* than Aristotle. They maintained that *animals simply*

Session at the Vivisection Laboratory, by Leon Augustin Lhermitte.

do not matter at all and that *humans can do with them whatsoever they wish.*

This view came to dominate Western thinking until quite recently. It had its origins in the writings of French philosopher, René Descartes. When laying down the foundations of modern physics, Descartes taught that the physical universe is essentially a vast machine. He considered animals to be mere *automata*, i.e. mindless machines incapable of thought and feeling. He stated that:

> *An animal screaming in pain is like a chiming clock.*

The early pioneers of modern *physiology*, i.e. the study of the way in which living bodies work, concluded that they could dissect living, unanaesthetised animals with a *total* disregard for the pain endured by their animal subjects. There followed a huge expansion in experimentation on animals during the twentieth century. Until recently, little interest was shown as to the impact on the animals concerned. Many were subjected to inhumane and wasteful procedures.

Today, however, it is quite clear that most kinds of animals possess some rudimentary form of thought and can experience both pleasure and pain to some degree. Indeed, there appears to be very little physical difference between the nervous systems of the human being and those of the higher animals, for example the ape. There is now a growing demand to end the callous treatment of animals. Some people even claim that, like humans, animals have rights that should be respected.

Do Animals Have Rights?

Many people use the term *rights* when discussing the need to protect animals from cruel and degrading

treatment by humans. In the context of animal welfare, however, the notion that animals have rights should be taken *metaphorically*, not literally. Even the noted animal welfare activist and author Peter Singer refers to the language of *animal rights* as 'a convenient political short-hand'.

Generally speaking, a species is acknowledged as having *rights* if its members can demonstrate a *capacity* to:

◆ make free and rational choices;
◆ recognise the rights of others;
◆ be aware of their obligations to one another;
◆ bear moral and legal responsibility for their actions.

It is clear from this that we *cannot* say that animals have rights in the same way as humans do because, as Roger Scruton points out, unlike humans, animals:

◆ do *not* possess the capacity for sophisticated thought or language;
◆ do *not* plan or make free and rational choices;
◆ do *not* accept moral and legal responsibility for their actions;
◆ are *not* critically self-aware.

Humans alone can have moral obligations and can accept responsibility for their actions. Rights are inseparable from responsibilities, therefore we cannot include animals as members of the Earth's moral community. But while there are clear differences between humans and animals, this does not mean that there is any justification for the claim that people are entitled to do with animals whatsoever they please. On the contrary, we *do* have moral responsibilities towards animals and should treat them with *respect*.

Why Respect Animals?

This question has stimulated a variety of answers.

Here are three of them:

1. Inflicting *unnecessary* pain on animals is wrong because it *diminishes* people morally. Caring for animals teaches us how to show kindness to other living things. This can translate into our dealings with one another, encouraging us to treat each other with compassion.

    (St Thomas Aquinas, *Summa Contra Gentiles*.)

2. We ought to show greater respect for animals precisely because they *are* different from human beings. All things have a role to play in the complex web of life. We must acknowledge and accept this if the biosphere is to remain viable and, by implication, the human race to have a future.

    (Stephen Clark, *The Moral Status of Animals*.)

3. God has instructed us to be stewards of the Earth: *Take care of all that has been entrusted to you.*

    (1 Timothy 6:20.)

We are *not* entitled to callously abuse or exploit animals. We have a duty of *care* towards them. Animals are not put here on the Earth purely, or even primarily, for human use. As one Christian veterinarian puts it:

> *Animals are not here for our use but for the glory of God, who delights in a differentiated creation and loves every individual being.*

(Andrew Linzey, *The Tablet* (1996).)

Questions

1. What criteria may be used to differentiate human beings from animals?

2. Can it be said that 'animals have rights'?
   Explain your answer.

3. Identify three reasons why human beings are called upon to respect animals and treat them with kindness.

4. Read the following extract:

   One can no longer flaunt the wearing of a mink coat in the way one could half a century ago. The range of alternative textiles that is now available to the average Westerner makes the slaughter of minks unnecessary. However it would be difficult to object to an Inuit killing a seal for clothing and food, as the Inuits' survival is on the line. (Adapted from P. Vardy, *The Puzzle of Ethics*.)

   In both of these examples, (a) the production of a luxury mink coat and (b) hunting seals, an animal is killed. Would you consider *either* of these examples to be morally justifiable? Explain your answer.

5. Read the following statement:

   It is contrary to human dignity to cause animals to suffer or die needlessly. It is likewise unworthy to spend money on them that should go to the relief of human suffering. One can love animals; one should not direct to them the affection due only to persons. (Catechism of the Catholic Church.)

   Do you agree/disagree with this statement? Give reasons for your answer.

Medical research

The question as to whether or not the use of animals in research is morally justified remains hotly disputed. Those who *oppose* any research involving experimentation on live animals sometimes do so by claiming that animals are so different from humans that no useful data can be successfully extrapolated from them to humans. However, those who *advocate* the use of animals in medical research say that it is regrettable, but *necessary*, to do so. They say that:

◆ humans contract many of the same *infectious* diseases as animals, e.g. humans and dogs have sixty-five such diseases in common;

◆ many *non-infectious* diseases, such as epilepsy, also affect other species.

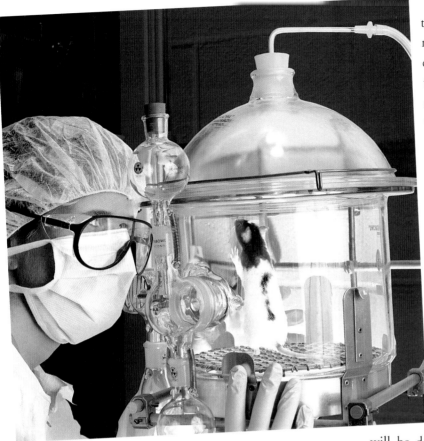

treatments for such diseases would be reduced significantly. But opponents of experimentation on animals remind people that such medical breakthroughs are achieved by subjecting animals to laboratory experiments in which they are injected with drugs, exposed to radiation or to toxic chemicals and infected with diseases—all of which inflicts *pain* on these creatures.

Many medical researchers favour the development of an *alternative* to the use of animals in medical research. The European Union agreed to implement a Europe-wide ban on the use of animals to test cosmetics from 2009. There is now a similar drive to produce alternatives to animal experimentation in the medical field.

There is some optimism that, in the near future, much testing and research will be done either by computer-modelling or by using cells grown in tissue culture.

However, many medical researchers have warned that, at least for the foreseeable future, some questions may *only* be answered by conducting experiments on live animals, in order to:

◆ better understand how diseases occur and to develop more effective ways of preventing, treating and curing them;

◆ test potential medicines by examining how they react in a living body and identify any unpredicted side-effects *before* they are tested on human volunteers in clinical trials.

Where animals are still used in medical research they should be *used sparingly* and *treated humanely*. There is now a growing consensus that the use of animals in biomedical research should be reduced to an *absolute minimum*, with the aim of eventually making such experiments completely *unnecessary*.

They go on to point out that medical experiments conducted on animals have, in the past, contributed enormously to several important breakthroughs in the treatment of human illnesses.

For example:

◆ experiments conducted on *dogs* were responsible for advances in kidney transplants and open-heart surgery;

◆ research on *monkeys* led to a vaccine against rubella and the development of life-support machines for premature babies;

◆ experiments on *rabbits* played an important role in the development of chemotherapy for leukaemia sufferers.

Currently, animals are being used for research into AIDS, Alzheimer's disease, cancer and cystic fibrosis. It is claimed that without the use of animals in laboratory experiments, the chances of finding successful

Questions

1. Many people are comparatively untroubled by the use of mice in experiments; an estimated 25 million mice are put to death in tests each year. However, the same people become very angry if rabbits, cats or dogs are used. Why does this happen? Is there *really* any difference?

2. Read the following extract:

Medical and scientific experimentation on animals, if it remains within reasonable limits, is a morally acceptable practice since it contributes to caring for or saving human lives.
(Catechism of the Catholic Church.)

What kind of restrictions should be placed on medical and scientific experimentation on animals? Explain your answer.

3. If someone you love were in danger of dying if doctors did *not* use a drug tested on animals: what would you want them to do?
Give reasons for your answer.

Picture Credits

For permission to reproduce photographs the author and publisher gratefully acknowledge the following:

Akg-images: 27, 30, 67, 82, 114, 185, 330L;

Alamy: 23L, 48, 62, 120R, 124, 211, 223, 246, 286, 306, 330CR, 350;

Art Archive: 41, 149, 181, 178;

The Bridgeman Art Library: 4, 5, 20, 23R, 42, 44, 53, 57, 64, 68, 78, 80, 103, 104L, 118, 129, 134, 135, 136, 138, 140, 147, 153, 154, 156, 158, 159, 162, 163, 164, 166, 167, 169, 170, 174, 176, 184, 187, 189, 191, 194, 196, 198, 200, 203, 207, 226, 228, 262, 264, 273, 274, 276, 280, 304, 326, 333, 342, 346, 349;

Corbis: 56 © Jon Jones/Sygma, 58, 76L, 269, 330R © Bettmann, 61 © Gianni Giansanti/Sygma, 100 © Patrick Robert/Sygma, 109 © Francis G Mayer, 122 © Jason Burke/Eye Ubiquitous, 144 © Todd Gipstein, 255 © Corbis, 258 © Corbis Sygma, 263 © images.com, 330BR © Joe McDonald, 334 © Reuters/Corbis;

Getty Images: 9, 32, 37, 39, 40, 54, 63, 72, 87, 91, 98, 107, 120L, 214, 215L, 215R, 219, 224, 229, 239B, 240, 247, 250L, 250R, 252, 267, 268, 277, 307, 308, 353;

Imagefile: 3, 14L, 18, 33CB, 33CT, 33T, 35, 47, 193, 231, 251, 297, 298, 343B;

The Irish Times: 52;

National Gallery of Ireland: 199, 347;

PA Photos: 76R, 92, 239T, 318;

Panos: 33B © Mark Henley, 33C © Tim Smith, 210 © Dieter Telemans;

Reportdigital.co.uk: 14R © Paul Carter, 150 © Stefano Cagnoni, 310 © Roy Peters, 311 © Duncan Philips;

Reuters: 21, 81, 104R, 285, 322, 336;

Rex Features: 233, 235;

Science Photo Library: 74, 115, 289, 338, 330TR, 339B, 339T, 343BL, 343TL;

UN Photo/Milton Grant: 209.

The author and publisher have made every effort to trace all copyright holders, but if any has been inadvertently overlooked we would be pleased to make the necessary arrangement at the first opportunity.